To my wife, Janet, who taught me what love really means, and my daughters, Jessica and Megan, who have allowed me to experience a second childhood.

The Art of Film Acting: A Guide for Actors and Directors

Jeremiah Comey

Focal Press

OXFORD AMSTERDAM BOSTON LONDON NEW YORK PARIS
SAN DIEGO SAN FRANCISCO SINGAPORE SYDNEY TOKYO

791. 43028

Focal Press is an imprint of Elsevier Science.

Copyright © 2002 by Elsevier Science (USA)

Library of Congress Cataloging-in-Publication Data
Comey, Jeremiah.
    The art of film acting : a guide for actors and directors / Jeremiah Comey.
        p. cm.
    Includes bibliographical references and index.
    ISBN 0-240-80507-0 (pbk. : alk. paper)
        1. Motion picture acting. I. Title.

    PN1995.9A26 C65 2002
    791.43'028--dc21

                                                                    2001058628

British Library Cataloguing-in-Publication Data
A catalogue record for this book is available from the British Library.

The publisher offers special discounts on bulk orders of this book.
For information, please contact:
Manager of Special Sales
Elsevier Science
225 Wildwood Avenue
Woburn, MA 01801-2041
Tel: 781-904-2500
Fax: 781-904-2620

For information on all Focal Press publications available, contact our World Wide Web home
page at: www.focalpress.com

10 9 8 7 6 5 4 3 2 1

Printed in the United States of America

791.43028

The Art of Film Acting

Contents

10. The Art of Giving and Receiving   131

11. The Senses   148

12. Intimacy, Empathy, and Intuition   167

13. The Audition   187

14. More on the Audition   209

Preface

Film acting, like all art, is a form of communication, a relationship with another human being on an emotional level. Vincent van Gogh's art is an inspiration because he put the most meaningful of ingredients into his paintings—himself. Just as great artists define themselves by their art, so do brilliant film actors communicate through their quality, which is personality combined with talent.

Acting is probably the most competitive business in the world because, for one thing, everyone thinks they can act. If you want to paint, sculpt, or compose music, everyone accepts the necessity for talent and training. No one in their right mind would think of being a professional concert pianist without having started practice at age four or five. But almost everyone thinks acting is easy. It is not; but we all can act if we first get out of our own way and forget all the social and personal inhibitions that have been laid upon us by our parents, our peers, and society. If you want to be a film actor, don't let anyone discourage you from your dream; but don't assume that it is quick and easy.

Acting is an art, and like the other arts, it demands that you study and master the craft. You also need to be able to expose your true feelings. It is easy to cry when you fight with a lover or watch a tearjerker. But it is another matter to cry in an audition or in a scene. In front of the camera, it can be a nightmare for an untrained actor simply to be believable and emotionally honest in a scene as simple as a quiet talk over a cup of coffee. In your everyday life it's hard to forget your inhibitions and, like a child, be your natural self. To become a good actor, you have to let the world see your emotions. Sir Laurence Olivier, one of the greatest actors, said, "This is not an occupation for adults."

Yet it is possible for a fifty-year-old woman who is inhibited to come into my class with no previous training and within weeks be giving a good film performance. She will have relapses and will have to keep working hard, but through the "Relating Exercise" she is learning how to override her intellect and show her emotions. It's not easy to take off your emotional clothing and show your real self, but this is what has to happen when you are in a film close-up. Experiences, family, friends, and everyone we have ever met have made a personal and permanent impact on our inner lives. The performances of great actors give us insight into these personal relationships and feelings by letting us see and experience their emotional impact.

This book explains how to make the transition to film acting from both stage acting and everyday life, and how to handle yourself in a professional situation. Reading this book alone will not make you a great actor; but it's a good place to start. Persistent application of its principles can guide you to the confidence and the skill you need to show your talent.

When you read this book, take your time. Borrow, rent, or buy all the films I use for examples. Study them and the performances I have talked about. Do the exercises in the book. When you work in other classes or workshops, try the principles of the Arts of Concentration, Acceptance, Not Knowing, Giving and Receiving, to help you in the Art of Relating. Relating is your way to attain emotional power. Every time you relate, you release a depth charge that explodes and shakes emotions loose from your inhibitions. Then your creative subconscious—the source of all great art—will force both these and unexpected emotions to the surface. You will find this process both a revelation and an inspiration, and so will everyone who watches you work.

Acknowledgments

I am happy to acknowledge help from Howard Gong, who gave me ongoing counsel and the will to begin this book and see it through. I owe thanks to Barbara Bowen for allowing me to use her scenes for workshop material; to Samantha Lane, who helped me put my thoughts in order; to Christine Mehner for her wide knowledge and support; to my friends and fellow teachers Mark Brandon, Dan Chernau, and Robert Winley, who graciously read the first drafts and helped me find direction; to Allan and Alicia Sirkin and Barbara De Prima for sponsoring my workshop in Miami; to Adam Stoner, who invited me to teach at the New York Film Academy; to Carol Hemingway, Jack Angel, DeeDee Michales, Robert Marcucci, Bob Brisco, and Robert Mckee for their support; to Helene Wong and Vicky Yiannoutsos, who were instrumental in bringing me to New Zealand as a Fulbright grantee to work with writers, directors, and actors.

I want to thank the professors and teachers who encouraged me to finish the book: Joy Rinaldi; Doug McHugh; Dunja Tot; Lynbarbra Mahler; Clay Banks; Nya Daigoa, a gifted artist who designed the cover; and my dear friend Patch MacKenzie, who supported my teaching from the beginning. I am grateful to every student I have had the pleasure to teach, for they have helped me learn.

I've had the privilege of studying with some remarkable acting teachers who helped me in my own personal journey—Rudi Solari, Guy Stockwell, Stella Adler, Sherman Marx, Cory Allen, and my first mentor, Charles Conrad, who generously started me on my way as a teacher. I especially want to thank Will Adams, a special friend and mentor, for without his expertise and help this book could never have been written. But my deepest debt is to Jan, my wife. Her love has sustained me throughout.

1
The Exercise

Jack Nicholson, in Five Easy Pieces, *single-handedly ushered in a new style of acting, a brand-new spontaneity that seemed to indicate he was performing without a script.*

Shirley MacLaine

My aim is to get you to relate to another actor as a real human being—woman to man, boy to girl, mother to daughter, man to man—and not as a person saying words from a script according to some logical idea as to how they *should* be said. I'm going to show you how I conduct my film-acting "Relating Exercise" to teach actors how to relate and how to concentrate. I teach more than the Exercise, but in it you learn the essential skill that sets you on your way to learning all the other skills that are fundamental to your becoming a great actor.

Here is a Relating Exercise scene as it was done in my class. A California Highway Patrol Officer, Chip, has stopped a beautiful woman, Mary, for speeding and is writing her a ticket. Mary, though a beginning actor, has no trouble relating to Chip. She is open, finds him attractive, and flirts with him. But the actor playing Chip, although he has been on a few auditions, has a problem: he's "in his head," which means that he intellectualizes the role and is acting with the *idea* that he's a cop, because the script and his logic have told him he's a cop. So he "acts" how he thinks a cop should act, which, of course, prevents him from relating honestly to Mary. As a result, he is pretty dull and uninteresting. I work with him to get him "out of his head" and to respond to what Mary is doing. When he finally does get out of his head, both he and the scene become interesting.

The two beginning actors face each other. Earlier, I had asked each to read the scene once silently, without making any judgments. (As in all scenes in this book, the directions in parentheses are descriptions of what the actors actually did.)

```
              CHIP
       (formal and official)
    May I please see your license
    and registration?


              MARY
    No.


              CHIP
    Excuse me?


              MARY
    I left in a hurry and forgot
    my purse.
       (flirting)
    And it looks like I'm going to
    miss my hair appointment.
```

(Chip is unresponsive to the fact that he is talking to a beautiful woman who is flirting with him.)

```
              CHIP
    Can I see your registration?
```

I interrupt the scene.

JEREMIAH: **What is she feeling?**

```
              CHIP
    (to Jeremiah)
            She's angry because she is
            getting a ticket.
```

(She is definitely not angry.)

JEREMIAH: **That's an idea you've got in your head. Look at her eyes and forget about being a cop. What is she feeling?**

(Mary is smiling, seductive.)

```
              CHIP
    (to Jeremiah)
            She doesn't like me.
```

JEREMIAH: **Are you kidding? Look at her face. Is she happy, sad, angry, afraid, or loving?**

> CHIP
> (to Jeremiah)
> > She is afraid.

JEREMIAH: **Where do you see any fear?**

> (Mary is still smiling and very appealing.)

> CHIP
> (to Jeremiah)
> > Well, she's getting a ticket.

JEREMIAH: **I'm not talking about what the script says. Look at her eyes. What makes you think she's afraid?**

> CHIP
> > Nothing.

JEREMIAH: **All right. Look at her mouth. Is she happy?**

> CHIP
> > She's smiling.

JEREMIAH: **Then is she happy? Is she loving? By loving I mean is she warm, caring, flirting, or anything that can be classified as loving?**

> CHIP
> > Yeah.

JEREMIAH: **Then deal with that. The script says she's angry, but she's not. That's all you have to deal with. Look at her eyes.**

> CHIP
> > She seems to be coming on to
> > me.

JEREMIAH: **You see it! Great! Then is she happy and loving?**

> CHIP
> > Yes.

JEREMIAH: **Then deal with those feelings when you say your lines.**

> (Chip is now concentrating his attention on Mary's emotions. She is flirting.)

```
                    CHIP
          (laughs, responding to her
          flirting)
     Is this your name? Mrs. Mary
     Brenco?

                    MARY
     It's Miss, not Mrs.
          (smiling)
     I hate that feminist stuff
     about women's liberation.
     There's only one place where a
     woman should be liberated.
```

(She laughs suggestively.)

(Chip gives her a coplike disapproving look. He goes back to acting the way he thinks a cop ought to act.)

JEREMIAH: **What is she feeling?**

```
                    CHIP
     She's loving.
```

JEREMIAH: **Are you dealing with that emotion?**

```
                    CHIP
(to Jeremiah)
          No. I'm maintaining my cool
          because a cop would never get
          involved. It would be out of
          character.
```

JEREMIAH: **Forget about how you think a cop should react. Deal with the emotion she is giving you. A movie scene is between people, not between robots.**

(Chip has trouble relating to Mary because the idea of being a cop still gets in his way.)

I ask Mary to stroke his face to break his paralyzing concept of being a cop. Touching stimulates intimacy, the exact opposite of Chip's idea. As we shall see, touching evokes the Art of Giving and Receiving.

(Mary repeats the lines as she strokes his face.)

                    MARY
          Yes it is. But it's Miss, not
          Mrs.
               (lovingly)
          I hate that feminist stuff
          about women's liberation.
          There's only one place a woman
          should be liberated.

(Chip gets turned on by her touching his face, and he reacts
lovingly.)

I interrupt the scene and play back this part of the tape for the class. We see
that he reacts to Mary instead of trying to act an idea.

JEREMIAH: **That works much better.** (to the class) **See how much more interesting they both are?**

(Return to scene)

                    CHIP
               (smiling, because she is
               stroking his face)
          Miss, you were doing 95 in a
          65. I'm putting it down at
          seventy-five.

                    MARY
               (laughing)
          I didn't know I was that fast.

(Now he's getting into it.)

                    CHIP
               (laughing)
          I'm also putting you down for
          driving without a license.

                    MARY
               (laughing)
          You're not going to take me
          into custody?

(Flirting, she kisses him.)

```
                    CHIP
               (ignoring the kiss)
          You don't look like a desper-
          ate criminal to me.
```

JEREMIAH: **What did she just do?**

```
                    CHIP
     (to Jeremiah)
          She kissed me.
```

JEREMIAH: **Why aren't you responding to her kiss?**

```
(Chip is back in his cop mode.)
```

```
                    CHIP
     (to Jeremiah)
          I don't think a cop would be
          turned on to someone he's giv-
          ing a ticket to. That would be
          out of character.
```

JEREMIAH: **Acting is about having an experience—so stop thinking and just respond to her. You don't have to grab her and throw her down on the seat. But you do have to react inside to what she is doing and feeling. The audience wants to see you feel something. Forget thinking that what you do is right or wrong. The experience you have inside you is more interesting than any of your ideas. Now, deal with her kiss**.

```
(Return to scene)
(She kisses him again.)
```

```
                    MARY
          Did anyone ever tell you you
          were handsome?
```

```
                    CHIP
               (He blushes, embarrassed—fear.)
          No, Ma'am.
```

Now he stops "acting" like a cop and deals with Mary as a woman. As a result, he experiences some real feelings.

```
(Mary strokes Chip's face and kisses him. Then, in a softer
tone)
```

                    MARY
         I am desperate. Why don't you
         give me your phone number?

                    CHIP
              (He responds, kissing her.)
         I'm on duty.

                    MARY
              (intimately)
         When do you get off duty?

(Chip is now relating to Mary and continues to relate to the
end of the scene. As he relates to her, he and the scene
become interesting.)

                    CHIP
              (smiling, softly)
         Late tonight.

                    MARY
              (smiling)
         Do you know Victoria's Secret?

                    CHIP
              (lovingly)
         Is it a nightclub?

(Mary, turned on, responds lovingly.)

                    MARY
         No silly, it's lingerie, and
         I'd like your opinion on some-
         thing. See you tonight. Here
         is my number. Got to run. Bye-
         bye.

END OF THE SCENE

                    CHIP
(to Jeremiah)
         But this would never work in a
         casting office.

JEREMIAH: **Don't underestimate casting directors.**

```
                          CHIP
(to Jeremiah)
                  They're not going to cast me
                  if I come on to this woman
                  when I'm supposed to be a cop.
```

JEREMIAH: **Casting directors, and particularly film directors, know when they see an honest response. That's what they're looking for.**

```
                          CHIP
(to Jeremiah)
                  But, what if there's no actor
                  to relate to, like in a cast-
                  ing session when the casting
                  director doesn't read with any
                  emotion or anything?
```

JEREMIAH: **Listen to the dialogue! Accept the imaginary situation. The combination of acceptance and real listening, along with the actual experience of reading in an office, will stimulate your creative process. If an unplanned spontaneous experience happens, go with it. If your response is honest it will work. Which did you enjoy the most? When you were playing the cop, or when you were relating?**

```
                          CHIP
(to Jeremiah)
                  When I was relating.
```

JEREMIAH: **And that's when you were fascinating to watch.**

In this kind of a situation it is easy to fall into the trap of playing the stereotype. If the role is a cop, an inexperienced or insensitive actor will play the scene like Chip did at the beginning, acting according to some intellectual concept of what a cop should be. If the role, say, is a priest, your intellect tempts you to speak in a clever Irish brogue. Mediocre actors always play the stereotype instead of the human being. In casting and rehearsing plays or films that have roles in which you have to speak in dialect, many good directors won't allow you to use a dialect until after you have worked out and understand the character you are playing. In the Exercise, I force you to relate, to concentrate your attention on the other actor, and then respond to his or her actions and emotions. This is the first step in not being trapped into acting the stereotype.

The Exercise is not intended to be a finished scene. I don't necessarily try to get you to go through a whole scene perfectly, but I work with you until you and the other actor experience some good moments. This way you understand the process of relating to and dealing honestly with another actor, and you have the experience of doing what Richard Brestoff calls "a precious exchange." As you continue to study and do the Relating Exercise, you get better and better and finally become, I hope, a brilliant actor.

In actual filming, you need a good performance only once. Two lines may be brilliant, and the rest of the scene may be boring. But those two good lines are not lost. In editing, the director often puts together a great scene by using the best moments from several otherwise dull or NG (no good) takes of the same scene.

Summary

1. Read the material once to eliminate ideas.
2. Forget what you personally want in the scene.
3. Concentrate and relate to the other actor's emotions: happiness, sadness, anger, fear, love.
4. Without judging, respond to anything and everything the other actor gives you.

Actor Practice

Talk to people. Observe and listen until your eyes are fatigued and your ears are numb. This is one of the main steps on the way to brilliant acting.

1. Hang around a cafe, a bar where cops hang out, any place where you can watch people, and without appearing suspicious, observe their social behavior.
2. Talk to a priest, a minister, a gang member, a cop, an elderly person. Forget what he or she is officially. Look for and talk to the real human being inside.
3. Think of the President of the United States and his main opponent. Forget about all your beliefs and feelings, political or otherwise, and imagine you are talking to him only as a person.
4. Talk to a local elected official. Watch him or her intently.
5. Think about and write down all the prejudices—racial, social, political, and cultural—you may have regarding certain people. Then put your prejudices and ideas on hold, and go talk to some of these people.

2

Stage versus Film Acting

Whereas you can—and many effective actors do—get away with faking, posturing, and indicating emotions on stage, it's difficult, if not impossible, to get away with anything false before the camera. That instrument penetrates the husk of the actor; it reveals what's truly happening—if anything, if nothing. A close-up demands absolute truth. It's a severe and awesome trial. Acting for the screen is a more honest trade.

Elia Kazan

"A more honest trade" does not necessarily mean "a better trade." Film acting and stage acting are different, and arguments as to which is "better" are pointless. Each has its own requirements, and good actors are good actors, stage or screen. Some actors are at their greatest on the stage, others in front of the camera, and some work brilliantly in both. Stage or film, the Art of Relating, which is the ability to relate to another actor, is indispensable. How and to what extent you relate depends on whether you are in front of the camera or on the stage. Successful actors know how to adjust in the crossover between the two mediums.

A friend of mine, who is a now a successful film actor, tells a story that when he was fresh out of college with his degree in theater acting, his first professional job was a role in a low-budget feature film. He determined to knock 'em dead. He studied and restudied the script, analyzed his character, and planned his performance and his choices line by line. As is the case on a depressingly high number of films, he got no help from the director.

Later, when my friend saw the finished film, he was surprised and embarrassed that in most of his scenes he was not believable. He looked especially bad in the scenes he had rehearsed the most diligently and in which he had carefully made his choices. Why was this? He knew he wasn't that bad an actor. He looked at the film several times to figure out why he came across as poorly as he did, and on the fourth viewing, he saw the light. He had prepared for and acted as he would have for a stage play. Here's what he had done.

He had planned ahead of time how to deliver each of his lines. His ideas stifled his natural delivery and turned his dialogue into line readings. Because he repeated his dialogue the same way on every take, the editor had no choice but to use my friend's line readings in editing each scene.

He had planned how he was going to react to the other actors' lines. As a result, his reactions appeared contrived rather than spontaneous.

He had projected his voice and his actions. He was unaware that the camera and the microphone were the audience. He did not realize that the camera was capable of intimacy and would record his feelings and thoughts without projecting.

He had thought that what he said was more important than what he felt, with the result that he communicated the wrong information. Dialogue is less important than what a character feels or thinks.

He had decided what emotions he should feel, and was working hard to express them, coming off as an actor "indicating" emotions that were not there. Without time for rehearsal, predetermined emotions can look forced and dishonest.

He had no idea that the camera was picking up his real feelings, which were nervousness and fear. The fear made him stiff and uncomfortable in front of the camera. At moments he even showed a nervous quiver.

He did not know that, with rare exceptions, a character in a movie is the actor's own self. He spent the entire movie trying to be the characterization of a policeman rather than just accepting himself as the policeman.

He did not know that his job was to see and listen to the other actors so intently that he recognized their feelings, and to say his lines intuitively according to what he saw and heard. He came across as an actor who was not giving to or receiving from any other character in the film.

The overall result was that he came across as a stiff, scared actor who was not participating in the story because he was not relating to his fellow actors. His ideas created line readings and made his performance unbelievable. He looked like an actor covering up his insecurity with overacting.

Preparing for a Role

For a stage role, you spend a lot of days rehearsing everything you are going to have to do every night for the run of the play. You and the director block your movement and action to make sure you and the other actors don't run into each other and that you always end up in the right place at the right time. Day after day, you rehearse your performance, your entrances, exits, timing, and stage business. You prepare for the reality that during the play's run you will have to repeat your entire performance every night. For film, things are different.

Actor Tom Hanks, in a TV interview, described how he used to spend the night before acting in a film scene by analyzing the scene, marking the key points, identifying the beats, making his choices, planning how he should do each line, and determining how he should feel and move. Then when he gets on the set the next morning, the director makes him throw out everything he planned, and perform by relating to the other actors. Frank Sinatra always refused to rehearse performance. Laurence Olivier said that in making the movie *Wuthering Heights*, director William Wyler told him to relate instead of "act." Gene Hackman said he learns his lines by rote without any planning, not allowing himself any emotional reaction, so that during shooting he can perform according to how he relates to the other actors. Meryl Streep said she usually reads the script once or twice and then performs by relating to and dealing with the other actors. Steven Spielberg said in an Actor's Studio interview that he never rehearses, because he doesn't want his actors to "act."

The Demands of Performance

In a stage play you know what you are going to do from the moment you first step onto the stage to final curtain. You often work from the emotions of other actors, but the camera's intimacy and truth are not always demanded of you. When the curtain goes up, there is no looking back. You must know all your lines, movement, stage business, and interpretations; and you are under pressure to carry through to the final curtain. Some nights you are brilliant, other nights not so brilliant, and there's nothing to do but approach the next performance with hope, determination, and good spirits.

For film, you are not expected to give a sustained performance for more than one shot at a time, and never for the whole screenplay. Restricted by costs, availability of actors, locations, and convenience, the director shoots her movie in separate chunks at different times and hardly ever in the same order as in the script. It is not unusual for the last scene to be shot first, followed by the other scenes, not necessarily in script sequence. The special character of motion picture production results in constant changes and altered points of view during actual shooting, so that director and actors rarely, if ever, rehearse for a sustained performance from the beginning to end.

All the good things, in any film, were a series of accidents.

Robert Altman

One Good Performance

For the camera, you have to give a good performance only once, and both you and the director concentrate on getting that one good performance. You may get it in one take, or you may have to do many takes before the director decides that you have done the right one. Your job is to perform under the pressure of Elia Kazan's "severe and awesome trial" of the close-up. Once your best performance is "in the can," it has been immortalized on film and you never have to do it again. Unlike for a stage play, film audiences in perpetuity will be able to see your best performance. For posterity's sake, let's hope it's a good one.

Your best performance in a film comes from living in the moment of the scene, which may or may not be what you or your director had planned or expected. You may or may not act the whole scene at one time, depending on its length and on how the director plans her shooting. It is certain that you will do several takes of the scene in close-up and from different angles. When a good film director calls "Cut and print" and then calls for an additional take of a shot you have just done, she is not looking for a repetition, even though your performance may have been brilliant. She is making one more try for something that she hopes will be knock-'em-out-of-their-socks brilliant.

In film, not rehearsing does not mean not preparing or not understanding the story. When a film director says she never rehearses, she is referring to dialogue and emotional relationships. Both you and your director rehearse blocking and camera movement, but the real performance comes when dialogue, emotions, and reactions are fresh and unrehearsed and the actors face each other with the camera running. The stage equivalent would be if the cast were to do its first rehearsal for performance on opening night. You don't see this in the theater, and I think you would be hard put to find a professionally produced play in which the first rehearsal for performance is on opening night.

Projecting

In film, you are acting for the camera and the microphone, whose only purposes are to record everything you do and say with relentless intimacy. Not until much later will audiences be allowed to see what you performed privately for the camera. My actor friend, unaware that the microphone and the camera were so close to him, had projected his voice and his actions. On the screen he sounds as if he is talking to someone on the other side of the playground. If he had been in a stage play, he would have sounded okay. In the film, his third-balcony voice projection while speaking to an actor standing fourteen inches away from him makes him look ridiculous. In a film scene, the camera and the microphone are as close as the lover you are whispering to, so you don't need to project your voice and actions. To avoid looking amateurish, talk naturally and don't project.

The chief requisite for an actor is the ability to do nothing well, which is by no means as easy as it sounds.

Alfred Hitchcock

Film and Theater Close-Ups

When you sit in the front row at a play, you are close to the actors and you can see them in what might be called a stage version of a close-up, but it's not anything like a movie close-up. In the front row, you are aware of the actors' loud, projected voices, their taut neck and throat muscles, and the tiny meteors of saliva streaking through the light. In contrast, a movie close-up shows you a quiet reality with its normal level of human interaction. It is easy to say that all you have to do in going from stage acting to film acting is to be what actors call "broad" in the wide shots and subtle in the close-ups." Not true. In a close-up, you have to be not only subtle but real, because it is in those close-ups where Kazan's "severe and awful trial" takes place. The camera sees everything and demands absolute truth. If you're scared or nervous or angry or sweating even a tiny little bit, the camera picks it up. It shows your insincerity, your truthfulness, your nothingness, your involvement, your emotions. You have to *be* there. The camera sees what you truly are at the moment. Good film acting teachers try to teach you how to successfully face that trial.

Film is a medium of images, and a movie close-up of you having an emotional experience is a wordless image even though you may be speaking dialogue at the same time. If you do not experience an emotion stimulated in you by the other actor and the circumstances, the scene dies. Your emotion, not your words, communicates to the audience what is really going on.

Emotions and Feelings

What's the distinction between emotions and feelings? There is no difference. Feelings are emotions. When you feel happy, you are experiencing the emotion of happiness. Feeling sad is the emotion of sadness. Your feelings and emotions originate in the right side of your brain and have nothing to do with the logic of its left side. You can decide what to think, but you cannot decide what to feel. That's why big macho football players cry and apologize for it when they are inducted into the hall of fame. They can't help it. When you are acting, your feelings have to be like that—you can't help it; they have to come from your true reaction to the other actor and to the circumstances of the scene. "I'm sorry," the football player apologizes at his display of emotion and tries to suppress it. You, the actor, must welcome your emotion and certainly never suppress it. You cannot fake emotion, but there are actors who try to all the time.

There are many working actors of the kind whom Constantine Stanislavsky called "mechanical actors." Although there are many fine actors in television, we see a perpetual parade of mediocre actors who try to "act" emotions. Stanislavsky said the mechanical actor uses his facial expression, mimicry, voice, and gestures to show us nothing but a dead mask of feeling that doesn't exist. "Indicating" means trying to express a feeling not from within but from without by using body and voice devices that supposedly represent some emotion or another. When you deliberately decide ahead of time to evoke a specific emotion, you can only indicate that emotion, not experience it. Sanford Meisner said, "you can't fake emotion." The camera knows the difference.

I don't believe in rehearsing the emotion of a scene: you can rehearse the mechanics of a scene. The actual thing happens when the camera goes.

George Cukor

Subtext

Subtext is what you really are saying regardless of what your lines are saying. It is the true meaning underneath dialogue, and it is what you communicate when you talk to anyone in the film. The words you say in film seldom convey an equivalent meaning to the words said on the stage, because the real meaning of a film scene is found mainly in the subtext created by what you experience at the moment, which has little or nothing to do with words. Stage actors do not have the close-up to let audiences see their emotions as intimately as on film. On the stage, there is little subtext because dialogue explains virtually everything. In a film, when the dialogue explains the story or the situation or feelings, it comes across as fake and boring. Your performance on film, mainly in close-up, depends on your true reaction to the feelings of the other actors and the situation. Unlike stage actors' preparation for their work on stage, most good film actors do not rehearse or plan exactly how they are going to react in a scene.

Subtext is that unspoken communication by way of your emotions or feelings. Regardless of what your script lines are, subtext is what you really mean and what the audience is really watching, even though it may not be logically aware of it. Through the subtext, the audience discovers your relationship to the other actors, and only when you are relating to each other can there be useful subtext.

People don't always express their inner thoughts to one another; a conversation may be quite trivial, but often the eyes will reveal what a person really thinks or feels.

Alfred Hitchcock

You communicate subtext through your tone of voice, body language, looks, and emotions, but only if they come from your emotional response to the other actors and to the circumstances and not from indicating, as with mechanical actors. Subtext is an undercurrent that allows the audience to understand what is really going on between the actors. Subtext is virtually impossible to rehearse because it is experiential and difficult to duplicate. The director usually tries to set the blocking to help the actors in creating subtext.

One example of how film director Mark Rydell blocks a scene to help the actors with subtext is in the film, *On Golden Pond*. To understand how this works, it is important that you view this film and watch this scene both with and without the sound. Chelsea, played by Jane Fonda, arrives on a visit to the summer cottage of her parents, Norman and Ethel, played by Henry Fonda and Katharine Hepburn. Norman is a crusty, often abrasive man who has a sense of humor but is unable to express his feelings very well. Chelsea desperately wants his love and approval. When Chelsea (J. Fonda) enters the cottage, the director frames her and Norman (H. Fonda) in a close two-shot: we see Chelsea full-face and the back of Norman's head. We see her feeling of happy expectancy. Here she encounters the close-up's "severe and awesome trial" of being absolutely honest.

```
INT. LIVING ROOM. EVENING.

CLOSE TWO-SHOT ON J. FONDA. The back of H. Fonda's head is
to us.

                        J. FONDA
                  Hello Norman.

(She goes to kiss him, but just before her lips touch his
cheek, he very slightly pulls his head back. We see her
extreme pain for an instant. She continues and kisses him.)

                        J. FONDA
                  Happy birthday.

(She is once again expectant and happy. Hepburn comes in the
door and stands behind them in the same close shot.)
```

Consider the dialogue to this point: four words, "Hello, Norman," and "Happy birthday." Not much for a great actress to knock us dead with, yet Jane Fonda does it. There is a lot happening emotionally, and Fonda, as Chelsea, lets us see how she feels. She is happy at the prospect of greeting her father, and it is clear by her feelings that she expects to be received by him in the same way even though she has been burned in the past. When Norman pulls his head back when she attempts to kiss him, we see, for a brief instant, the intense pain it causes her. Then she is back to her feeling of happy expectation for a short moment when Norman gives his next line:

```
CLOSE-UP, H. FONDA


                        H. FONDA
                 (to Hepburn)
            Look at this little fat girl,
            Ethel.
```

Rydell blocked this scene so that Jane Fonda faces us in a close shot over Henry Fonda's shoulder. We see exactly what is going on inside her. With the back of his head close in the right foreground, we see his slight unplanned movement backward that tells us what he is experiencing. The least bit of untruth on Jane's part would kill the scene, but she truly experiences the emotions so honestly that we experience them with her. What she does is impressive. This is a good scene for film actors—and film directors—to study.

On stage it is almost impossible to achieve film's intense intimacy. The same scene as it was done originally in the stage play with other actors is effective, but not as compelling as it is in the film close-up. Chelsea hugs her father, who hesitates briefly before returning the hug. The dialogue and body movements predominantly indicate the feelings of the actors, particularly when Chelsea's father, instead of pulling back from her kiss as in the film, hesitates before he returns her hug. The actors doing this scene in the stage presentation show the proper discomfort and awkward hugging the scene requires, but without the power of a film close-up, it takes Norman's line, "Look at this little fat girl, Ethel," to give the scene its full impact. In the film scene the impact comes earlier, when in close-up we see Chelsea's emotions so intimately that it seems we are guiltily eavesdropping, which is exactly what the camera is doing.

On the stage, an actress has to make sure the entire audience sees her response. Subtext nuances are not as discernible, especially for someone sitting several rows back in the theater. In a play, subtext, or the author's hidden intention, comes from the text. On film, subtext becomes clear to the audience through the actors' emotional experiences while relating to another actor. The stage actor has to look for the author's intent by interpreting the emotional undercurrent, explicit or hidden, in the words. Eugene O'Neil experimented with conveying subtext to the theater audience in his play *Strange Interlude* by having his characters speak their true thoughts and feelings in asides to the audience. It is an interesting play, but its asides are not as effective and unobtrusive as the film close-up.

All acting in film takes place in close-up. In a wide shot, anyone can look believable taking a gun out of a drawer or fluffing up the sofa cushions. You earn your money in close-up, where the camera sees your emotions. You can't hide anything because the camera sees everything—fear, happiness, anxiety, lack of confidence, nervousness, whatever is going on inside you. On film you cannot "act" in love, you have to *be* in love. Sanford Meisner said that your greatest source of creativity as an actor is concentration of attention outside yourself. The way to get in touch with this creative source is to concentrate on the other actor. The camera will pick it up.

Some very good actors in the theater play parts that don't reveal themselves, whereas in films, some actors who may not be as great have some quality that gets revealed.

Paul Mazursky

Camera and Proscenium Arch

The camera can take your audience anywhere. It can present a panoramic view or an extreme close-up. It can range from the spectacle of *Braveheart* and *Gone with the Wind* to the simplicity of *Strangers in Paradise* or *Clerks*. Film has the ability to take us visually from distant galaxies to the microscopic world of neurosurgery, from an aerial shot of a lake to a close-up of the lily pad.

The size and design of a theater dictate what the set will look like and how the audience sees the play. Most theaters have a proscenium arch through which the audience sees the play from a single point of view as if through a transparent fourth wall. In some theaters, the stage thrusts out into the audience, and in arena theaters, the audience completely surrounds the acting area.

The location of your seat in a theater determines how you see the play. Your point of view is different from that of any other position in the house, except that everyone in the audience can see the whole stage and the whole set. At a play you may watch the entire action or any part of it you choose. You may study the set, look at any actor on the stage, or watch the actors who are speaking—whatever you choose to look at.

On the film or TV screen, you may only see what the director wants you to see. She dictates what each image will be, how much of the screen it will fill, and from what distance and point of view you see it. If the picture is a big-head close-up of an actor, that's all there is for you to look at. If it's a wide shot, the camera shows you only as much as the director wants you to see. Though the stage audience sees the entire set, it does not have the ability to move closer or farther away. The film audience sees an assortment of close-ups and wide shots created and selected by the director. She, in effect, moves the audience closer to or farther away from the action in the movie.

Personality and Character

In both film and theater, there are two kinds of roles: personality and character. Your personality is who you are mentally, physically, emotionally, and spiritually. Almost all the roles in film are personality roles in which you play yourself as if you were actually the character called for by the script. Jimmy Stewart, for one, was a personality actor who always played himself in someone else's shoes. Most stars are personality actors and do not try to transform themselves into someone else. In most film roles, actors let their individual selves filter through the role to exploit their respective personalities. Milos Forman, who directed great films such as *One Flew Over the Cuckoo's Nest* and *Amadeus*, was once asked what it means to be professional in films; his answer was that what is important are the talent and the personality.

In a Character role, you play the fictional personality of someone else. Character roles are traditional in the theater, and we read about the great actors of the past who transformed themselves into the famous roles of characters who were completely different from themselves. When you play a character role, you have to hide your personality so that you are perceived as someone who is different from you both physically, psychologically, and mentally. The great Michael Chekhov, a character actor in both stage and film, transformed himself so completely in many roles that the real Chekhov disappeared.

Film is a personality medium, but character roles have been created by some film actors like Chekhov and others. In the 1949 film *Kind Hearts and Coronets*, Alec Guinness plays the eight character roles of the people his main character has to eliminate to gain a royal title. Each character is completely different from the others and is not just Guinness in a different costume. Paul Muni transforms himself as Zola in the film *The Life of Emile Zola*. More recently, there was Daniel Day-Lewis in *My Left Foot*; Tom Hanks in *Forest Gump*; Dustin Hoffman in *Tootsie, Little Big Man,* and *Midnight Cowboy*; Leonardo DiCaprio in *What's Eating Gilbert Grape*; Billy Bob Thornton in *Swingblade* and *U-Turn*; Gary Oldman in *Hannibal*; Judy Dench in *Shakespeare in Love*; all create wonderful film character roles in which they are not recognizable as their own personalities. Jon Voight is such a great character actor that no matter what his role, he always seems to be someone other that Jon Voight. His Howard Cosell in *Ali* is virtually unrecognizable as Voight.

There are a number of leading men and women who have done or could do character roles: Anne Bancroft, Jennifer Jason Leigh, Meryl Streep, Helen Bonham Carter, Cicely Tyson, Jodie Foster, Marlon Brando, Samuel L. Jackson, Robert Duvall, Tim Roth, and a few others. They have the ability to filter the assumed character through themselves and make it believable. There are many women actors who could do character parts brilliantly, but such parts are hardly ever written for them.

You make use of your personality. That's why some have lasted such a long time. They have something you can use.

Howard Hawks

A few of the prominent personality actors who have lasted a long time are Humphrey Bogart, Cary Grant, Robert De Niro, Susan Sarandon, John Wayne, Danny Glover, James Caan, Gene Hackman, Morgan Freeman, Paul Newman, Henry Fonda, Jane Fonda, Harrison Ford, Sidney Poitier, Kirk Douglas, Bette Davis, Robert Redford, and Kathy Bates.

A leading actor who fits a role playing his or her own personality is more efficient for film than hiring an actor who doesn't look the part and having him transform himself into the character. We still have character actors in film, but they are mostly personality actors who themselves are interesting or unusual characters. The Academy Award for best supporting actor was originally created for the character actor, the type of actor who would never be a leading man but who did an excellent job in a lesser part. Character actors for film, both men and women, usually differ from leading actors by a wide range of traits and characteristics that are physical: fat, thin, bald, specific accent, tall, short, unusual facial features, odd physical build, unusual voice. Each is usually cast for his or her respective characteristic physical traits, but the true character actors transform themselves into a character having any one or more of such specific traits. The Academy categories for men and women, as distinct from the categories Leading Men and Leading Women, are Character Men and Character Women.

There are good reasons why character-transformation roles are not common in film acting. Most important is that it takes a long time for an actor to create a great character. It took Dustin Hoffman nine months to work on his character Dorothy for the movie *Tootsie*. Eddie Murphy creates a whole family in *The Nutty Professor*. He plays the Mother, Father, Grandmother, Uncle, and Brother. When I saw the picture, I thought each was a different actor until my daughter told me he was playing all the parts. The time spent creating a character for film costs a lot of money that producers are unwilling to spend. It is cheaper and easier to hire personality actors that fit the role. There are exceptions, like the two above, because where would you find ready-made personality actors like Dustin Hoffman or Eddie Murphy? They don't exist and have to be created. The time it takes for character transformation costs lots of money, so only leading actors with marquee value get a chance to do it. To the accountants, the expense of creating a transformed character other than a star would not be cost-effective.

Film is all about personality. Robert Duvall has been around for years and his character work is exceptional, but we still see the Robert Duvall personality with an accent and changed mannerisms. James Woods was brilliant in *The Ghost of Mississippi*, but he was still James Woods, the person. Character acting takes a skill many actors do not have, and producers are wary about hiring an actor who tries to get too far away from his type.

The stage is more suitable for creating character roles. A thirty-five-year-old actor may have the chance to play a twenty-year-old young adult or a man of sixty-five. During the relatively long stage rehearsal, he discovers the character's traits that are different from his personal characteristics and has the time to blend these into his performance. The actor may have a month of rehearsal to find the different ways the character reacts, and how to bring these traits closer to himself. Immersion into a character is a challenge; it is also part of the satisfaction and fun of working on the stage.

In the film *On Golden Pond*, Katharine Hepburn and Henry Fonda are perfect as a sixty-nine- and seventy-nine-year-old married couple. They are such skillful actors that we believe they have been married forever. They play themselves, even though Fonda has made a few subtle character choices, like being a little hard of hearing and a little senile, but he is the same Henry Fonda we have loved through many films. Had this role been available when Fonda was a young actor, I doubt he would have been cast as Norman and then aged to eighty with makeup. Using age makeup to make a young actor look old on film can sometimes be effective, but it is expensive because of the time it takes. In *Citizen Kane*, Joseph Cotten played the part of Kane's friend both as a young man and an old man. In this film, it was necessary to make up Cotten as an old man to cover the time span. The makeup was pretty good, but even though the transformation is not very great, there is no doubt it is the young Cotten playing an old man. On film, we are aware of Joseph Cotten's makeup job, but on the stage he would have looked like a genuine old man. Undetectable age makeup can be created for film, but it is more demanding and time-consuming for both the actor and the makeup artist, which costs more. For the stage, actors are expected to do their own makeup.

It is physically demanding to rehearse a play and then perform the lead role night after night. I don't think Henry Fonda, or any man at his age, could have made it through rehearsals and a run of the play. To get the play rehearsed and performed, it is more practical to cast a younger actor for the role of an eighty-year-old.

Dialogue

Film is mainly visual, and a film script usually contains about one-tenth the dialogue of a stage play. Compare a stage play to most screenplays. You can immediately see the difference. A leading actor might have a hundred lines in an entire movie. In a play, he may have a hundred lines in four pages. Dialogue is the essence of a play, and actors tell the story through the playwright's words and instructions. The story is advanced in words. The audience comes to hear what the playwright has written. In a good film, the story advances through the subtext created by the actors' emotions.

I try to avoid talk at all cost. You lose that spontaneity when you realize somebody's thinking the hell out of their part.

James Bridges

Monologues

Monologues are rarely used on film because the camera can take the audience into a character's mind through flashbacks and voice-overs and in close-ups that reveal what is going on inside the character. Film can present scenes that enact what in a play would be offstage action and have to be explained in words. The monologue is a device for the audience to understand what can only be communicated by words of explanation, such as the back story or a character's thoughts and feelings. A monologue in a film is most often a misguided attempt by an inept writer or director to solve a dramatic problem. There are exceptions.

In the film *On Golden Pond*, Hepburn sends Henry Fonda out to pick strawberries. We see shots of Fonda wandering around the woods. He can't find his way. He turns and runs in the opposite direction. He is out of shape. He sits on a log to catch his breath. We can see that he is confused, lost, and frightened. In this scene, the camera shows us Fonda's experience, but in the stage play, it has to be explained later in a monologue or expository dialogue.

On stage, monologues can be used for exposition, back story, or for understanding a character's thoughts. In modern theater, they also need some reasonable motivation. In a film, a monologue needs a strong dramatic motivation. Katharine Hepburn has a monologue in the film version of *On Golden Pond*. She delivers her monologue to a doll her character has had since she was a little girl. She is alone in the cottage.

```
(She takes her doll, Elmer, down from the mantel and hugs
him to her.)
```

```
          HEPBURN
Oh, Elmer, isn't he awful?
Elmer, Elmer, Elmer.
```

(She stands for a moment, lost in thought. The sound of a motorboat on the lake interrupts her. She turns and walks to the window. She waves to it and sits on the steps.)

```
          HEPBURN
    (to Elmer)
They say the lake is dying,
but I don't believe it. They
say all those houses along
Koochakiyi Shores are killing
Golden Pond.

See, Elmer, no more yellow
tents in the trees, no more
bell calling the girls to sup-
per. I left you in this win-
dow, Elmer, sitting on the
sill, so you could look out at
Camp Koochakiyi, when I was
eight and nine and ten.

And I'd stand on the bank,
across the cove at sunset, and
I'd wave. And you always waved
back, didn't you Elmer?
```

This monologue allows Hepburn to reminisce about her life as a child on the lake and what she shared with her imaginary playmate, Elmer. The monologue gives the audience insight into Ethel's character, thoughts, and feelings. You might say that it is not a monologue because she is talking to someone: her doll. But the doll is really not a participant and serves the same purpose for her as did Wilson, the basketball, for Tom Hanks' character in the movie *Cast Away*. The basketball and Elmer are pretty good excuses to allow the actors to speak monologues when there is no other live person to talk to.

What I'm looking for instead of actors is behaviors, somebody who will bring me more.

Robert Altman

Film Experience versus Stage Experience

The close-up offers emotional exposure. It reveals your inner feelings through your eyes and face. It uncovers your personality by revealing your deepest thoughts. In the climax of *On Golden Pond*, Jane Fonda confronts her father, Henry Fonda:

```
                    J. FONDA
          . . . it occurred to me that
          maybe you and I should have
          the kind of relationship we're
          supposed to have.


                    H. FONDA
          What kind of relationship is
          that?


                    J. FONDA
          Well, you know, like a father
          and a daughter.


                    H. FONDA
          Oh, just in the nick of time,
          huh? Worried about the will,
          are you? I'm leaving every-
          thing to you except what I'm
          taking with me.


                    J. FONDA
          Oh, stop it, I don't want any-
          thing. It just seems like you
          and I have been mad at each
          other for too long.


                    H. FONDA
          Oh? I didn't know we were mad.
          I thought we just didn't like
          each other.

(This hits J. Fonda hard. She starts to cry.)

EXTREME CLOSE-UP ON J. FONDA's FACE.


                    J. FONDA
          I want to be your friend.
```

The intimacy of this close-up on Jane Fonda as she says the last line brings the audience in to where it is standing next to her and participating in her feelings. Finally, Henry Fonda lets her in, not much but a little bit. We know their relationship will improve.

The stage actor has to project the dialogue and use larger-than-life movements to reach the back row. The experience of an actress on stage may be as deep as Jane Fonda's in the close-up, but the distance from the stage to the audience makes that experience less visible and intimate. Onstage intimacy has to be heightened to convey its meaning to the audience. Paradoxically, however, when you heighten intimacy, it diminishes. Intimacy is close, personal, and quiet. The back row is not close or personal, and it cannot be reached with quietness. So on the stage, some of the intimacy, maybe most of it, is lost.

An actor who is truly heroic reveals the divine that passes through him, that aspect of himself that he does not own and cannot control.

John Patrick Shanley

Reacting

One interesting and important characteristic of film is its use of the reaction shot, which is just that—a close-up of an actor reacting, with or without words, to something that has been said or done. It is a valuable shot that is intimate, revealing, and fascinating. There is nothing like it in a stage play. In editing, the director and the film editor select scenes and bits of scenes and assemble them in the order they think makes the best final film. To acquire all these bits and pieces, a conventional and safe way to direct a scene is by "coverage" shooting, which refers to blocking and shooting every scene in such a way that there are sufficient shots and angles of every line for the editor to assemble the final film creatively and in continuity.

Let's say you are at a table with another actor in a dialogue scene. The director first shoots the scene in an establishing shot, generally a wide shot that shows most of the table and the two actors. She follows this with a medium shot of the two of you. Then she has you repeat the dialogue while she shoots "over-shoulders" (OS), which are close shots of each of you with the camera looking at your face from behind and over the other actor's shoulder. Then she shoots individual close-ups of each of you as you speak and listen to the other actor who is off-camera. The director ends up with a group of shots that allows her and the editor to edit the scene in many different ways. This is not the only way to shoot a scene, but I refer to it here to point out the nature of the reaction shot.

Of these shots, several will be close-ups and over-shoulders of you just listening and reacting to the other actor. These reaction shots are very important to the editor and especially to you. Editors love good reaction shots because they can put them anywhere in a scene to change the pace or set a mood, or use them to get over an awkward or unusable cut. The point for you, the actor, is to always be participating in the scene and to not be out to lunch during the other actor's lines. Concentrate and listen. If you are interesting and involved, you may get a lot of screen time in reaction shots. There are times when the reacting actor is on screen longer than the actor speaking. It depends on who is the most interesting.

An Emmy-Award-winning film editor told me of the time she was editing an episode of one of the biggest prime-time TV dramas whose guest star was one of film's biggest stars. (For obvious reasons, I can't name the star or the show.) His performance was so bad that after she had edited out his bad scenes, the guest star ended up with a minute and a half of screen time on an hour show. You can be sure that there were a lot of reaction shots in this episode.

Stay with it. Be totally involved in your scene even if you do not have a single line of dialogue. You will be surprised at how many of your silent reaction shots make it into a film when you keep concentrating on the other actor and stay in the moment.

Acting in film requires a different orientation and training than for acting in theater, not that one is better or more valuable than the other. Some assume that the tricks of acting for the camera alone distinguish film acting from stage acting. These include tricks such as not blinking your eyes, hitting your marks, looking steadfastly at the actors' eye nearest the lens, matching your movements, and so on. You do have to learn these things, but the distinguishing essence of film acting is that you have to bring up your emotions not through psychological or physical gimmicks but through the concentration of your attention on the other actor's emotions and the circumstances (see Chapter 5, The Art of Concentration). All significant acting in film takes place in close-up, and learning film acting is the task of learning how to successfully meet the "awesome trial" of the close-up. This is what I teach.

Summary

1. The Art of Relating is essential for all acting, especially for film acting.
2. Novice actors often overanalyze a character and pre-plan every move in a performance. This often leads to line readings.
3. Do not anticipate or plan how you will react.
4. You don't need to project your voice or gestures; the camera is capable of recording the subtlest intimacy.
5. Dialogue is less important than what you feel.

6. Predetermined emotions can make you look forced and dishonest. Predetermined emotions inhibit you ability to relate with your fellow actors.

7. The character you play is your own self. Good film actors reveal their true feelings and personality. React as yourself, not as you think your character would or should react.

8. On film, rehearsal for performance happens during shooting. Each take is basically a rehearsal.

9. The audience discovers your relationship with the other characters through subtext.

10. The camera can take the audience anywhere, and is not limited to the size of the stage or the sets.

11. On film, monologues are rarely used. Flashbacks or voice-overs are generally used to reveal the back story.

12. On film, the close-up records exposed emotions.

13. The reaction shot on film is necessary for the director to tell the story. What he wants to say can come from subtext, thought, or inspiration.

14. The director and editor decide what the audience will see on screen.

Actor Practice

Join a theater group. Act in plays.

Ask a friend who is working in a movie if you can observe her when her scenes are being shot.

Go see a live play that has been made into a movie. Read the stage play and the script before you see the film version. This is a great way to start understanding differences between stage and film. Examples: *Other People's Money, Butterflies Are Free, Glengarry Glen Ross, One Flew Over the Cuckoo's Nest.* If possible, compare the screenplay to the actual play. See where they differ and why.

3

Becoming a Great Actor

It took me years to fully understand never to plan how I would say a line, and always to listen to the other actors.

Vanessa Redgrave

The Actor's Responsibility

Your responsibility as an actor is to entertain by communicating your real feelings to an audience. "Phoning it in"—performing a scene without experiencing real emotion—does not communicate. Just by having an emotion, you communicate it to your audience, the members of which in turn experience their own emotions. When you experience real emotion, you become interesting. This is called entertainment.

Casablanca

Casablanca, the 1942 film with Humphrey Bogart and Ingrid Bergman, is Number Two, right behind *Citizen Kane*, on the American Film Institute's list of the one hundred best American films of all time. Why has this Warner Brothers movie, which had neither a high budget nor a brilliant climax, been such an evergreen for generations? Because of great acting, acting where the actors experience genuine emotions that their audiences clearly see and feel. In their performances, Bogart and Bergman demonstrate the Five Arts of film acting. Their final scene, in which their characters say good-bye forever, is a perfect example of how they applied these arts. The scene as written is not unusual. It is short, cliched, and predictable, a scene that mediocre actors would reject as not having enough "meat" to it. But the situation is real—actors supply the "meat." View this scene and see what Bogart and Bergman do to make it work.

ILSA (Ingrid Bergman) and RICK (Humphrey Bogart) are saying
good-bye on the airport ramp. In the background, the
airplane, its engines running, waits to carry Bergman away
forever.

>   BERGMAN
>   What about us?

>   BOGART
>   We'll always have Paris . . . .
>   It doesn't take much to see
>   that the problems of three
>   little people don't amount to
>   a hill of beans in this crazy
>   world. Someday you'll under-
>   stand that. Not now.

(Bergman drops her eyes. It is too painful to look at
Bogart. He gently touches her face to raise her tear-filled
eyes to meet his searching look.)

>   BOGART
>   Here's looking at you, kid.

Bogart and Bergman wouldn't call what they were doing the Five Arts of
film acting, and they probably would have laughed themselves silly if someone
had suggested that was what they were doing. But they are brilliant in this
movie and in this scene because they were talented enough to Concentrate; to
Not Know what they were "supposed" to do; to Accept the given circumstances; to Give and Receive; and to Relate. Don't be fooled. The depth of the
performances in this apparently simple scene is camouflaged by the artistry of
these fine actors. To learn film acting, a good place to start is with what Bogart
and Bergman do in *Casablanca*.

Acting Is Being and Awareness

Good actors know that *being* is the essence of believable performance. *Being* means that you totally accept the given circumstances and are
aware of moment-to-moment reality. It means actually living in the reality of
the scene—not pretending, not waiting for your next cue, not thinking of how
you're going to "act," not thinking of choices, and not speculating on how good
a job you are doing. *Being* focuses your attention so you are not living in the
memories of the past nor the fantasies of the future. In front of the camera,
being helps you to become aware of the realities of every moment. It is not

logic, supposition, or philosophical discussion. It is experience. It is simply being there, dealing with everything that faces you.

Awareness is the foundation of *being*. It is learning to see, listen, and be mindful of every moment in your life. It is having trust in your "child-mind," living in the moment, not knowing, and centering your mind through concentration. You need these abilities of awareness to become a great film actor, and they are used by great actors, knowingly or not. They are fundamental to my teaching.

The Five Arts of Film Acting

The Five Arts of film acting are the Art of Concentration, the Art of Not Knowing, the Art of Acceptance, the Art of Giving and Receiving, and the Art of Relating.

The **Art of Concentration** focuses your attention, not on yourself but on the emotions of the other actor. Concentration is knowing where to place your attention. In the farewell scene at the airport, Bogart knows where his attention has to be. Bergman is looking down, so he gently raises her head, which lets him concentrate on her face and deal with what she is feeling.

When you practice the **Art of Not Knowing** you are free from ideas or judgments in your acting. You experience everything as if for the first time. Not Knowing keeps you alert and aware. A box of assorted chocolates is more exciting than a box of *all* butter creams because in the assorted box every piece is different; not knowing what you are going to get until you take that first bite puts you in a state of anticipation. In the same way, the Art of Not Knowing makes you an interesting actor because you are continually in a state of anticipation. During production, *Casablanca* was shot day-to-day without a completed script. At one point, Bergman asked Michael Curtiz, the director, "Please, please, who do I love, Humphrey Bogart or Paul Henreid?" Curtiz would not tell her, so Bergman was unwittingly practicing the Art of Not Knowing, and it showed in her performance. Everything she did and said came across as if for the first time, and we, the audience, saw and felt her emotions.

The **Art of Acceptance** allows you to completely believe both the other actor and the imaginary circumstances without pretending.

```
(In a scene in my class, Sally's dormitory room has been
vandalized. Her stereo smashed against the wall. Drawers
emptied on the floor. Bed overturned. Obscene words written
on the wall. John, her roommate's brother, has just come
into the room.)

                        SALLY
              Someone wrote on my wall.
```

```
(She is not accepting the circumstances. She says her line
to John as if she were commenting on the weather.)
```

JEREMIAH: **Sally, your logical thinking is telling you that you are not in a vandalized dorm room and this is not your roommate's brother.**

To get Sally past her logical thinking, which says "I'm not in a dorm room and he is not my roommate's brother," I ask her to scream to put her into the emotional state of the situation—"as if." Sally lets out a scream.

> SALLY
> (screams her line)
> SOMEONE WROTE ON MY DORM WALL.

```
(She becomes believable and instinctively reaches over to
touch John.)
```

JEREMIAH: **Sally, grab him, pull him in.**

John is observing, not responding, but I don't want to stop the scene now. Grabbing him is a way to get him involved. You have to commit to the imaginary circumstances. She is now committed. He is not.

```
(Now she is into it. She is on the edge of tears, shouting
at John, trying to get him to get into the situation.)
```

> SALLY
> Now I'm paranoid. I think
> everybody is following me . . .
> and he even knew my name.

> JOHN
> (as if he's reading a
> classified ad)
> We should call the campus
> police.

> SALLY
> They already dismissed it as a
> prank.

```
(John still is observing, not participating. He reads his
lines, eyes on the page.)
```

                    JOHN
          Then let's go to the police.
          They'll know how to handle it.

JEREMIAH: Sally grab him, keep pulling him toward to you, don't let him get away from you.

(Sally's physical action involves her more fully in the scene. She becomes more honest, pleading with John for help.)

                    SALLY
               (crying, yelling)
          I CAN'T SPEND THE NIGHT IN MY
          ROOM. I WON'T SLEEP, AND
          FINALS START TOMORROW.

(She really shakes him to get his attention. But he acts like a rag doll, unwilling to participate. This does not stop Sally. She becomes more committed.)

                    SALLY
          I'm afraid. What should I do?

(Sally is into it. She is involved, believable. John is out to lunch.)

                    JOHN
          Don't you have any friends?

                    SALLY
          Only you?

                    JOHN
          I'll call my sister, she'll
          let you stay with her.

(Sally shakes her head in disbelief at John's lack of participation.)

JEREMIAH: Class, notice Sally's reaction. She looks at John in disbelief and shakes her head.

Sally has turned in a believable performance because she accepted the circumstances of her dorm room being violated and John as her friend.

JEREMIAH: **Sally, good work.** (to the class) **Sally did a good job when she completely accepted the situation and forgot she was acting. But when the scene ended, see what she did? She realized that no matter what she did, John was not going to participate So she shook her head, thinking to herself, "what a jerk." That's the subtext we're looking for on film. It was an unplanned comic reaction that came out of the moment and was real.** (to John) **John, you said the lines, but you didn't accept the circumstances. Your logic and fear got in the way.**

At this point, I worked with John to get him to accept the circumstances and relate to Sally.

JEREMIAH: (to the class) **For Sally, the situation became real. You can see how she had several different experiences—anger, sadness, fear—all in less than twenty lines. That's how you act on film. You don't pretend. You accept the imaginary circumstances as real and go with them. And her experience after the scene was over, when she shook her head in exasperation at John. It was an honest impulse, real and funny. Always express your impulses, because they make film scenes fascinating, and they make you look good. And don't stop acting the instant the director says, "Cut." Some of your best reactions happen when you least expect it. Film editors love to use shots like that.**

Without thought, Sally became sad, because her acceptance of the vandalism brought her to the present moment, and the scream brought out the anger and tears. Acceptance stimulates genuine feelings. In *Casablanca*, Bogart and Bergman accepted—not just pretended to accept—the circumstances of their scene and their romantic feelings for each other, and thereby experienced real emotions.

In the **Art of Giving and Receiving** you give your entire emotional experience to the other actor and are receptive to all feedback. Say you are in a scene where the other character gives you a wedding ring. Experience the ring. Look at it, feel it. See, really see, *his* experience as he gives it to you. At that moment, discover how you feel about receiving the ring. Do you or do you not want to marry him? Now give the actor that very experience, rather than some experience you think you should have. The Art of Giving and Receiving stimulates genuine feelings.

The **Art of Relating** is responding to an actor, object, or situation verbally, nonverbally, or physically. Visualize the following scene. Your character is in love with the other character. Here is the way the scene was written:

TOM
Will you marry me?

> AMY
> I'm sitting here thinking what
> a great dad you'd make.

> TOM
> I was thinking what a great
> mother you would make.

> AMY
> I love you, but I want to fin-
> ish grad school.

> TOM
> I could help you study for
> your exams.

(He kisses her.)

> AMY
> That's scary. You helping me
> study.

> TOM
> I'm a great teacher!

> AMY
> All right, I'll marry you.

> TOM
> You must be crazy.

The following script is the way the scene was actually played. As in all scenes in this book, the directions in parentheses are descriptions of what the actors actually did.

> TOM
> Will you marry me?

(She laughs.)

> AMY
> I was just thinking to myself
> what a great dad you would
> make.

(He's serious.)

```
                    TOM
        I was thinking what a great
        mother you would make.
```

JEREMIAH: **Tom, what is Amy feeling?**

```
                    TOM
    (to Jeremiah)
            She's not taking me seriously.
```

JEREMIAH: **I understand that, but what is she feeling?**

```
                    TOM
    (to Jeremiah)
            She is laughing at me.
```

JEREMIAH: **Stay away from judgments. She is laughing. But not at you. Don't make it personal. Deal with her laughter.**

```
    (Amy is still laughing.)

                    AMY
        I love you, but I want to fin-
        ish grad school.

    (He starts laughing.)

                    TOM
        I could help you study for
        your exams.

    (He tries to kiss her. She continues laughing and pushes him
    away. Her rejection makes him feel angry. Tom ignores his
    anger.)

                    AMY
        That's scary, you helping me
        study.

    (Amy laughs hysterically at the line and at Tom's reaction.)
```

JEREMIAH: **Tom what did Amy do to you?**

```
                    TOM
    (to Jeremiah)
            She rejected my kiss.
```

JEREMIAH: **And you felt what?**

```
                        TOM
              I felt . . .
                   (he thinks)
              . . . angry.
```

JEREMIAH: **Then let it out. Get angry at her.**

```
(Tom yells at Amy.)
```

```
                        TOM
              I'm a great teacher!
```

JEREMIAH: **Tom, louder! Do it again.**

```
                        TOM
                   (yelling his anger)
              I'M A GREAT TEACHER!
```

```
                        AMY
              All right, I'll marry you.
```

```
(By now, he is angry and really yells his next line.)
```

```
                        TOM
                   (very angry)
              YOU MUST BE CRAZY . . . !
```

The script tells Tom that she accepts his proposal. Conventionally, all should be sweet and lovely. But he relates to her actions, which make him angry even though he loves her. He will continue to love her, but right now he is angry. His anger is colored by her hysterical laughter, and he surrenders to it. To ignore the anger would make the scene dishonest. The Art of Relating means that you respond to all feedback: every emotion, action, and expression of the other actor. Respond without judgment or preconceived ideas as to what the script or your logical mind tells you. Your logical mind tells you how you *should* feel and, consequently, how you *should* respond. In good film acting there are no *shoulds*.

The Power of Relating

The movie *Dersu Uzala*, directed by Akira Kurosawa, is set in the wilderness forests of Siberia. Munzuk, an old hunter, tracks his prey. Staying alive depends on how well he concentrates on and relates to the signs and footprints in the earth. He relates to the tiniest bits of information that tell him the kind of animal he is tracking: its health, size, speed, and direction. Through relating, he sees and responds to every detail and nuance.

Be a hunter. Seek out every detail and nuance of the other actor's actions and feelings as if your life depended on it—in truth, your professional life does depend on it. Do it by concentrating on the other actor and relating to everything about him—his physical condition, his appearance, his movements, his way of speaking, and his emotions. Relating eventually becomes internalized and sharpens your intuition. This develops your emotional power and makes you fascinating on film.

Acting "On the Nose"

Cause-and-effect is the basis of relating. Be aware of any emotional, physical, or vocal change (cause) in the other actor so that you can be influenced (effect) by him. Most actors are concerned with "acting," not relating. Lines like "I love you" or "You son of a bitch," for example, can easily become acted cliches. The meaning of the dialogue can be so strong that it denotes a specific emotion (sadness, happiness, anger, fear, love). An actor, often because he knows his line is "I love you," gets ready by becoming tender and "acting" sincere. On "You son of a bitch," he tightens his muscles, enlarges the veins in his neck, pretends to be angry, and shouts the line. Playing lines in this cliched way is called "acting on the nose," or acting according to the literal meaning of the script's words and not according to the emotions of the moment.

In real life, you may hear "You son of a bitch" said quietly and gently with great effect. Sometimes, you'll hear "I love you " shouted angrily with great truth. It depends on the emotions of the other person. Look at your partner and genuinely relate to his emotion on his *preceding* line. Then, when you say, "I love you" or "You son of a bitch," you will be relating and responding to his emotion, and your acting will never be cliched.

Listen to the Other Actor

Watch yourself closely to see how often in a scene you make mental comments and think of your next line instead of listening to the other actor. You may find yourself thinking about answering even before the other actor speaks. Most of the time the scripted dialogue controls what you think, but not what you feel. To feel emotions, be aware of what the other actor feels. You then become free to react with genuine feelings rather than simply restating the scripted dialogue with an automatic, on-the-nose response.

Bad actors line-read. That is, they use the literal meaning of the line to convey the experience. They use obvious ideas, which have nothing to do with feedback from the other actor. Mediocre actors presume the cause ahead of time and only pretend to relate. Great actors actually relate. The essence of great acting is honest relating. In the chapters that follow, I shall discuss the Five Arts and how you can master the craft of acting.

Acting Is a Profession

If acting is the journey you have chosen, approach it without time restraints, judgments, or ideas as to results. Develop your talent, your technique, your self-confidence. Set realistic goals. Accept, surrender to, and enjoy every experience. Accept yourself as you are, and you will begin to understand your infinite connection to the universe. Life will flow from you into the universe and back, constantly rejuvenating your creative energy.

Summary

1. The purpose of acting is to communicate.
2. The Five Arts of film acting are Concentration, Not Knowing, Acceptance, Giving and Receiving, and Relating.
3. The essence of great acting is Relating.

Actor Practice

Selected Films and Scenes

If you want to be a great actor, study the great actors. Student artists learn color, composition, form, and techniques from the works of the masters by studying and actually copying them. When a student artist can't achieve a desired effect in his work, he goes to the masters to see how they solved such problems. Once an artist understands what the masters have done, he is free to create his own personal form of self-expression. It is the same with acting. Study the performances of the great actors to see what they do. I have referred to films and scenes to illustrate a way of looking at the performances of great actors so that you may learn to make evaluations for yourself.

Study both the films and the scenes I have used in this book as well as other films. They will show you what the best actors do and what I teach. Learn from the best.

How to Watch Films and Videos

1. Look at the complete movie.
2. After watching the complete film, study the performances in selected scenes one at a time. The more times you look at a scene, the more you are going to see.
    a. Listen to the dialogue. If you have a copy of the script, read the scene.
    b. Study each performer separately. Determine the emotion each one is feeling. Does it change? When? Be specific.
    c. Are they listening?
    d. Are they practicing the Art of Not Knowing? When?
    e. Does Acceptance of the other character and the circumstances color the actor's performance?
    f. Are both actors Giving and Receiving? How? Are they physical with each other?
    g. Does their Giving and Receiving add to the relationship?
    h. Are they Relating?
3. Now, with the sound turned off, view the selected scene. Notice what is really happening between the actors, not what the dialogue says is happening.
4. View the selected scene again with the sound turned on.

Reviewing Workshop Videotapes

In my workshops, I use video cameras to record, on your own tape, every scene you do. This tape becomes a record of your progress.

Your workshop video is not intended to be shown to anyone, especially your boyfriend, girlfriend, best friend, husband, wife, or agent. A third party who sees you on tape outside the workshop context is unaware of what is happening and can misunderstand what you are doing, to your detriment. An old saying warns, "Never show an incomplete work to an idiot." This does not necessarily imply that your spouse, friends, and agent are idiots; but it does mean that unless other people understand thoroughly what you are doing and are personally involved in, they will invariably come to the wrong conclusion about your work.

Don't let your ego lead you into showing anyone a performance that has not been done specifically to be shown to an audience. Your tape is for your own development. Do not show it to an agent, manager, casting director, producer, or director. I assure you, they will always come to the worst conclusion about your acting ability.

In one of my workshops, an actress in her late 40s did a scene with a man in his 30s. She showed it to her husband who commented, "Why did Jeremiah cast you with him? You're too old to be his wife." In the next workshop session, she stopped in the middle of the scene because this younger man kissed her. She said, "He would never kiss me in real life." She told us what her husband said, and I explained that being affected by his comment unnecessarily involved her in an idea, which interrupted her learning. She watched her video again and saw why the younger man kissed her. She realized that it did work for the scene. The workshop and tapes of your work are for your personal development, and unqualified outside opinions only do you harm.

How to Watch a Video of Your Workshop Scene

1. Watch the video alone. We are always fascinated with ourselves, but don't make this a session in self-admiration.
2. Look at the complete scene. Don't worry about how you look. The lighting is not set up for glamour, so put your ego and hang-ups aside. If we were making a movie we would take the time to make you look as beautiful or as handsome as possible. The video's only purpose is to help you improve your acting.
3. Concentrate on the other actor.
   a. What emotion is he or she feeling?
   b. Are you responding to that emotion? If not, you should be.
   c. When your partner changes emotion, do you respond?
   d. If your partner does something physical, does it affect you?
   e. Are your emotions coming from the script or off your partner? Don't let the script dictate your emotions.
4. Are you listening?
   a. Are you responding? Good. Are you thinking about responding before your partner finishes talking? If you are, you're not listening.
   b. Are you on the same vocal level as your partner? Above? Louder? Below? Softer?
5. Sight reading (see Chapter 4).
   a. Are you reading your lines to the page or to the other actor?
   b. When sight reading, are you reacting to your partner or are you too busy reading?
6. Are you practicing the Art of Not Knowing?
   a. Are your responses unplanned? They should be.
   b. Are you stuck on the ideas from the script? Don't be.
   c. Are you thinking about the past or the future instead of Concentrating on the present?
7. Are you Accepting the character and the circumstances?

8. Are you Giving to the other actor and Receiving from him or her?
   a. Are you on the same level of energy? Is your partner above you, using more energy?
   b. Is your partner below you, using less energy?
9. Are you Relating?

Look for and see what you are doing so that you can improve. Study your scenes carefully, and don't fall into the trap of admiring yourself and overlooking what you are really doing.

4

Sight Reading

The enjoyment I get out of acting is the risk factor—that feeling of flying without a net.

Michael Douglas

How Sight Reading Works

Alicia arrives at her audition without being "prepared." Her normal habit on the night before an audition is to memorize the scene and analyze her character in sufficient depth for her to make the creative "choices" that enable her to plan exactly how she will perform the role the next day. But this time she was not able to prepare as usual because her dog had suffered an injury and she had taken him to the veterinarian—the shock and stress of which left her exhausted and upset. In the excitement, she had misplaced her sides. (Sides are pages from the script. The character you are auditioning for appears on these pages.)

The next morning, Alicia set off for her audition. "I'll get there early," she said to herself, "and memorize and study the script." At the casting director's waiting room, she picks up a fresh copy of the sides and has just finished reading the scene through once when she hears the casting assistant's voice: "Come on in, Alicia, the casting director wants to see you now."

Alicia goes into the casting director's office with few expectations. From reading the scene once, she knows what it is generally about, but that is all. She reads the role with the assistant casting director without ideas or planning. She glances at the script when she needs lines and watches the assistant for cues. First she laughs. The casting director looks stern, and tears come to Alicia's eyes. She feels fear, which translates into an unplanned experience. She is in jeopardy without any of her usual carefully planned defenses. The experience becomes real, and, consequently, she gives a truthful performance that is refreshing and creative.

The casting director sees that Alicia is having an experience and immediately takes her in to the producers. This has never happened to her before, and she is both surprised and delighted. She has stumbled on to a creative approach to auditioning. But the question is, will she recognize what she has done? Or will she go back to her old method of rehearsing and planning how she is going to deliver every line, saying to herself, "I'm really going to knock 'em dead on this one!"

Sight Reading and Cold Reading

Sight reading is often mistakenly called "cold reading." They appear to be similar, but there is a significant distinction between them. A cold reading is an audition for a scene in which the actor has not studied the script or done any preparation. Sight reading is a way of doing a cold reading and making it appear as if you had actually studied and prepared the scene beforehand. Sight reading is the process of glancing for less than a second at the script page, picking up a line, or even a whole paragraph of lines, then delivering them honestly and spontaneously while you look directly at the other actor. Learning to sight read skillfully frees you, gives you confidence, and allows you to trust your intuition. In this chapter, I am going to tell you how to become a skilled sight reader. It is the fastest way for you to have an emotional breakthrough and to showcase your personality. Developing this skill makes you emotionally available and capable of making any adjustments the director or casting director suggests. It makes the audition process not only exciting but enjoyable.

What Sight Reading Does

Becoming an effective sight reader allows you to concentrate on the other actor. When you look directly at her as you deliver your lines, your subconscious instantly captures any expression or physical change in her, letting you respond at will to anything and everything. It sharpens your awareness for nuances in the other actor's performance, and gives you freedom from dependence on the page. Mastering this ability will make you look professional in the audition.

Many times in my acting class, two actors will perform a scene so brilliantly that it looks planned and rehearsed. A visitor will ask, "How long did they work on that scene?" When I answer, "They read it just once, and we don't rehearse," the visitor looks at me in disbelief. When you realize that you are capable of doing the exact same thing through sight reading, you will have a whole new perspective on acting. But like any art it takes practice.

How to Sight Read

To sight read, glance at the dialogue for a second or less and immediately return to your point of focus on the other actor. In my class exercise, I ask you to glance at the line. No matter how little you grasp in that fraction of a second, immediately focus your eyes back on the other actor. Then say the words. It is unimportant whether you remember one word or a complete sentence. At this stage of the learning process, glance at the page, grasp as many words as you can, then quickly focus on your partner and say what you remember. When you have said all that you remember, take another glance and continue. Do not start saying a line until you have focused your attention fully on the other actor.

To practice sight reading, open a book to any page and hold it in front of you. Do not lay it in your lap. Pick a spot on the wall or some object as a point of focus at eye level. The preferred way to practice is to stand in front of a mirror, glance at the line in the book for a millisecond, then bring your eyes back to your point of focus, which is you. This forces you to make eye contact. Only when you are focused on that point, your eyes, say exactly what you have picked up from the page. Do not ad lib. Be exact. Do not try to comprehend the meaning, or grab more than you are capable of reading in a glance. Practice extends the number of words you can absorb each time. Remember, you cannot speak a single word of the line until your eyes are focused back on the reference point.

To be a good sight reader, practice ten minutes every morning and ten minutes every night. Sight reading is comparable to exercising any muscle in your body. If you want to stay in shape as an athlete, you work out three times a week. If you want to improve, you work out four times a week. If you want to be world class, you practice seven days a week, probably twice a day.

Actors, Artists, Athletes, Musicians, Writers

Disciplined practice makes you proficient. The late Walter Payton, a running back for the Chicago Bears, held the record for most yards gained in a season. He would run up a hill every day while dragging a log behind him to increase the strength of his leg muscles. Opposing players paid a price to tackle Walter Payton. Great musicians became what they are by practicing daily for hours. Writers do nothing but write. Artists are famous for living at the edge of starvation just so they can paint without interruption. All creative artists study and practice constantly. But, curiously, most aspiring actors do not seem to think they need the same kind of dedication and disciplined practice. But you do. There are many skills you need to practice every day to become a professional actor. Sight reading is just one of them.

A Word of Caution

When you practice your sight reading, your concentration tends to wane. You may find yourself engrossed in the book, rather than practicing the sight reading. Don't get discouraged or angry with yourself. Just bring your focus back to your point of concentration, and keep going.

Material for Practice

Read books when you practice sight reading. Do not practice with scripts, newspapers, or magazines. Novels are best because the sentences are longer than the lines of dialogue in a script, which forces your eyes and mind to work harder because you are picking up more information.

Importance of Sight Reading

If you have mastered sight reading, the casting agent or director quickly can determine that your film personality is right for the role, that you can take direction and relate. They want to know that are you a professional who can handle the job. Remember this: developing your talent depends on sight reading more than anything else I teach.

Sight reading can tap into your creativity. Reading the material only once coerces your logical brain to practice the Art of Not Knowing. This sharpens your intuition, which is the impetus that releases your creativity. Not Knowing puts you emotionally on the edge and gives you insight into the character that neither you nor the director knew existed. Only after the experience will you logically recognize the brilliance that occurred on an intuitive and spontaneous level.

Many actors think they can give a better audition performance by memorizing the sides. False. If you memorize the script, you often set or limit your intuitive performance. What happens when a director asks you to read for another role, right now? Can you work off the page? He may need the part cast in the next half-hour. That's not much time to prepare, but your job is to give the director a performance that will impress him. If you are fearful of sight reading and become anxious, your mind loses focus and you appear unprofessional. Mastering sight reading makes you self-confident and gives you the edge in auditions.

In a high-pressure sight-reading situation, a director can quickly learn a great deal about you as an actor and as a person. Are you spontaneous? If you are a skilled technical actor, you might look spontaneous the first time. But repeating the performance in the same way is a sign to the director that you are not relating. You are just a pretty good technician.

Second-Guessing the Director

You cannot second-guess the director. You may have had the script for a day or two, but the director on a feature film has probably worked on it for over a year. Any ideas you have about what the director wants can only be guesses. The best thing you can do in an audition is to relate spontaneously to the person you are reading with by concentrating on nuances and emotional changes. Trusting your sight reading allows you to relate and to respond to a director's adjustments.

Multiple Auditions

If you are scheduled for several commercial auditions a day, it's impossible to memorize, or even prepare, for that many parts. Sight reading is crucial. What do you do if the sides are available only at the casting session? If you arrive and are immediately escorted in with no time to prepare? If you have worked hard at your sight reading, you have nothing to worry about.

Let's return to Alicia and her experience at the beginning of the chapter. She discovered dramatically how effective sight reading is in a cold reading. But in all probability, she will go back to her old way of working, not understanding what happened in that audition. She may think it was luck, not talent, that brought her to the producers. But the casting director saw that she had an experience—a real experience—and that's what movies are all about.

Helpful Hints

1. To keep you from becoming engrossed in the book you have selected for sight-reading practice, set a kitchen timer at three-minute intervals to remind you to bring your focus back to sight reading. As your concentration improves, extend the time by thirty-second intervals.
2. Sight read books, not magazines or scripts.
3. Sight read material that interests you.
4. Discipline yourself to practice sight reading every day. Remember, this is your career.

Summary

1. The skill of sight reading is crucial to developing your intuition.
2. Sight reading gives you the edge over the competition in an audition because you can concentrate on the other actor instead of the page.
   a. It makes you look professional.
   b. It increases your self-confidence.
   c. It requires less time to prepare for the audition.
   d. It is the most effective way to stimulate your creative impulses.
   e. It helps you develop your Ability to Relate.

Actor Practice

Practice sight reading every day for ten minutes in the morning and ten minutes at night.

5

The Art of Concentration

It's the unpredictable. That's what Brando had. The ability to surprise you with whatever he would do. From moment to moment you never knew. But it always made sense.

James Caan

Concentration

The Art of Concentration means giving your full attention to what you are doing. Concentrating on the other actor lets you experience the moment without thinking about your emotions. This is the creative source of acting. Your audience enjoys and believes you only to the extent that you are emotionally connected to the other actor. When you feel an emotion, you are interesting, but when you pretend or act an emotion, you lose credibility.

To concentrate, fix your attention on the other actor. The extent of your concentration sets the limit of how good you will be. When you can't—or won't—concentrate fully, your performance will be boring. When you do concentrate with your whole being, your performance will be interesting. Learn to concentrate with your whole being. Whatever you do—javelin throwing, painting, racecar driving, acting—concentration puts your attention where it has to be for you to achieve excellence. It gives you access to your intuitive knowledge and energy, which results in spontaneous and creative performances. All the intellectual and logical garbage sloshing around inside your head is the stuff of poor performance, but you can control it through concentration.

Internal Rap

Internal rap is that constant conversation you carry on with yourself inside your head. It goes on all the time, except when you concentrate directly on a point of focus. It sounds like—"That red Porsche is sensational. I sure wish I had it." "What would you do with it?" "I'd put the top down and get that guy in the beer commercial and drive to Malibu." "Look at that sexy woman." "Well, suck in your stomach." "You should put more feeling in your lines." "What a cute guy." "My hair's a mess." "Knock 'em dead on your next speech, you can't miss." "I wonder how I'm coming across?" "When we do that scene again, I'm really gonna blow him out of the water." "Wow! I'm sure a good actor." "Wow! I'm sure a rotten actor." The rap goes on and on, and most of the time you're not aware you're doing it. Internal rap is the enemy of the Art of Concentration.

Call internal rap whatever you want—daydreaming, reminiscing, mental planning, thinking, solving problems—it stops yakking when you concentrate on the other actor. Internal rap is like one of those trick birthday candles that re-lights itself when you blow it out. The instant you allow the tiniest crack in your concentration, your internal rap jumps back in. That's when the prizefighter goes down for the count; that's when the runner knocks down the hurdle, the swimmer flubs her turn on the last lap, the race car driver crashes and burns; and that's when the actor looks fake. Champions—artists, writers, racecar drivers, musicians, athletes, actors—all became champions by learning to concentrate so intensely that their internal rap didn't stand a chance. When you halt the internal rap, your concentration becomes directed, and you are free to get on with giving a great performance. This is the Art of Concentration in film acting.

Interest Is the Focal Point of Concentration

The greater your interest in the other actor, the greater your awareness and the more directed your concentration. As your internal rap diminishes, the more truthful and intuitive you become.

It is possible, and we have all done it, to carry on a face-to-face conversation with a person to whom you are oblivious because you have not concentrated all your attention on him or her. This non-interest lets your internal rap babble on, and that's one reason we instantly forget people's names after being introduced. From now on, as a part of your actor's discipline, use your concentration to remember the name of every person introduced to you. When your interest is enhanced, the more aware you become of another person's hair, eyes, teeth, lips, complexion, clothing, attitude, emotions, body language, and name. You become sensitive to tone of voice, facial expressions, and physical being. Intense interest carries relating to a deeper level than speech alone; so, if you are to succeed at acting, at some point you have to tell your internal rap to shut the hell up.

When you truly concentrate on the situation and the other actor, you are "in the zone": your mind and body function intuitively instead of logically, and your performance seems to come from "inspiration." You are simultaneously relating on two levels—the conscious and the intuitive.

Feedback

What Richard Brestoff calls "the most precious exchange" with reference to fine acting is a description of the actor's version of what modern science refers to as a "feedback loop." He writes, "When actors have an effect on each other; when one action causes a reaction in the other, which causes a reaction in the first character, then the most precious exchange in the theater is taking place."

Your dialogue stimulates the other actor's responses—emotions, appearance, and actions—which are then fed back to you on the separate paths of seeing, listening, and touching. Then your responses are fed back to the other actor, and so on. With actors who concentrate, these responses affect each actor's subsequent responses throughout the scene. Remember what James Caan said about Marlon Brando: "From moment to moment you never knew. But it always made sense." That is, it always made sense to the actor who concentrated on Brando.

Emotions

Concentration of attention on the other person's emotions is the creative source of film acting. Through the Art of Concentration you experience the other actor's emotions with clarity. Human beings are always in some state of emotional experience, and your job is to deal with that experience:

1. Recognize the emotion that the other actor is experiencing—sadness, happiness, anger, love, fear.
2. Respond appropriately to that emotion.
3. On a subconscious level, don't let your logic or internal rap interfere with feedback from the other actor and the situation.

Yoshiko, a talented, bright actor, and Harry, a beginning student, are doing a scene in class. We see how Harry lets his internal rap turn his concentration away from Yoshiko.

```
(We pick up towards the end of the scene.)

                 YOSHIKO
        . . . the feeling is mutual. I
        mean it's not like we're
        engaged or anything . . . I
```

```
                    just want to be with you go to
                    a movie or dinner every now
                    and then . . .

                            HARRY
                    Hey! Let's get married. I'll
                    buy you a ring and give it to
                    you on Valentine's Day.

                            YOSHIKO
                    Valentine's Day, yeah . . . I
                    remember, making little heart-
                    shaped cards out of red con-
                    struction paper and mixing
                    water with flour to make glue.
                    Then everybody would exchange
                    candy. All the little boys
                    gave the girls candy kisses
                    and these little candy pastel-
                    colored hearts. . . .
```

(Tears begin to run down her cheeks.)

```
                            YOSHIKO
                    . . . and as usual, I didn't
                    get anything.
```

(Harry punches his next line.)

```
                            HARRY
                    TOUGH TIT!

                            YOSHIKO
                       (still crying)
                    You know that growing up was
                    different than . . .
```

JEREMIAH: **Harry, what is Yoshiko feeling?**

```
                            HARRY
              (to Jeremiah)
                    She is loving.
```

JEREMIAH: **Is she? If you were concentrating on her instead of on what's going on inside your head, your internal rap, you would see what she's feeling. Look again.**

```
(Harry looks at her, carefully.)

                    HARRY
(to Jeremiah)
          She's crying. But in the
          script, "TOUGH TIT" is in cap-
          itals. Meaning I should punch
          the words.
```

JEREMIAH: **Great! . . . and every other idiot who reads for the role is going to do exactly the same thing. How's the casting director going to see you as different? "Tough tit" is a cliché, but you don't have to play it as a cliché. Now if Yoshiko were three years old and crying, what would you do? Beat her up?**

```
                    HARRY
(to Jeremiah)
          I would probably give her a
          hug. Reassure her.
```

JEREMIAH: **Good, do that. Then say your dialogue.**

```
(Harry hugs Yoshiko. He closes his eyes and shakes his
head.)

                    HARRY
              (gentle and sad)
          Tough tit.
```

JEREMIAH: **Great!** (to the class) **This time he saw her pain and dealt with it. Harry says that line with the subtext of sadness that little boys can be real bastards. At the beginning, if he had been concentrating on how she felt instead of getting caught up in an internal rap about the script, he would have seen her pain.**

When actors concentrate on the feedback from each other's actions and emotions, the performances of both actors immediately improve. Actors become more in-the-moment and honest. It's simple, as Sandy Meisner says, it just takes years to get it.

Happiness, Sadness, Anger, Fear, Love

Although everyone is always experiencing one of the five emotions—happiness, sadness, anger, fear, love—each emotion can have variations. Love can be caring; it can be motherly love; it can be friendliness, sexual attraction, flirting, lust, or passion. Each is a manifestation of the emotion love.

The five primary emotions are the source of all your experiences, and it is possible to experience one or more emotions at a time. Recognizing another person's emotions can be difficult, but to be a good film actor, you have to develop the art of seeing and identifying emotions.

You cannot know what another person is thinking, but you can be aware of what he is experiencing. If he is crying, you don't know the reason for the tears, but you can see that he's crying. In this next scene, Michael is relating to Jane, but she is not responding to him.

```
                    MICHAEL
               (laughing)
          I've been here over an hour.
          The bus was supposed to be
          here 30 minutes ago. This is
          . . . Damn it.


                    JANE
          It's always on time.


                    MICHAEL
          This is not my day. I lost my
          cell phone. I think I left it
          with my mother. And I've got
          to meet somebody in 15 minutes
          and there's no way of getting
          in touch with him. Dang it.
          You never find a pay phone
          when you need one. I can't
          look because I'll miss the
          damn bus.


                    JANE
          It'll be here any minute.


                    MICHAEL
          I hate this. I haven't had any
          sleep. I'm on edge . . . I
          just left the hospital, my Mom.
          She's not doing very well.


                    JANE
          What's wrong with your Mother?


                    MICHAEL
          Cancer . . .
```

> JANE
> I'm sorry. Here, use mine.

She hands him a phone.

> MICHAEL
> Thanks.

JEREMIAH: **Jane, what is Michael feeling?**

> JANE
> (to Jeremiah)
> Well, I think he is angry that
> he's late, and emotionally
> upset. He is sad that his
> mother is dying of cancer.

JEREMIAH: **Can you read minds?**

> JANE
> (to Jeremiah)
> No, but I wish I could.

JEREMIAH: **So does everybody else. But acting isn't an exercise in psychic revelation, and it isn't a guessing game. If an actor is crying, you don't know what he's crying about unless he tells you why. You're guessing. What's important is that you see what he's feeling. I'm not concerned with what you think he *should* feel. Jane, do you see sadness on his face?**

(Jane pauses and looks at Michael, who looks lovingly at her.)

> JANE
> (to Jeremiah)
> Not now. But he was sad a
> moment ago.

JEREMIAH: **Jane do you remember hearing sadness in Michael's voice?**

> JANE
> (to Jeremiah)
> Not really.

JEREMIAH: **Or were there tears in his eyes?**

(Jane thinks and looks at the page.)

> JANE
>
> (to Jeremiah)
>> No. Maybe that's what I was
>> feeling—my mother just died of
>> cancer.

JEREMIAH: **I'm sorry to hear that. Do you want to continue with the scene?**

> JANE
>
> (to Jeremiah)
>> Of course.

JEREMIAH: **Then forget what you think. Allow yourself to deal with what is going on with Michael emotionally, not what you think should go on because of what the script says. What is Michael feeling?**

> JANE
>
> (to Jeremiah)
>> He is caring.

JEREMIAH: **Good! Caring and love are the same emotion. Now see his love, and forget about the dialogue.**

(Skip to end of scene.)

> JANE
> What's wrong with your Mother?

> MICHAEL
> Cancer . . .

> JANE
> I'm sorry. Here, use mine.

(Jane starts to cry.)

> MICHAEL
> Thanks.

> JANE
> I'm glad to help.

JEREMIAH: **Wow!** . . . (to the class) **When Jane saw Michael's love for his mother, she had a real emotional experience and started to cry.** (to Jane) **When you** concentrate on the other actor's emotions and stop thinking about the script, the dialogue takes you to another level. That was great. (to the class) Also, what if Jane hadn't told us her mother had just died of cancer? We would still get the idea that her tears were empathetic feelings about Michael's reaction to his own mother's cancer. You can't really know the reason for the other person's emotion. The only thing you can do is see and recognize it.

Learn to see and recognize which emotion is going on, and then respond to it. It is easy to recognize extreme emotions, like violent rage or roaring laughter. But it is more difficult to recognize and identify the subtle ones. An actor may be experiencing a strong emotion, yet outwardly showing only subtle signs. Don't be trapped into thinking she is not feeling anything, because there is always some sign: the eyes, the expression, the tremor or stillness in hands or muscles, physical position, the color and tone of the skin, even your intuition. There is always a clue to what a person is feeling, so concentrate and find it. To become a great actor, develop the skill of recognizing emotions to the point where you can recognize the emotions of a marble statue.

One emotion can successively give way to another and back again rapidly to the first emotion or to yet another emotion. Being a good film actor means seeing, identifying, and responding to these changes. When talented actors put their attention on their partners and are open to experience, then fasten your seat belts.

Two advanced students, Katy and Gary, are doing *The Closer*, written by Louis La Ruso and Robert Keats. Gary has found out that Katy has been seeing another man. Most actors would play the scene at high volume.

We pick up in the middle of the scene. Each has read the scene only once.

```
(Gary is intensely angry, but the anger is very subtle. You
can see it only in his eyes.)

                    GARY
              (extremely angry)
          Are you going to live with him?


                    KATY
              (angry, not loud)
          Yes. You stay here, if you
          want to.


                    GARY
          You did this the day we met.
          Let me hang myself for your
          amusement. Why didn't you tell
          me the second I walked in the
          door?
```

                    KATY
               (crying)
          I was scared. Because you're a
          coward.

                    GARY
               (starts to smile)
          You spoiled bitch. Are you
          dressed because you thought I
          might hit you? What do you
          think I am?

                    KATY
               (sobbing)
          I've been hit before.

                    GARY
          Not by me. Is he good?

                    KATY
          Don't do this.

(Gary's smile is sadistic. He is enjoying her pain.)

                    GARY
          Just answer the question. Is
          he good?

                    KATY
          Yes.

                    GARY
          Better than me?

                    KATY
          Different.

                    GARY
          Better?

(Katy, still crying, is affected by Gary's being amused at
her expense. She sneers at him. Then with glee in her face,
she fights back.)

                    KATY
               (smiles through the pain)
          Gentler.

```
                    GARY
          What does that mean?


                    KATY
          You know what it means.


                    GARY
          Tell me.


                    KATY
               (angry)
          No.
```

JEREMIAH: **Terrific!** (to class) **That's what you should be able to do in an audition. This scene looks like it has been rehearsed and planned out moment by moment. But they only read it once.**

```
                    KATY
     (to Jeremiah)
                    All I did was look at his
                    face. He was incredible. He
                    was feeling so much.
```

JEREMIAH: **That's the point. Both Gary and Katy are responding to feedback from each other. What each receives is stimulating their responses. It has nothing to do with making logical choices. Without rehearsal you don't have time to plan exactly what you are going to do.** (to Katy and Gary) **Did either of you know what you were going to experience in the scene?**

```
                    GARY
     (to Jeremiah)
                    I knew I was probably pissed
                    at her when I read the
                    material. But the moment she
                    said the first line and
                    smiled, I went postal.
```

JEREMIAH: **I can understand that, but what I found interesting is how she evoked other emotions in you. You seemed to get sadistic pleasure from the feedback you received from her.**

```
                    GARY
     (to Jeremiah)
                    I knew I was smiling, but I
                    didn't know that it was coming
```

```
across like that . . . Come to
think about it, I was enjoying
her pain.
```

Differentiating between the Emotions

Love, fear, and anger are each capable of stimulating a release of adrenaline into your body. When you think of or see your lover, adrenaline flows. Your heart rate goes up, you get excited, your hormones start pumping, and you become aroused. When you make an illegal U-turn and a flashing red light confronts you in the rear view mirror, your body gets a shot of adrenaline. Your heart rate goes up, you experience fear, and you want to flee. When the cop takes out his ticket book, you get angry. Such anger is usually directed inward—"Damn, why did I hang that U?" But it can also be directed outward, which is why police officers sometimes get shot writing traffic tickets. A police car chase starts with a red light in the rear view. Adrenaline pumps, the driver's instinct for fight-or-flight takes over, and away he goes. Adrenaline also fires up the batter's fight-or-flight instinct, and with murderous intent he goes after the pitcher who has just dusted his ear with a 98-mile-an-hour fastball.

Love, fear, and anger, which we classify as separate emotions, each puts us through the same adrenaline-induced physiological responses. Since we live in a civilized society, we have been taught from childhood not to act on our impulses. How you react depends on your personal situation and the circumstances. Good actors cultivate their intuition so they *can* act on impulses. This gives them great emotional resources in their film acting.

Love

Love is affection towards another person; warm feelings, caring. This feeling can range from kindness to intense sexual desire.

Anger

Anger is hostility towards any person or object, or towards oneself. This hostility can range from simple frustration to blind rage.

Fear

Fear is the fight-or-flight emotion that arises in the presence or anticipation of danger. It can render you unable to respond or it can put you into panic. Fear exists at a primitive level to protect you, and it can sometimes override the logical part of your mind. In acting, you experience fear in two ways: personal fear and character fear.

1. Personal fear. This is your own fear as a person, and you do not want it to be visible to the audience. Unlike the other emotions, which work on any level, personal fear can inhibit you. Personal fear comes from your concentration on yourself instead of on something outside of you, and it blocks you from feeling other emotions. If the other actor is personally afraid, help alleviate his fear so he can respond emotionally to you. Support him emotionally. Extend yourself with a hug. Hold his hand, stroke him, or talk to him softly. His focus will change. He will become more aware of you and less self-conscious. He will start to relate to you, and his performance will improve. When you embrace him emotionally, he will experience a level of shared feelings (intimacy) that allows the scene to work.

   When you are personally afraid, no matter how you act, the camera will unerringly pick it up, and on the screen you will look like nothing more than a scared actor. To get rid of personal fear concentrate on the other actor and turn it into workable energy.

2. Character fear. This is the fear your character experiences. To do this on film, you have to be truly afraid. If you try to fake it, the camera sees you as an actor trying to look frightened. Accept the circumstances.

Laughter and Sadness

Laughter and sadness both relieve emotional tension. Laughter relieves tension by explosion; sadness by surrender, letting go. The end result of both is to relieve tension, unlike the other emotions, which stimulate.

Laughter, which is an expression of being happy, is a fully extended emotion, ranging from a simple smile to uncontrolled laughing. In a scene where you have a slight smile but are not really laughing, "happy" is a more appropriate description. Of all the feelings, laughter is unique. It is a shared, contagious emotion.

Sometimes people laugh to avoid experiencing some other primary emotion. A man stumbles on the edge of a carpet and laughs. A newscaster bobbles a word and laughs. A girl giggles when she is called on to recite before the class. An actor chuckles when he looks into the eyes of his serious partner. All are using laughter to turn aside embarrassment or an uncomfortable emotion.

Brittany is a talented actress with a ready and natural smile. In the next scene she works with Joshua, whom she comforts after his father's death. The first time they do the scene, she smiles all the way through, which keeps her from dealing with the reality of the death of the father.

```
                    BRITTANY
          Would you like to take a walk?

(She is smiling supportively.)

                    JOSHUA
          Sure.

                    BRITTANY
          I'm very sorry about your
          father.

                    JOSHUA
          He had cancer. Everybody knew.

(She becomes sad but is smiling.)

                    BRITTANY
          I really liked him.
```

JEREMIAH: **Brittany, why are you smiling?**

```
                    BRITTANY
     (to Jeremiah)
          I want to be sympathetic.
```

JEREMIAH: **That's fine. But when you smile, smile only because you relate to Joshua, not because you're trying to be sympathetic—that's your logic at work. You were smiling even before you started. You're avoiding the reality of the death. If you have the impulse to smile because of what you get from Joshua, smile. You can even laugh if that's what you feel. Take it again from your last line.**

```
                    BRITTANY
          I really liked him.

                    JOSHUA
          Everybody did. I'll miss him,
          but I'm glad that it is over.
          He didn't suffer much.

                    BRITTANY
          He was lucky.
```

> JOSHUA
> He really liked you. He always
> thought that I should have
> married you, instead of
> Joanna. He liked you better.

> BRITTANY
> You should have married me. We
> would have had beautiful kids.

(They both start to laugh. It is spontaneous and comes from their relating to each other.)

> JOSHUA
> I hate ugly kids.

> BRITTANY
> So do I.

> JOSHUA
> Thanks for coming to the
> funeral.

(Tears come to her eyes. She has acknowledged the death and her own emotion.)

> BRITTANY
> I needed to tell you that I
> love you. I loved your dad
> too.

> JOSHUA
> I still love you.

JEREMIAH: (to the class) **Once Brittany stopped smiling for no reason except to protect herself, she had nowhere to hide. Then Joshua's father's death hit her right between the eyes. She dealt with it and had a strong emotional experience.**

Sadness is the emotion of sorrow, unhappiness, or pain, usually followed by tears. It can range from slight disappointment to uncontrollable crying, which is difficult to do when you want to do it. Some actors have more access to their tears than others. Sometimes chemicals are used to induce tears, or glycerin to make tear drops. These tactics work at times, but nothing can substitute for the real experience.

The emotions you experience can and will vary in intensity, energy, and spontaneity depending on your personality. Some actors have logical control over most of their emotions, but great actors don't have any constraints.

Focused Concentration

Concentration of attention on the other actor's emotions—happiness, sadness, anger, fear, love—is the creative source of film acting. Placing your concentration on the other actor's emotions gives you a specific point of focus. David Mamet said that the actor who thrills the viewers is the one who "behaves with no regard to his personal state, but with all regard for the responses of his antagonists." When you disregard concentration, you lose your connection with the other actor. You then stop relating and become mediocre, or worse.

How to Increase Your Concentration

Seeing

See and respond to the other actor's emotional changes. If your partner changes emotionally, react with an equal or greater level of energy to her change. This doesn't mean that you should go through a lot of gyrations or facial expressions. If you have an emotional experience, you don't have to *do* anything, because that experience will come through to the other actor, and, more importantly, to your audience. As you get better at seeing with a child's eyes, you will respond more and more intuitively.

One of my favorite moments is in the film *Legends of the Fall* with Brad Pitt. Pitt's character, returning after the first World War, rides up the hill toward the ranch. The ranch hand sees him in the distance and calls to the colonel, played by Anthony Hopkins; Julia Ormond and Aidan Quinn, who plays Pitt's brother, each experience an emotion that we see and understand. They do this without words, facial gymnastics, or silly indications. They actually experience the emotions, and we see them.

```
(Close-up. The Indian ranch hand hears the horses. He turns
and looks over the hill. The other ranch hand sees the
Indian and also turns.)

                    RANCH HAND
          Colonel.

(He points out the distant figure on horseback, and they
look with anticipation as Pitt approaches the ranch house.)
```

CLOSE ON JULIA ORMOND

(She watches Pitt through the screen door. We see the internal experience she is having, and we know that she is in
love with Pitt. Quinn comes down the steps, unaware that his
brother has returned.)

CLOSE ON QUINN

                         QUINN
        I'm going to town . . . it's a
        . . .

(He stops in midsentence when he sees Ormond staring out the
window. He sees what she is feeling and realizes she is in
love with his brother.)

(Quinn feels disappointment, and we see it. When Ormond
becomes aware of his presence, she turns and looks at him.
She is ashamed of her feelings, lowers her head, and runs up
the stairway. Quinn looks out the screen door toward his
brother.)

This scene is a perfect example of truly seeing. Each actor intently sees
what is going on with the other, and, without words, each has an emotional
experience that is clearly communicated to the audience.

Listening

Sharpening your listening sense almost instantly increases your
effectiveness as an actor. Listen, really listen, to everything the other actor says.
Force yourself to listen. Hear the tone of his voice. Is he louder or softer than I
am? Am I responding to his emotional tone? Listen as a young child listens.

In *As Good As It Gets*, Jack Nicholson plays an obsessive-compulsive man.
He is sitting alone in a restaurant and takes out his plastic eating utensils.
Helen Hunt, who plays a waitress in the restaurant, interacts with Nicholson.
When you view this scene, watch how the talented Nicholson is absorbed in lis-
tening to Hunt's tone and inflection.

                         HUNT
        Are you afraid you'll die if
        you eat with our silverware?

>   NICHOLSON
>   We're all going to die. I'm
>   going to die, you're going to
>   die, and it sure sounds like
>   your son is going to die.

(Hunt stares at Nicholson. Silence. Nicholson looks up,
realizing he has made a mistake.)

>   HUNT
>   If you ever mention my son
>   again you will never be able
>   to eat here.

(Watch Nicholson's reaction as he listens to her. He is
frightened. He can't talk. But he listens.)

>   HUNT
>   Do you understand?

(Nicholson listens to her so intently that he is transfixed.
We have no doubt that he really and truly hears her every
word and sees her emotion.)

>   HUNT
>   Do you understand me you crazy
>   . . . ?

(Nicholson is speechless. He listens so intently, it is a
struggle for him to speak.)

>   HUNT
>   Do you?

>   NICHOLSON
>   (struggling)
>   Hun . . . Yes

>   HUNT
>   Okay . . . I'll get your eggs.

Touching

Touch relaxes you and invokes intimacy. Touch heightens your
awareness of the other actor and allows you to believe what she is saying or

doing. Often, in class, two actors doing a scene will be a little stiff or un-relating. Then one of them touches the other on the arm, and you can see them both instantly relax and become intimate. Almost always, a scene goes better if in some way you touch the other actor or she touches you. Touching focuses your concentration and releases your inhibitions. The actual root meaning of "acting" means "to do," "to carry out an action." Physical movement, which includes touching, can evoke an emotional response.

At the climax of *As Good As It Gets*, Nicholson kisses Hunt. It is an unemotional kiss and not very exciting. Nicholson takes a moment, then—

NICHOLSON
I can do better than that.

Nicholson's second kiss is spontaneous; he caresses her hair and shoulders. The touch tells us that he cares for her. The touch works on a subconscious level and tells the audience more than the kiss.

Physical and Emotional Copying

Mimicking another actor by exactly duplicating his emotional and physical responses as he experiences them keeps you focused on him. It stimulates you. Copying like this is extremely effective when you are first learning the Relating Exercise because it forces you to concentrate and relate. In *Duck Soup*, Groucho Marx does a vaudeville act with his brother, Harpo. Both of them are dressed identically and stand facing each other; between them stands an empty frame representing a mirror. As Groucho moves, Harpo exactly mimics his movements to make it appear as if he is a mirror reflection. It is a brilliant piece of comedy. They copy each other's movements perfectly until the payoff when Groucho drops his hat.

Mimicking makes you a participant, not an observer. It forces you to engage the other actor, physically and emotionally. Trying to mimic exactly another actor's every movement and expression makes you concentrate on that actor to the total exclusion of everything else. In every scene you do, concentrate to that extent when you see, listen, and touch.

Summary

Concentration of attention on the other person's emotions—sadness, happiness, anger, fear, love—is the creative source of film acting. Learn to differentiate between these emotions through the Art of Concentration.

Actor Practice

Seeing

1. In class, watch each scene and identify what the other actors are feeling.
2. Watch movies. Pay attention to how actors express feelings without words.

Listening

3. At night when everyone is asleep, turn out the light and listen for as many different sounds as you can.
4. During the day shut your eyes and see how many sounds you can hear and identify.
5. During conversation, listen to yours and your partner's vocal levels. You will probably find that your vocal level matches that of the person you are with and that of the situation. Purposely raise or drop the level and notice the difference in response.
   a. In bed
   b. In a living room
   c. In a ball park or football stadium
   d. In a movie theater
   e. In a car (parked, driving)
   f. In a restaurant
6. In comedies, watch when an actor imitates another actor. It usually evokes laughter.
7. Stand in front of a mirror and do a mirror exercise with yourself. Do it long enough for the image in the mirror to lead you.

Touching

8. Sit with a loved one and say something intimate like "I think you are beautiful." Now touch the person and say the same thing. Notice the response.
9. Study the body language of others when they are feeling emotions—sadness, happiness, anger, love, fear.
10. Constantly watch people, and develop the ability to recognize the emotion that each individual is feeling.
11. From now on, concentrate on and be interested in anyone you are introduced to—and remember the name.

6

The Art of Not Knowing

In acting, it's best if you really don't know.

Jack Nicholson

Everything Happens As If for the First Time

The Art of Not Knowing is reacting to every experience *as if it were happening for the first time.* Even though you think you know what is going to happen in a scene, you don't know, and you don't want to know. Because when you figure out ahead of time how you are going to act in your scene, you put a limit on your own creativity and will most likely give a mediocre performance. So don't try to figure it out ahead of time.

A personal idea is any bias not directly related to the reality of the scene, and it will stifle your potential for having a creative experience. Through Not Knowing you become free of personal ideas. Judgment, which is one form of a personal idea, stops you from clearly seeing what the other actor is feeling or doing. When you judge, you prevent yourself from getting emotionally involved. And when you are not emotionally involved, your performance suffers.

Judgment

Personal judgment ruins a scene. Kim, a volatile and generally open actress, is doing a scene in the workshop. She is working on *Demo* by Barbara Bowen, with Adam, an outrageous actor. By outrageous I mean you never know what he is going to do next, a great quality that makes for great actors. At an intense point in the scene, Adam makes an obscene gesture. Kim (the person, not the character) is offended, but she ignores her real feelings.

                              KIM
                        (caring)
                . . . I think that's the cause
                of our problem.

                              ADAM
                Do we have to talk about this
                now?

                              KIM
                        (caring)
                When are we supposed to talk
                about it?

                              ADAM
                        (angry)
                Later, okay?

JEREMIAH: Adam, what is Kim feeling?

                              ADAM
        (to Jeremiah)
                She is being a bitch to me.

        (He looks at her for a moment.)

                              ADAM
        (to Jeremiah)
                Damn it! You're right, I'm in
                my head. She's loving.

                              KIM
                        (loving)
                No, it's not okay. You keep
                saying later and later never
                happens.

                              ADAM
                        (coming on to Kim)
                Kim, this report is due by
                tomorrow morning.

        (Kim keeps her eye on the page and reads her lines. Kim
        never looks at Adam. Adam yawns.)

```
                    KIM
        I'm having a tough day, a
        tough week, a rotten month,
        and I need you . . .
```

JEREMIAH: **Kim, what did Adam just do?**

```
                    KIM
        He is putting the moves on me.
```

JEREMIAH: **Your concentration was on the page, not on Adam. You missed what he did. He yawned.**

```
(Adam, continuing the scene, picks up her hand and kisses
it.)
```

```
                    ADAM
              (coming on to Kim)
        I'm not like you, I don't ana-
        lyze things to death.
```

```
(Kim smiles then continues. But when she says her next line
she gets angry and pulls her hand away.)
```

```
                    KIM
        You're supposed to be my best
        friend, you're my husband. I
        need to talk to you, but
        you're never available.
```

JEREMIAH: **Kim, what did Adam do to make you angry?**

```
                    KIM
(to Jeremiah)
              He never communicates. He's
              always too busy working.
```

JEREMIAH: **Forget that. That's coming from the script. I want you to relate to Adam. What is he feeling. He's loving, right?**

```
                    KIM
(to Jeremiah)
              Yes, but my mother has breast
              cancer and I'm not interested
              in him being loving. I want to
              talk.
```

JEREMIAH: **I understand that, but respond to his feelings.**

(Scene continues.)

> ADAM
> (loving)
> I'm available, just not now.

> KIM
> Then when?
> (pause)
> You're never there for me.
> It's taken this long to real-
> ize it. You wouldn't need to
> talk about your mother having
> breast cancer?

> ADAM
> No way, that's personal
> between you and your mother.

> KIM
> That's my point. It is
> personal. It's part of my
> life. I'm upset about it. I'm
> on eggshells when my mother
> and I talk.

> ADAM
> You'll figure it out. You
> always do.

> KIM
> It's getting to me, Adam. I
> need to off-load some pressure
> and I want to do it with you.
> I need to talk. It's who I am.

(Adam goes to kiss Kim, but she rejects him by putting her
hand on his chest and pushing him away.)

> ADAM
> (angry)
> Sure you do. But I can't right
> now. This report is due by
> tomorrow. You're just overre-
> acting.

(Kim reads her lines without looking at Adam. Her performance is bad.)

                    KIM
          Overreacting?

(Adam responds by making a masturbation gesture. The class laughs.)

                    KIM
          Do you remember when your
          brother got hit by the car?
          Your mother was calling at all
          hours. You were there for her.

(She is still not looking at him. Although he is not saying anything, his action tells us how he feels about Kim's directing her lines to the page instead of to him.)

JEREMIAH: **Kim, what is Adam doing?**

(Kim looks up. It registers. The class laughs. Kim picks up on the laughter.)

(Even though she is laughing, she is angry and suppressing it.)

(Kim continues. She's still not dealing with Adam, and she's still not dealing with her anger.)

                    KIM
             (not looking at Adam)
          Maybe, but you coped at the
          time. You needed sex, I gave it
          to you. Now I needed you to
          listen. Can't you do what I'm
          asking? Don't you love me
          enough? What if, God forbid,
          something should go wrong, my
          mother is your family too . . .

JEREMIAH: **Kim, what is Adam doing?**

                    KIM
       (to Jeremiah)
          He's being obscene.

JEREMIAH: **How does it make you feel?**

```
                        KIM
    (to Jeremiah)
               I'm not going to work with him
               anymore. It's degrading.
```

JEREMIAH: **You're letting a personal idea take control. Use your lines and take out your anger on Adam. Let him have it!**

```
                        KIM
    (to Jeremiah)
               I'm not angry.

    (We can see her seething anger, but she tries to ignore it
    instead of using it.)
```

JEREMIAH: (to class) **See how angry she is?**

The class can see her anger. It's obvious.

JEREMIAH: **Kim, I want you to yell your next line at Adam.**

It took several tries before Kim touched the core of her anger. The anger forced Kim to deal with Adam and get past her personal reaction of "I'm not going to work with him anymore. It's degrading."

Practicing the Art of Not Knowing often leads to unexpected brilliance. Your subconscious mind, along with the material, can take you to some wonderful places. Kim did not know that Adam was going to make the gesture he did. It was a great opportunity to be brilliant by truly reacting through her lines as her character, not as herself.

Kim took herself out of the scene by letting her personal judgment block her emotional response to Adam. She has a belief system; part of her identity is tied into it. Her personal opinion of that obscene gesture took over and stifled her emotions. I know she is religious. Some of the anger could have been self-directed because she was laughing at Adam, which, in her mind, would not be an appropriate response. Had she immediately dealt with the situation as the character—using the words of the script and responding emotionally—it would not have become personal. She then would have had an unplanned experience. But she bogged down with her self-restricting personal judgment of Adam's action. When an actor does something in a scene that is offensive to you, let your character acknowledge it, allow it to affect you, respond to it as the character not as you yourself, and then forget it.

Being Intimate without Taking It Personally

Be intimate without having your own personal ideas, opinions, beliefs, stereotypes, generalizations, or judgments override the present experience. Make all your reactions in response to the content you receive from the other actor's dialogue and action. In the preceding scene, Kim, the actress, allowed Kim, the person, to take over the scene by making an irrelevant personal judgment about obscene gestures. She ignored Adam's emotions. The result: Kim came across as unbelievable and amateurish.

Beginner's Mind and Logical Mind

You have two minds—your beginner's mind and your logical mind. Your beginner's mind sees, smells, hears, touches, and tastes everything with curiosity, wonder, and excitement. It is clear and uncluttered. Your logical mind has rules and always tries to be in control. Your beginner's mind is curious. Your logical mind thinks it knows everything. Your beginner's mind does not know, but is willing to discover. Your logical mind has a history, which means that everything it thinks is tainted by the past. Your beginner's mind has no preconceptions and sees things as they really are. It is childlike in the best sense, just as children under the age of two are totally experiential. A baby who is attracted to a tin cup looks at it without judging it, picks it up, smells it, tastes it, drops it, grabs it again, loses interest, and moves on to another object. In her first year, a baby, through pure experience, learns half of everything she will learn in her entire life. Think of your beginner's mind as the mind of a child, open to all the possibilities, nonjudgmental and playful. Your beginner's mind has all the qualities you need to be a great actor.

Let your beginner's mind make you a good actor. Get rid of personal ideas—opinions, beliefs, judgments, or generalizations based on your past experiences—and anything related to your thinking. Personal ideas hinder you from using your beginner's mind, and they limit your potential emotional experience.

After the Scene, Forget It

In the 1977 television series *Roots*, Marlon Brando plays Norman Rockwell, the former head of a Neo-Nazi party. He is a cruel, hate-ridden racist, and Brando, doing his usual brilliant job of acting, makes us believe him. In real life, Brando is a fighter against injustice and has vigorously opposed the discrimination and mistreatment of American Indians and African Americans. But for the demands of his role, unlike Kim in her scene, he disregards his own personal ideas and allows racial hate and prejudice to fuel his role. He plays counter to his own professed belief. Then forgets it.

Put aside all your personal ideas unless a specific emotion or result is demanded from you. This is a business. Show Business. On demand, you have to give what directors ask of you. To trigger an emotion, use anything and everything—a physical action, your imagination, even a past experience. But if you do use a past experience, let go of it the instant you start relating to the other actor, because in recalling an experience, you may become so involved with yourself that you stop relating. I'm sure someone somewhere can use emotional memory effectively. But in film scenes, I ask my actors for intimate, personal, and unplanned experiences. Don't let opinions and beliefs affect you to the point where you are closed and unreceptive to anything that may happen in a scene.

Opinions and Beliefs Will Destroy You

Opinions are conclusions you hold with confidence, but not necessarily substantiated by positive knowledge or proof. Opinions are changeable. Kim's opinion of Adam was that he acted like a degenerate when he made that obscene gesture. Her opinion might have changed had she realized that he was angered by the nasty tone of her voice and her ignoring him, and he impulsively reacted with an obscene gesture.

Beliefs are convictions you hold as true. Your mind is made up with no room for variation. Beliefs are usually based in religious, political, racial, or cultural ideas that have become part of your personal identity. Beliefs leave you without options and are death to your creativity. Let's say that Kim is strongly religious and believes that anyone who uses an obscene gesture has no moral character. By refusing to work with Adam because she believes he is immoral, she limits her potential. The Japanese Kamikaze pilot of World War II believed he would go to heaven if he intentionally crashed his airplane into an American warship. His belief left him no option. When you are locked into a belief, you eliminate all other creative alternatives. Whatever you do, don't let opinions and beliefs affect you to the extent that you are closed and unreceptive to anything that may happen in a scene.

Play the Character, Not the Stereotype

Stereotypes and generalizations are oversimplifications: all American businessmen are ugly Americans; all Italians are great lovers; all Japanese males are Kamikazes; white men can't jump; black men can jump and have good rhythm; all Arabs are terrorists; all Irishmen are drunks; everybody from Sweden has blue eyes and blond hair; all lawyers are lying scumbags. These are stereotypes and generalizations, and they are wrong. Prejudices are based on stereotyping and lead to categorizing people as a whole, rather than individually. When you stereotype a person and don't see him as a unique individual, you see him as an unchangeable block of characteristics. Each person in this world is an individual with his or her own unique character. Play the character, not the stereotype.

Go Beyond the Stereotype

Two actors are doing a scene from *Raging Bull*. Harry plays Jake La Motta (played by Robert De Niro in the movie) and Michael plays his brother. Harry decides to do a New York accent along with his imitation of Robert De Niro.

HARRY
What is this kiss on the mouth
shit?

MICHAEL
What? I just said hello. Since
when I can't kiss my sister-
in-law?

HARRY
Ain't a cheek ever good enough
for you? I never even kissed
Mama on the mouth.

JEREMIAH: **Harry, that is very interesting—are you from New York?**

HARRY
No, I'm from Illinois. But I
spent two week there about
three years ago.

JEREMIAH: **A whole two weeks—Wow! You must be an expert on a New York accent.**

HARRY
Well, the character is from
New York.

JEREMIAH: **That's true. If you can do a New York accent or any accent off the top of you head with no preparation, do it; but it shouldn't interfere with your**

acting. The accent must be believable, and not clash with your ability to relate to another actor. And another thing—stop trying to imitate De Niro.

```
                    HARRY
        Well maybe De Niro was trying
        to imitate me.
            (class laughs)
        I can't get De Niro out of my
        head doing this role. I keep
        seeing his performance.
```

JEREMIAH: **De Niro did an excellent job in this role, but I'm trying to get you to be emotionally expressive. You're doing a stereotypical New York character. You have an image of how Jake should act. Let's see if you can forget that and relate to the imaginary character and the situation with your brother. What is he feeling?**

```
                    HARRY
        He is angry.
```

JEREMIAH: **Then forget about the accent and De Niro and deal with you brother's anger.**

When Harry did the scene again he expressed genuine anger at his brother Joey, and the scene worked.

JEREMIAH: (to the class) **What Harry was doing was a stereotypical characterization of a New York tough guy. If we want a New York tough guy, we will hire De Niro. But if you give me a guy from Illinois who emotionally relates to his brother, I might think of changing the character from New York to Chicago.**

Actors tend to stereotype when they play priests, nuns, police officers, professors, psychiatrists, and ethnic characters. And why not? It's easy to let the broad Irish brogue or the uniform or the beard carry your performance. The audience may sometimes think you're clever even though you lose the emotional essence of the real person and give a mediocre performance. Stereotypes and generalizations simplify the massive amount of information you are faced with in life. To avoid stereotypes, intently observe all kinds of individual people as they work, as they go about their working and playing. Stereotypes save you time and energy, but they cause you to overlook the essence of everything.

Judgment Is a Trap

Judgment is your ability to use your logic and common sense to make decisions based on past experiences. It is your mental capacity to discriminate, and it protects you from repeatedly making mistakes. For you, the actor, judgment restricts your ability to see all the choices open to you. In both life and acting, your judgment may not always be correct. In acting, judgment limits your ability to use your beginner's mind.

Let's say you are doing a serious scene and the other actor has the giggles. He giggles when he starts a line and sometimes giggles in the middle of one. He delivers his lines as if reading them. He doesn't look at you. You make the judgment that he is ruining the scene. But don't look at the director and say, "Can we start this scene over?" Deal with the actor as he is. If he makes you angry, don't ignore it. Let the anger come out in your lines. If you think he is funny, laugh. React to him the same way you would react to the same behavior in life, but use the lines of the script.

Become Aware of What Is

Put aside all your personal judgments and interpretations and become aware of what is. See the reality of the experience. When you judge the other actor, or when you are closed to his emotional experience, your performance will be mediocre, or worse. Kim's performance in the earlier scene was bad because she did just that—she judged Adam and was closed to his experience. Disbelieving what your fellow actor is doing in a scene is a judgment. If he gives you line readings, or you do not believe his acting, accept the response as if it were really happening. It *is* happening, so use whatever you are getting. Would you laugh, be sarcastic, get angry? Do what comes instinctively. Respond immediately, and do not judge your response. Deal with what he is giving you, because disbelieving him is trying to make him responsible for your inability to accept his feelings.

Leave Your Feelings on the Set

When you fall in love in a scene, you have experienced genuine feelings for the other actor. Everything you do while you are acting then becomes personal. The pain, happiness, sadness, anger, fear, and love are real. But because acting is your art form, with your imagination and creative talent at work, give up your feelings when the scene is over. You cannot take it home or take it personally. Keep your ego out of it and leave all personal experiences on the set when you walk off.

Self-Criticism

Self-criticism inhibits your creative thinking. When you think to yourself or hear yourself say to someone about your performance, "That's no good. That will never work," you inhibit both the other actor's creativity and your own. You are not allowing yourself the possibility of that experience. Self-criticism is a form of judgment—self-judgment—that stifles your imaginative flow.

Two students finish a scene.

JEREMIAH: **That was excellent.**

(Zahn, a talented actor, turns toward me and makes a face.)

JEREMIAH: **Zahn, what is that face for? Why are you acting so disappointed?**

> ZAHN
> My work sucks. Don't tell me it was any good. I didn't feel any emotion. I missed the whole thing.

JEREMIAH: **Zahn, when do you know that you have been burned, when you pick up the frying pan or when you have dropped it?**

> ZAHN
> After you let go of it.

JEREMIAH: **That's right. You have already been burned by the time you let go. You don't register the experience until after the fact. That's the same thing with acting. If you are truly experiencing the moment, you won't know until after the experience. Oftentimes we think what we did didn't work, but our own personal judgments aren't always accurate. Go and look at the video and you will see that although it was not a dramatic scene, you and your partner Patricia were emotionally connected and worked moment to moment. The work was interesting and professional.**

Professional actors don't make negative comments about their work, so stop judging and accept your experience. It is what it is, nothing more or less. You did it and you did your best. Nothing is perfect. Strive for perfection in a positive way by accepting your experience. So, when a director says, "Cut! That was great!" accept it. The director and the producers have enough to worry about. They don't need an insecure actor. Always smile and say thank you.

Use Your Beginner's Mind to Not Know

The Art of Not Knowing means experiencing the beginner's mind. Your every experience in a scene should be *as if for the first time*. By clearing your mind of all personal ideas, you begin in the state of *tabula rasa*, the unwritten slate. Not Knowing is the ultimate approach for achieving spontaneous acting. It allows your subconscious to surprise you. Not knowing ahead of time how you are going to play the scene lets you discover moments in acting you could never conceive of logically. It is these moments that carry you through to a great performance.

Summary

1. Eliminate all outside personal ideas: opinions, beliefs, stereotypes, generalizations, and judgments.
2. Look at the other actor—really look—and ask yourself, "What is she experiencing?" Then deal with that.
3. Be open to all creative possibilities by using your beginner's mind.
4. Do not know ahead of time. Stop planning.
5. Observe people.

Actor Practice

Great actors spend a lot of their time watching other people. Regularly go out and observe people—in a restaurant or bar, at a party, in school, at the theater, or wherever. Choose an individual and mentally jot down the following: Who is that person, really? Race. Nationality. Age. Height. Weight. Eye color. Occupation. Status (money, society, occupation). Car. Where does he/she live? How do you react to him/her and why? What is your opinion of him/her? What are his/her personal characteristics? How does he/she move, walk, talk, work, interact with other people? Both see and imagine who he/she really is as a person. Don't allow yourself to judge or stereotype. Imagine what it would be like to be that person. Be discreet, because some people are touchy about being scrutinized and may act unpredictably.

7
More on the Art of Not Knowing

The thing is to become a master and in your old age acquire the courage to do what children did when they knew nothing.

Henry Miller

The First Time

The Art of Not Knowing means experiencing something as if for the first time. You may have memorized a scene and know what is going to happen, but you mustn't know. You have to experience the scene's events and dialogue as if for the first time. In a state of Not Knowing, your true emotional responses become stimulated by using the other actor as a catalyst.

I was working with a writer who wanted to see how a few scenes from his new comedy screenplay would work. Brena played the part of the widow who had just returned from a funeral after burying her husband. John played a young man who accompanies her home. The writer considered his play a comedy. He thought this was a really funny scene.

```
(The two actors laugh as they walk into the apartment. John
follows the script direction and is laughing. Brena is shak-
ing and seems fearful.)

                      JOHN
           How do you stop people from
           bugging you about getting
           married?

                      BRENA
               (laughing)
           Do I have to answer? Old Aunts
           used to come up to me at
           weddings, poke me in the ribs,
```

```
                    cackle, and tell me, "You're
                    next." They stopped after I
                    started doing the same thing
                    to them at funerals.
                        (starts to cry)
                    Okay, how can you tell when a
                    blond is making chocolate-chip
                    cookies in your kitchen?
```

(John reaches over and hugs Brena.)

```
                         JOHN
                    I don't know.
```

```
                         BRENA
                        (crying)
                    You find M&M shells all over
                    the floor.
```

(John starts to laugh and Brena's tears change to a smile.)

```
                         BRENA
                    Thanks for the ride.
```

```
                         JOHN
                    You're welcome.
```

(Brena breaks out of character.)

```
                         BRENA
        (to Jeremiah)
                    This is a comedy. I shouldn't
                    be crying.
```

JEREMIAH: Yes, it is a comedy, but stop judging and trust your intuition. You didn't expect to cry. Did you? Then trust yourself, let us see your pain.

```
                         BRENA
        (to Jeremiah)
                    But the material should be
                    light and fun.
```

JEREMIAH: Who says? Now let's look at the scene dramatically. Your husband has just died. That's a traumatic experience for any wife.

                          BRENA
(to Jeremiah)
              But she's trying to seduce
              John, not cry all over him.

JEREMIAH: **That's correct. But intuitively something deeper is going on. The seduction is on the surface. Underneath is your character's pain, your loneliness, and fear. Which is exactly what a woman who has been married for several years would feel being with a strange man. What's going on in your character's mind? Is she afraid? What is she thinking? "Does he think I'm attractive? Is he going to make the first move or should I? What if he rejects me? He's handsome. I need someone." Brena, keep going—trust yourself.**

(They continue the scene.)

                          BRENA
              What would you like to drink?

                          JOHN
              No. I'm fine.

                          BRENA
              I'm going to have a scotch on
              the rocks, and you?

                          JOHN
              Nothing, thanks. I have to be
              going.

                          BRENA
              Please stay for a few moments.
              You smell like Harry. That's
              why I let you pick me up.

                          JOHN
              But you asked me for a ride. I
              thought you needed a lift.

(Brena moves very close to John and strokes his face.)

                          BRENA
              I need a lift.

(Brena kisses John.)

                        BRENA
        Harry.

                        JOHN
        Harry?

                        BRENA
        Your eyes remind me of Harry.

                        JOHN
        I'm John.

                        BRENA
        And you smell just like him.

                        JOHN
        Who, Harry? . . . wait a
        minute, isn't he the guy we
        buried?

                        BRENA
            (laughing)
        Yes.

(John interrupts the scene.)

                        JOHN
        (to Jeremiah)
            Why is she laughing?

JEREMIAH: **Just go with the laughter. Don't judge.**

Again, Brena's subconscious is leading her in the right direction. The laughter is an escape from pain and depression.

(John starts to laugh along with Brena.)

                        JOHN
        Holy Smokes . . . Harry is
        your husband. We just buried
        Harry. I was doing a favor for
        my mother, escorting her to
        the funeral. I had no idea
        that he was your husband. You
        were the one who hinted you
        needed a lift.

> BRENA
> I am very grateful.

(Cut to end of scene)

> BRENA
> (to Jeremiah)
> But why was I crying?

JEREMIAH: **Once you have read the material, your subconscious mind knows how you should feel. Your logical mind doesn't care how you feel and it doesn't have a clue, because it's only concerned with logical results. Your subconscious gives creative answers that you don't expect. Your subconscious—your intuition—gave you your tears. That's the Art of Not Knowing, Brena. Remember, you just buried your husband. I think you were brilliant. Thank you.**

> BRENA
> (to Jeremiah)
> But it's a comedy.

JEREMIAH: **So.**

> BRENA
> (to Jeremiah)
> But in the script it says I
> married him for money.

JEREMIAH: **That's a fact. But what we are interested in is your feeling for Harry, not what you think about the script. The writer does the thinking, you do the experiencing.**

This is a perfect example of the Art of Not Knowing. It is the subconscious leading your performance. Scary isn't it? That you can read a piece of material once and come up with a performance that surprises you. It's because, one, you have been acting all your life, so you have a reservoir of emotions and experience stored away in your subconscious. And, two, the subconscious is much more creative than your logical brain. The only problem is access. Not Knowing is one way to touch your subconscious. Not Knowing puts you in danger, heightens your awareness, and stimulates your emotional reservoir. This is what happened to Brena. She let her intuition override her ideas, and the result was a brilliant performance. Her tears gave us insight into her relationship with her dead husband. The laughter on the line, "We just buried your husband," allowed her to break the heaviness of the situation by laughing, which led her into the seduction of John. That's the creative process. It happened without her thinking about it. It's automatic and came from her subconscious, not the logical part of her brain. You could work for days trying to logically construct how to play the scene, yet still not arrive at an answer that will work as creatively as Brena's did.

In the scene below imagine that you are Susan Sarandon. How would you prepare and what would you plan to do? In the movie *White Palace*, Susan Sarandon and James Spader are talking. Spader tells her his wife died. (Here and everywhere in this book, actions in parentheses are not script directions. They are what the actors actually did.)

```
(Sarandon and Spader are sitting at the bar, drinking.)

                    SARANDON
          Sorry about your lady dumping
          you.

                    SPADER
          She didn't exactly dump me.

                    SARANDON
          Oh yeah? What did she do then?

                    SPADER
          She died.

                    SARANDON
          Died. You mean died?

                    SPADER
          Yeah.

(Sarandon starts to laugh.)

                    SARANDON
          How'd she do that?

                    SPADER
          Car turned over.

                    SARANDON
             (still laughing)
          Oh, I'm sorry. I can't believe
          . . .
```

                  SPADER
It's all right.

                SARANDON
I don't know why I'm laughing.
Your wife died.

                  SPADER
I guess no one ever died on
you before.

                SARANDON
  (smiling)
No. Charley died.

                  SPADER
Charley? Is that your doggie?

                SARANDON
No. Charley, my kid.

(She becomes sober and serious.)

                  SPADER
Your kid?

                SARANDON
I know. I know.

                  SPADER
How did he die?

                SARANDON
Leukemia. What can you do. The
world spins around.

If a lesser actor than Susan Sarandon were preparing for this scene, she would probably try ahead of time to imagine what it would be like to lose a son, and then, in the scene, try to experience the *proper* painful emotion and attitude of grief. Sarandon obviously did not plan what she *should* feel or *should* act. Without opinions and expectations, she took what was written in the script and turned it into a brilliant performance by dealing with the moment and letting her laughter come through. We see her pain, and we believe her. She lets her intuitive response inform her emotion and color her dialogue. Sarandon, being the great film actor that she is, probably hadn't planned to laugh at that point.

She probably did not know beforehand how she was going to react. Her response seemed intuitive, and she went with it.

Don't Plan What You Expect to Experience

Discovery means becoming aware of something for the first time. The Art of Not Knowing is the art of rediscovery. Not Knowing keeps you from striving for a specific result. Sarandon could have gone directly for cliched sadness, which, happily, she did not. On every take and in every performance, make your experience as if it is happening for the first time.

First Reading of a Scene

On first reading a scene, absorb the material and don't think up any ideas about how to perform it. When you read it for the first time, read it by rote with an empty mind, which will then open you to the possibility of a variety of experiences. When you completely eliminate preconceived thoughts and ideas, you will perform more effectively on film.

Bad Acting on Film Is the Triumph of Logic

The less you depend on ideas, the stronger your emotional experience. When your intuitive process takes over, it dictates the colors so rapidly that your painting (your performance) is complete before you have time to think or judge. It seems to have just happened. It is choiceless and effortless.

In a scene from the movie *Threesome*, Lara Flynn Boyle angrily confronts Josh Charles in the hallway. The actors do a good job of relating, not thinking.

                    BOYLE
        Why are you so standoffish
        with me? Why won't you kiss
        me?

                    CHARLES
        Why? You see . . . I can't
        tell you.

(He is struggling. Boyle has tears in her eyes.)

                    BOYLE
        Tell me.

```
                    CHARLES
        I am—I'm sexually ambivalent.


                    BOYLE
        Ambivalent about sex in
        general, or ambivalent about
        sex with me?

                    CHARLES
        Ambivalent about sex with
        girls. I like them. I just
        don't want to have sex with
        them.

  (Boyle, in pain, intuitively explodes with a laugh.)

                    BOYLE
        I suspected it.
```

Both the pain and the laugh drive her line, "I suspected it." The laughter is an unexpected response that is real, adds creative color, and gives us insight into Lara's character. Her acting is brilliant. She realizes that it is not her fault that he is homosexual. At the same time, the tears signify her loss of his love. Remember, the Art of Relating is the basis of film acting. Once you lock onto a result or an idea you're in trouble, because then it is almost impossible to relate and be responsive to the other actor's performance.

Forget about History

Only by looking at the world with a child's eyes can you see what actually exists. To discover your acting partner, look at him as if for the first time, with your mind uncluttered by ideas and logic. The Art of Not Knowing means subconsciously absorbing information from the script and, at the same time, disregarding thoughts and ideas derived from your life. Forget about history, let your intuition tell you what to do, and discover the present moment through being aware of what is happening right here and right now.

Don't Be Safe

Make every moment count as if it were your last. Not Knowing gives you lots of energy by heightening your awareness, which then adds excitement to your performance. Everything the other actor does is significant, no matter how small. Every twitch of the eyebrow, every movement of the lips, every change in the tone and timbre of the voice. Let whatever it is engender a response inside you. The more acute your awareness, the better your response—and the better you look on film.

Nothing stimulates your awareness like being in danger or jeopardy. Not Knowing does just that. Why do you suppose film editors love to find a scene in which you have "gone up" (forgotten your lines)? Editors like this kind of shot because when you forget your lines, you are no longer acting—you are in danger. You are real. If you don't do something stupid like looking at the director, and saying, "I'm sorry, can we do that again?", the editor will have a shot of you that she can use as a reaction shot in this or some other scene. You'd be surprised at how many close shots of actors who have "gone up" are used by editors for reaction shots. When you forget your lines, if you maintain your concentration on the other actor, you look believable and real because you are in danger and your situation *is* real.

Fear Is Your Friend

Say you are lost on a snowy dark night and you come to an old, spooky farmhouse. A sign says, "Trespassers will be shot." No answer to your knock. Without shelter, you could freeze to death. It's life and death. You break the window and crawl in. You try the light switch.

Which is more exciting? You flip the switch and the lights go on. Or, you flip the switch and nothing happens. The longer the lights are out, the keener your senses are to detect what might be there. Rats? Bats? An escaped psycho? A scared farmer with a shotgun? A dead body? It's scary, but it's exciting! You are in jeopardy, and because you're in a state of Not Knowing, your alertness is excruciating.

Once the lights go on, your imagination quits working so hard. The more you know, the fewer feelings of jeopardy and fear you have. Remember, the less you know, the greater the chance for you to have an emotional experience and, consequently, the better your performance.

Every Scene Is Life or Death

Two students are doing a scene. Jesse plays the bartender. Devon plays the detective, who is about to accuse the bartender of complicity in a murder. After a few lines, we can see that the actors are relating but not putting themselves in jeopardy. They're "phoning it in."

JEREMIAH: **Class, does anyone see anything wrong with this scene?**

Several students speculate. Finally Michael speaks up.

> MICHAEL
> (to Jeremiah)
>> It's boring. I'm not going to
>> spend seven bucks to watch
>> that.

JEREMIAH: Right! They don't have anything at stake. You two guys are having a friendly conversation as if you were on a coffee break. Jesse, you wouldn't want a detective accusing you of murder would you?

> JESSE
> (to Jeremiah)
>> Hell no.

JEREMIAH: Devon, your job is to get a reaction out of Jesse. You are the catalyst in the scene.

> DEVON
> (to Jeremiah)
>> But I didn't want to do the
>> stereotypical cop thing. Isn't
>> that an idea?

JEREMIAH: You have to make every scene a life and death situation. If nothing's at stake, your audience is bored. Any scene you do has to be the most important thing in your life at the time. Passionately accept the fact that you need information from this bartender. I don't mean "act." I mean believe. Accept the circumstances. The more meaningful the situation is to you, the greater the jeopardy. Focus on and respond to the way he reacts to your questions. You don't know how he's going to behave—that will keep you in the moment.

> (Skip to end of the scene)

> DEVON
>> What? Do I look like an idiot?
>> Somebody made a call from
>> here, to the shooter.

> (Jesse responds to the grin and starts to laugh.)

> JESSE
>> It's a public phone. People
>> make calls all the time.

```
(Jesse's laugh makes detective Devon respond with anger.
Jesse, frightened, jumps back.)

                    DEVON
                (intense)
            You want to take the rap. Good.
            A witness ID'ed Gardino. I'm
            going to pick him up, and I
            personally know you made that
            call. And if you don't cooper-
            ate right now, I'll offer him a
            deal to give you up and I'm
            gonna enjoy taking you down.

                    JESSE
                (shook up)
            I'm out of this . . . Veto was
            looking for him, that's all.
            The call was just a favor, but
            I didn't know they had a con-
            tract on him. I swear.
```

JEREMIAH: **Devon and Jesse, Great! When you guys accepted the circumstances and put yourself in jeopardy, you created dramatic excitement, and the scene worked. At the end there, we were fascinated.**

The Power of Not Knowing

An anthropologist once told me of the intuitive sense of the Eskimos in the days before we destroyed their traditional way of life. In 1922, director Robert Flaherty, the "father" of documentary filmmaking, was shooting *Nanook of the North,* a famous documentary about Eskimos. Flaherty's camera malfunctioned several hundred miles from civilization, and a fourteen-year-old Eskimo boy who had never seen a camera fixed it for him. How could he do that? Here's how:

1. The Eskimo boy was skilled in the Art of Not Knowing and had no preconceived ideas as to how mechanical things did or did not work.
2. He found cameras to be of great interest, which brought about intense concentration.
3. He was not afraid and was willing to take action.
4. The age-old ability of his people to survive successfully in the Arctic wilderness had given him an unshakable confidence in himself.
5. He understood simplicity, and his perceptions were uncomplicated.
6. He was intuitive.

Be an Eskimo

Great film actors all have the same abilities the Eskimos had. They operate from the state of Not Knowing. They enhance awareness through intense Concentration. And they Relate to what they receive from others. These are three of the Five Arts of film acting. They also overcome personal fear, are willing to take necessary action, and are intuitive. These are additional arts of acting.

Acting a Scene before Reading It

Some teachers try to induce a state of Not Knowing by prohibiting students from reading the scene before doing it in class. Occasionally, this results in brilliance. This approach will certainly cause you to respond spontaneously, but only by luck, not creativity. It is not the answer. You have no information. Not reading the script is unreliable. Your subconscious needs information before performance.

Memorizing and Not Knowing

When you read or memorize, put yourself in a state of Not Knowing. Let your subconscious assimilate the information without letting logical ideas lock you into results. Spontaneity is not necessarily creative, but creativity is almost always spontaneous—because creativity in acting comes from your intuition and from relating.

Reading a Scene for the First Time

Here is what I ask of my students before doing a scene in the workshop: read the script to yourself once only. This allows you to experience the material spontaneously. Without the facts, the creative process cannot always come up with answers that will work for you. Subconsciously absorb the information, but don't start planning how you are going to act. For the Art of Not Knowing to take place, read the script by rote. Absorb and then forget what you have read. Rote reading keeps you from implanting ideas in your conscious mind. While you are reading the script for the first time, don't put feeling or interpretation into the lines. But if you should have a feeling, acknowledge it and don't fight it. Put the script down until the emotion subsides.

Here's what may happen if you allow an emotion to develop fully during your first reading. If you become infused with sadness, you are having the experience before you start acting. Then when you work in class, the experience has changed. It is weaker or has vanished altogether. If you read comic material and laugh, it dissipates your potential acting experience.

In both situations, stop reading until the emotions dissipate. Then finish reading. It is exciting to read a script that engenders feelings. But protect the creative process by curtailing your emotions before your performance. When you are acting, disregard all your previous feelings so you can experience the dialogue as if for the first time.

Repeating an Emotional Experience

The craft of being a stage actor is learning how to repeat experiences night after night while remaining fresh and spontaneous. In film acting, it is necessary to give a good performance only once. On film, the scene becomes permanent. The director may shoot additional takes, but the good directors do not want repetition—they expect something different and hope for something better. In editing, the director and the editor choose the performance the audience will see in the completed film.

Experience every moment for the first time. Your emotion can even go in a different direction: you might cry on take One, cry and laugh on take Two, cry and get angry on take Three. This diversity gives the director and editor choices. Even when you are overwhelmed by an emotion such as sadness, the good director expects additional takes of your scene to vary. If you repeat each experience exactly the same way, the director and the audience see that your performance is being controlled by you instead of being controlled, as it should be, by both the situation and the other actors.

In *Waking Ned Devine* the actors are trying to manipulate the dead man's face into a smile when his false teeth fall out and drop onto the bed. Both actors respond with unplanned laughter. Whether the teeth falling out was planned or unplanned—it could have been either—doesn't make any difference. We see their reaction. Both actors deal with the situation brilliantly. It becomes a true and spontaneous moment.

Discover Facts by Concentrating on the Other Actor

As you play the scene, your job is to discover what the facts of the script mean by concentrating on your partner—the intonations of her voice, and her physical and emotional experiences. This is the Art of Concentration. When you discover the facts from your partner, you will then be relating and in the moment, and you will give a good performance.

An Emotion Can Become an Idea

Marsha, a good actress, is doing an emotional scene (written by Barbara Bowen) with Daniel, who plays her husband.

```
              DANIEL
. . . I'm sorry, I was putting
the pictures away. I was being
cagey. I thought it would be
best.
```

(Marsha, looking at a picture of her daughter.)

```
              MARSHA
I tried to forget that day
would ever come. I had to stay
sane. I packed your bag when-
ever your Daddy came to town,
but this little clause in our
divorce decree was waiting
like a time bomb. Then your
first tooth fell out. I should
have seen the handwriting on
the wall but I didn't . . . I
wasn't looking. I couldn't
bear to, even when your Daddy
called to remind you. Your
birthday was coming, apparently
the magic legal age, to be put
on a plane, two hours to
Daddy's new house. You got all
excited. Then we had to shop
for books and games to enter-
tain you. I had to answer a
thousand questions about your
very first flight on an air-
plane. I should go with you
just in case you need your
Mommy, if you're scared or get
sick or someone misplaces you
like a piece of luggage. I can
only pray that you will be all
right. And that Judges will
have to take Mommy classes so
they will understand some day.
You waved good-bye and I
smiled back and you disap-
peared down the ramp. I didn't
```

```
                         want to upset you. That's why
                         I held my tears for almost a
                         month and why I cried all the
                         way home.
```

It is obvious to me that Marsha has obligated herself to the emotional content of the scene. She is feeling sad but isn't experiencing her tears. Her idea is stifling her believability.

JEREMIAH: **Marsha, this material is very leading, and instead of being open to an experience, you are anticipating tears.**

```
                         MARSHA
          (to Jeremiah)
                         When I read it the first time
                         I started crying. Then I get
                         in front of the class and the
                         experience goes away.
```

JEREMIAH: **Your expecting to cry turns into an idea, not an experience. I want you to do the last page again. This time I want you to laugh.**

I ask her to laugh in contradiction to the experience she thinks should happen because I want her to separate the logic of the idea from her actual experience. She and Daniel do the scene again, forcing laughter through the entire scene.

JEREMIAH: **Now do the scene from the top.**

```
          (Marsha starts out smiling. Her concentration is on Daniel,
          who is still laughing while saying his next line. Suddenly
          she breaks down and cries. It becomes an honest
          performance.)
```

Keep Your Emotional Responses from Becoming Ideas

Say you are doing a scene in a film. You have an experience and cry on the first take. The director customarily shoots scenes more than once. Don't expect to cry on every take. When you think, "I hope it happens . . . It's close . . . I can feel the tears," you lose contact with the other actor and become self-absorbed. When tears or any emotion become more important than the other actor, the emotion becomes an idea, not an experience, and it looks fake on film.

Judgments Ruin Your Acting

A judgment is a comment, spoken or unspoken, about yourself, the script, or other actors. When you first read a script, a light bulb may go on. You like or don't like the dialogue. The words suggest an image, a situation, an emphasis. Anything you think, no matter how small, is an idea and a mental comment. You can't completely avoid commenting, but you can reduce its effect on your performance. Acknowledge your comments, accept them, and let them pass. If you try to block them, they will only grow in importance.

Don't Indulge in Self-Criticism

Wanting to be brilliant creates demands. Concentrate on the work, not the results. Be content that you are doing your best, and don't be swayed by internal or external opinions. Stop considering your acting as good or bad. Is the glass half empty or half full? Remember, you decide how to look at the glass. Lose the concepts of good and bad, right and wrong.

A Genuine Experience

Anna, a student who had never acted before, was doing a scene with Fred, one of my experienced actors. She started off not looking at him. I had her focus her concentration on Fred, and I told her to forget about anything she thought she *should* do. Anna's performance immediately improved. (The scene was written by Barbara Bowen.)

>   ANNA
>   I want you to be responsible
>   and get a steady job.
>
>   FRED
>   I can make more money working
>   two days than if I worked in
>   an office all week.
>
>   ANNA
>   We're always broke, we have no
>   savings, and I don't see a
>   future living with you.
>
>   FRED
>   You do okay, we have enough to
>   eat, and I always pay the rent
>   on time. What are you so wor-
>   ried about?

> ANNA
> I'm pregnant.

> FRED
> Really? Wow. If you want to
> have the baby, I'll support
> you in every way.

(Fred starts to cry.)

> FRED
> I'll do whatever you want me
> to do. I don't want you to
> worry about a thing.

> ANNA
> Do you mean it?

> FRED
> Yes. I love you.

(Anna starts to cry. Real tears.)

JEREMIAH: **Great!** (to class) **How could Anna turn in a creative performance like that without knowing anything about how to act? First, she had no idea that she would have an experience in the scene—Not Knowing. Second, she Concentrated on and Related to Fred. The other thing she did was Accept him and the imaginary situation of being pregnant. And she accepted Fred's response when he cried, which surprised and overwhelmed her. She responded to his emotion, which is Giving and Receiving. Through Not Knowing , she had a genuine experience.**

Summary

1. Practice the Art of Not Knowing. Use the beginner's mind to minimize all ideas from the script and personal ideas such as opinions, beliefs, generalizations or stereotyping, and judgments. Respond to the unexpected.
2. Before performance:
   a. Read the script once only. Absorb and forget.
   b. Do not comment on the script.
   c. Memorize the script by rote without having ideas or emotional experiences.
   d. Place no demands on your performance. Do not judge it as good or bad.

e. Don't let your emotions become ideas.

f. Place your concentration on your partner.

g. Look on every moment as if it were your last (jeopardy).

Actor Practice

We generally assume that by knowing the name of an object, we know that object. But knowing a name is not enough, because we only know something through actual experience. Not Knowing means experiencing all the many aspects of something with an open mind free of preconceptions.

1. Put four drinking glasses on a table. While you are out of the room, have a friend pour a different brand of cola soft drink in each glass. Then come back in the room and, by tasting, try to identify the brand of cola in each glass. You are now in a state of Not Knowing. There are no labels, just cola. What does each glass have in common? Use all your senses—taste, smell, feel, hearing. Are the bubbles different? Stickiness? Viscosity? What are the differences? Make your decisions based on your experience of each drink. Add a little jeopardy by knowing that you are to be executed at dawn if you do not identify the drinks correctly.

2. Fill a glass with water from the kitchen sink. Look at it. Is it clear or cloudy? Does it have anything in it like, dirt, particles, or bubbles? Is it warm or cold? Does it smell? How does it taste? It seems that only when water has a strange taste do we notice it. Now take a mouth full and move it around with your tongue. Is it wet? What is wet? A symbol meaning what? Not dry? What is dry? Language conveniently keeps us from discovering the experience.

   Now you are experiencing the water, not just drinking it. Become aware of water. In our fast-paced society we absorb with little or no experiencing. We need to slow down, stop, and start discovering the essence of everything. The Art of Not Knowing means to discover by using all your senses—taste, smell, touch, hearing, and seeing. It also means rediscovering and reexperiencing everything, not as an intellectual exercise, but as a reawakening of your senses to the magic of this world. That's what great actors do.

3. Get videotapes of the films I have referred to—not only in this chapter, but in the whole book—and view them, especially the scenes I discuss.

8

Still More on the Art of Not Knowing

Directing is about seeing twenty moves ahead while you're working on the next five.

Steven Spielberg

The Director's Ideas

The director is the storyteller who sees the past, present, and future. He has probably read hundreds of stories and scripts to find a worthwhile screenplay to turn into a film. He has spent months, sometimes years, studying the script. He is responsible for conceiving the images, getting them on film, and giving himself and the editor sufficient coverage to put together a good movie. He is responsible for the overall look of the film, and with his camera and his actors he creates the pieces that make up the whole movie.

There is more to acting than just learning your lines by rote and then walking onto the set and working from the emotions of others. Acting a role *as if* for the first time and relating to the other actors does not mean that it's okay to go into a scene with nothing. Both your conscious and subconscious minds need information to feed your intuition. You can't exclude ideas from the creation of art, but the director, not you, directly handles the ideas and logic of the scene by figuring out what the actors would logically be doing in these particular circumstances; then he figures out how to add interest, or drama.

Before shooting starts, you and the director have talked about and understood the characters, the given circumstances, and the goal of the story. You have rehearsed camera positions and movement. During shooting, your job is to go through the actions the director wants you to do, to deal directly with the other actors, and to let yourself experience whatever feelings come to you. My goal is to teach you to learn to relate in the present to the other actors, to practice the Art of Relating, to rely on your intuition, and to forgo the left brain stuff that actors often mistake for acting. But there *is* left brain stuff to do: like memorizing lines, knowing the director's intentions, knowing who your character is and who the other characters are, and knowing all the given circumstances. Listen to and absorb what the director wants, because he hired you to communicate his vision.

Ideas and the Actors

Certain roles require more left brain work than others. I am sure that Marlon Brando, Jon Voight, and Tom Cruise all studied the lives and problems of paraplegics who must spend their days in wheelchairs when they prepared, respectively, for the films *Men, Coming Home,* and *Born on the Fourth of July.* Anne Bancroft studied the ways of nuns and the church for *Agnes of God.* Gene Hackman had to have studied the mores of nineteenth-century farmers and marital expectations for his role in *Zandy's Bride.* In these films, and in all the motion pictures we respect, actors have to learn beforehand what the director wants, what their characters want, and how real people function in whatever culture the characters are supposed to be living in. Performance occurs when the camera rolls and each actor does what the director asks him or her to do, while at the same time being motivated by the actions and feelings of the other actors.

Pre-Production

Much of a movie's production time may be spent on pre-production. The director of photography, the assistant director, the camera operator, the production sound engineer, the script supervisor, and the crew are all responsible to the director, who is the problem solver. The producer controls the business, leaving the aesthetics (we hope) up to the director, who selects the locations and has the final say on costumes, sets, props, and most of the casting. He participates in budgeting and scheduling, on set and costume design, and makes the final decisions on locations, sets, script rewriting, and the hiring of key people. After a long while, he casts the actors. As one producer put it, "The actor is the last hair on the dog's ass." Remember that the time you spend on a movie as an actor is short compared to the time it takes the director just to be ready to start making the movie.

The Director's Vision

The director wants, among other things, to create scenes and performances that are interesting and moving.

In Chapter 1, "The Exercise," I referred to lines like "I love you" and "You son of a bitch" as lines that can easily become acted cliches because their strong dialogue can denote a specific emotion (sadness, happiness, anger, fear, love). On "I love you" actors tend to "act" what they think is loving and sincere. On "You son of a bitch" they pretend to be angry and shout. Don't get caught in that trap. But if sincerity, anger, and love come from genuine feelings, your actions, though apparently incongruous, will be honest and believable. The point is this: to avoid being mediocre or worse, react only from real feelings, not solely from what is "expected," or from what has worked for you in the past, or what you have seen other actors do.

Let us see how a director might guide an actor into going beyond the expected. In my advanced workshop, we worked on the following scene, which depicts a moment where the boss tells an employee that he is fired. There is nothing that is apparently exciting about this scene. The two actors are experienced and able to work with a director's adjustments.

```
INT. ADVERTISING AGENCY. THE BOSS'S OFFICE - NIGHT.

(The Boss and Matt are sitting on opposite sides of the
desk.)

                    BOSS
          This came from upstairs.

(Boss hands Matt a letter.)

                    BOSS
          I have to let you go.

(Matt is at first shocked, then indignant.)

                    MATT
          Because of the Thornton
          account. Isn't it?

(Matt stands up to leave.)

                    BOSS
          Probably had something to do
          with it. A very generous
          offer. Six months severance
          and medical until you get set-
          tled. Plus . . .

(Matt walks to the door. He turns. He is controlled. He
speaks with accusatory anger.)
```

<pre>
                    MATT
          How can you sleep at night.
</pre>

JEREMIAH: (to the workshop) **What emotion do you think Matt was feeling?**

<pre>
                    JENNY
     (to Jeremiah)
          He's angry.
</pre>

JEREMIAH: **That's one. Another?**

<pre>
                    LOU
     (to Jeremiah)
          I think he might be sad or
          afraid.
</pre>

JEREMIAH: **You're being creative. What else was he feeling?**

<pre>
                    JENNY
     (to Jeremiah)
          At first, he looked kind of
          stunned.

                    LOU
     (to Jeremiah)
          I think his last line is
          angry. "How can you sleep at
          night."
</pre>

JEREMIAH: **Yeah, he was first stunned. Then he got indignant, and then angry. He did all right—they both did all right—we believed them. But their performances and the scene were not very interesting. How do we make it interesting? What if he were happy at getting fired?**

<pre>
                    LOU
     (to Jeremiah)
          How could he be happy? It
          wouldn't work for the scene.

                    JENNY
     (to Jeremiah)
          Not after losing his job.

                    JANIE
     (to Jeremiah)
          No way!
</pre>

JEREMIAH: **You guys are stuck with an idea—the idea that he can only feel one way. Let's play *what if* just for this scene. Matt, you've been wanting to quit, but you've been putting it off because if you quit, you get nothing. Today the boss has done it for you. But now, instead of nothing, you will collect severance pay and still be on a medical plan.**

```
                        KRISTINA
        (to Jeremiah)
                    I don't see how that could
                    work. The dialogue implies
                    anger.
```

JEREMIAH: **Yes, it does imply anger. Most audiences and actors expect Matt to do just what he did—show shock, indignation, anger. In an audition, most actors would read the scene that way. That's what everyone expects. The same old thing. Sure, we the audience believed it, but we weren't fascinated.** (to the actors) **Try it again. Matt, the firing saves you from quitting and getting nothing.**

They repeat the scene, only this time Matt's performance surprises and delights us. We were expecting something like the first performance, but he fooled us. He is slightly amused when the Boss tells him he's fired. He has a twinkle in his eye when he says, "How can you sleep at night." The Boss doesn't get the joke. The subtext? Matt has the last laugh, and the audience will not know how he arrived at his performance.

JEREMIAH: **That worked great. Notice that I didn't tell Matt how to feel or how to react. I only suggested different circumstances for this scene only. He accepted those new circumstances, and his feelings determined his performance. A director's adjustment doesn't have to change the story or the given circumstances. It just gives you another element to work with.**

A good director, instead of telling actors precisely how to act, makes suggestions that stimulate discovering the experience for themselves and coming up with (the director hopes) something completely different and fascinating. In this scene, I gave Matt a suggestion that everyone could hear because it was a teaching situation, but in actual production, the director talks to actors privately. Good actors create their own adjustments that lead to interesting, unpredictable performances. Try it. Don't wait for the director. Think up your own "as if" circumstances and see where they take you, especially when you relate to the other actor.

                    CHARLES
(to Jeremiah)
                    Doesn't casting have a lot to
                    do with it? If the boss were
                    pushy and arrogant, the rela-
                    tionship would be different,
                    wouldn't it?

JEREMIAH: **Sure would. Any scene will be different, depending on which actors are cast and their respective states of mind. A director plans his casting so that each actor's own nature tends to carry both the scenes and the film toward fulfilling his vision. What if the Boss is elderly and is Matt's mentor? How about a beautiful woman who is the Boss. Or a kindly mother figure. The character of the Boss determines how Matt will relate. Let's change actors and see how it goes. Jenny, you play the boss. Bruce, you play Matt. This is a cut-and-dried situation—the firing of an employee who will probably react with shock and anger. So how do we make it exciting, or at least more interesting?**

(Here and elsewhere in this book, the actions in parentheses are not script directions. They are the actual actions of the actors as they performed them.)

Before the scene I say quietly to Jenny, "You're in love with Bruce."

INT. — ADVERTISING AGENCY — NIGHT, CLOSING TIME.

Bruce and Jenny are sitting in her office.

                    JENNY
          This came from upstairs.

(Bruce glances at the letter, and in disgust tosses it back
onto Jenny's desk.)

                    JENNY
          I have to let you go.

(Bruce gets up and starts to leave. Jenny stands up, walks
around the desk, and stands in front of him. She looks lovingly directly into his eyes.)

                    BRUCE
          It's the Thornton account.
          Isn't it?

```
                    JENNY
          Probably had something to do
          with it.
```

(She continues looking him in the eyes, and says her next
lines with a hint of seduction in her voice.)

```
                    JENNY
          They're making a very generous
          offer. Six months severance
          and medical until you get set-
          tled. Plus . . .
```

(Jenny touches his hair. He ignores it.)

```
                    BRUCE
               (puzzled)
          How can you sleep at night?
```

JEREMIAH: **Bruce, I want you to do that line again.**

I whisper to Jenny to kiss him.

JEREMIAH: **Bruce, pay attention to her touching you.**

```
(Jenny touches his hair. Then she kisses him lovingly on the
cheek. Bruce takes her in his arms and kisses her passion-
ately. Then holds her by her shoulders at arm's length.)
```

```
                    BRUCE
               (mock disapproval, as if
               she's a naughty little girl)
          How can you sleep at night.
```

(He leaves the office.)

JEREMIAH: **Jenny, doing a specific physical action can change the relationship. When you kissed Bruce, he changed and finally participated in what was going on. Then, by holding you off and saying his line the way he did, he gave us something different. We expected the two of you to profess love for each other. But instead of letting it go that way, he responded to your love, but came up with something different. What each of you did made the scene unpredictable and interesting. Nice work.**

Good Actors Make Things Happen

Good actors always find something in themselves to help make the scene exciting. In interviews and in writing, many of our best actors have said that one of their fears is that they will not be able to get in touch with whatever it is that will let them go beyond believability and come up with an exciting and unexpected performance. It takes a lot of work, but try to find something in yourself relative to the circumstances that both you and the director haven't thought of before. One advantage of film is that the director can always reshoot until he gets a scene that works.

JEREMIAH: **Debra, you play the wife, and Harry, you're her husband, who's coming home after being fired. Don't rehearse with each other, just memorize the dialogue.**

While they are memorizing, I block the camera movement with other actors. Debra doesn't know that I told Harry that there is a pistol in the pocket of the coat in the closet.

JEREMIAH: **You guys ready? Okay. Action.**

```
INT. BEDROOM. DEBRA.

(Harry enters the bedroom. He stumbles through the door,
slumps on the bed. He knocks an open suitcase off the bed.)
[The workshop laughs.]
```

JEREMIAH: **CUT! What are you doing Harry?**

```
                    HARRY
(to Jeremiah)
          It says he just had a car
          accident.
```

JEREMIAH: **But the accident wasn't that serious. You're not hurt. Start it again.**

```
(Harry re-enters. His wife, Debra, is packing her suitcase.)

                    HARRY
          Where are we going?

(Debra says nothing, keeps packing. Harry walks to the
closet, roots around, and turns around with a gun in his
hand. She turns to get something out of a drawer and sees
him.)
```

                    DEBRA
          Harry . . . ?

(Harry sticks the gun's muzzle up to his neck. Debra stays
with the scene. She takes a couple of careful steps toward
him.)

                    DEBRA
          Give me the gun please, Matt.

JEREMIAH: (softly) **Debra, be careful! The gun contains blanks. If it goes off it
could seriously hurt him. Don't jerk or touch the trigger when you take the gun.**

                    DEBRA
     (to Jeremiah)
          I can't. What if something
          happens? I hate guns.

JEREMIAH: **Debra, focus on the situation. You're an actress, this is your job.
You can do it.**

(Debra approaches slowly with caution. She reaches for the
gun. Her hand trembles.)

                    DEBRA
          (fearfully)
          Please Harry. Don't do this.
          We can work this out. Listen
          to me. Stop. Think about this.

(Harry smiles and turns his head. Debra's eyes fill with
tears.)

                    DEBRA
          (crying)
          Why are you doing this?

JEREMIAH: **Excellent! That's a Print.** (to the workshop) **I expected her to be
frightened when I told her how dangerous the situation was. But I didn't know
she would cry. The tears are a bonus. Okay, do the rest of the scene.**

(Harry takes the gun from his neck and points it at Debra.
She backs away.)

```
                      DEBRA
                 (frightened)
            Harry . . ..
```

(Harry starts to laugh. Debra, frightened, stares at him.
She realizes that he is just playing with her. Then she
becomes angry.)

```
                      DEBRA
                 (angry)
            You're so immature. You're a
            spoiled little boy who always
            gets his way. Not this time.
            It's over.
```

(She continues packing her bag furiously.)

JEREMIAH: **See how a director, by controlling the situation with suggestion and
through blocking the actors, can help you get honest performances. Notice I
never told them how to act. I just changed the circumstances.**

```
                      LOU
            (to Jeremiah)
                 I'm curious. Debra cried by
                 accident, but how would you go
                 about making her cry if the
                 scene called for it?
```

JEREMIAH: **It's difficult. One of the things you look for in casting sessions is
whether or not she can deal with the emotional stuff in the script. But your job
as an actor is to learn how to come up with tears. Let's see if we can get something different. Debra, see Harry's desperation and get him to stop. This time,
you know the gun's not loaded and it can't go off.**

```
                      DEBRA
            (to Jeremiah)
                 Why didn't you tell me that in
                 the first place?
```

JEREMIAH: **I was helping you to accept the situation.** (to the workshop) **When
Debra thought the gun was loaded it frightened her. In the movie** *At Close
Range,* **there was a scene where Sean Penn was holding a gun on Christopher
Walken. Penn stepped out of the scene and said to the prop person, loud enough
for Walken to hear, "Give me the loaded gun." Then he stepped back into the
scene. This put Walken in a different frame of mind. He wasn't sure if the gun**

was real or blank, and that gave him more to work with. Debra, after we're done, look at your tape and see the difference between the two takes.

>   DEBRA
> (to Jeremiah)
>   I could feel the difference.

JEREMIAH: **Good. Now Debra, try to take the gun. You love Harry. The last thing you want to see him do is commit suicide.**

> (Harry is sitting on the bed, gun in hand.)

>   DEBRA
>   (loving)
>   What are you doing?

JEREMIAH: **Kneel down next to him and touch him gently. Now, say it again.**

>   DEBRA
>   (lovingly, touches his arm)
>   What are you doing?

JEREMIAH: (to the workshop) **See the difference? See how the physical action of touching makes the scene better. Good directors, especially in emotional scenes, put the actors in physical and mental positions to evoke feeling. She is kneeling, which puts Harry in a stronger position. When she puts her hand on his arm, we can see them become intimate, and the scene becomes more real. Her loving gesture adds feeling to her line. Much of acting is simply relating. It keeps you honest, gives you a point of focus, and brings out the appropriate feeling.**

Directors Use Blocking to Elicit Responses

The good director knows what kinds of responses he wants in the scene, and he blocks the actors to help bring out the scene's emotional content. Debra has no idea how the director wants her to play the line, "What are you doing?" Everything she thought, every idea she had, is now invalid because the director is having her kneel beside Harry. The honesty of her acting will depend on the circumstances and the feedback from the other actor. Successful directors know what they need and will spend the time and film to get it.

In film, ideas come originally from the writer and then from the director, who has to understand each character from every point of view. He has lived with the script and its characters; and, like the writer who plays God when writing, the director becomes omnipotent when directing. He alone is responsible for the outcome. He has figured each camera angle for the scene. He understands every aspect from costuming to special effects. He knows the purpose behind every physical and emotional change, and how each scene furthers the story. But the director does not give the performances. The actors do.

I heard that when Robert Altman directed $M*A*S*H$ the two stars, Elliott Gould and Donald Sutherland, were apparently confused about their roles and asked the studio to let them out of their contracts. They had no initial concept of the overall picture and were apprehensive that this director would hurt their careers. $M*A*S*H$ turned out to be an artistic and commercial success. The two actors became stars. From the beginning, Robert Altman knew what he needed and brought it off by setting up circumstances that turned into great performances by both actors.

A Director's Scene Preparation

For film, performance rehearsal is often short or nonexistent. This does not mean that the director has not rehearsed the scene. In pre-production, he has worked with a storyboard artist and set designer to create a believable way to capture each scene. The director discusses each scene in detail with the director of photography, and they work out how the picture is to be shot. A tremendous amount of planning and preparation has been going on for many months, and the ideas are in motion before you ever arrive on the set. The director has the overall picture; your job is one part of the whole—to communicate the director's vision to the audience. To help you do this, the director may adjust your performance as he sees fit. Ideas are secondary for the actor and primary for the director. Emotions are secondary for the director and primary for the actor.

Physical Movement Influences Emotion

In one workshop exercise, we do a scene that shows how physical movement and proximity can affect actors' emotions. The actors, Ben and Mary, are beginners who are self-conscious and a little embarrassed. I have them stand at opposite ends of the room and say the line, "I love you."

BEN
(self-conscious)
I love you.

MARY
(without conviction)
I love you too.

JEREMIAH: **Mary, take that bed pillow off the chair and hit Ben. It's soft. You're not going to hurt him. Ben, when she hits you, say your line.**

(She hits him on the side of the head with the pillow.)

                              BEN
                       (laughs)
                    I love you.

                              MARY
                    I love you too.

(Mary also laughs. Then she turns to me and waits with a look on her face that says, "So I hit him, now what?")

JEREMIAH: **Keep doing it. Ben, every time she hits you, say your line. And Mary, say yours. That's it! Hit him harder. Keep saying your lines and mean it.**

(She keeps hitting him. They say their lines. And she finally gives him a good rap in the face that gets him angry. He pushes the pillow away and Mary almost falls to the floor. Now she is angry. She hits him again.)

                              BEN
                       (angrily)
                    I love you.

                              MARY
                       (very angry)
                    I love you too.

(She stops swinging and they both stand there breathing hard and looking at each other. Then they break out laughing and hug each other.)

JEREMIAH: **That was good.** (to the workshop) **Did we believe them?**

                          ANNETTE
(to Jeremiah)
                         At the end. I believed them
                         after they got angry. Even
                         when they said, "I love you"—
                         especially when they were mad.

                            BRUCE
    (to Jeremiah)
                    Yeah. After she hit him two or
                    three times, I believed them.
                    Funny, how you can say you
                    love somebody when they hit
                    you in the face.

JEREMIAH: **After a few hits, they forgot about us and about being self-conscious and embarrassed. It was just the two of them. They became intimate, even though she was swinging and he was dodging. Now, Ben, walk over and hold Mary's hand and say the line.**

    (Ben takes her hand. After all their activity, they feel
    closer, but they now are a little awkward.)

                            BEN
                        (matter-of-fact)
                    I love you.

                            MARY
                        (unconvincingly)
                    I love you too.

JEREMIAH: **Mary, turn and face me. Ben, get behind her and put your arms around her waist and your head next to her head. Now say the line.**

    (Ben puts his arms around her, and we can see that they are
    much closer emotionally.)

JEREMIAH: **Ben, now kiss Mary's neck.**

    (Ben kisses her.)

                            BEN
                    I love you.

                            MARY
                        (giggles)
                    I love you too.

    (This time we really believe they are in love.)

It's the same dialogue, but the physical distance and action between the actors change the subtext behind the line. As long as the two actors relate to each other, they will have a different experience depending on the distance and the position. That's one reason why the director's work is so important—he determines the ideas, the blocking, and movement, often with the participation of the actors. He sets the scenes so that the actors work from the circumstances and from each other's feedback, which makes them emotionally available and interesting.

Importance of the Art of Not Knowing

If ideas are so important, why must new students disregard their ideas? Most actors are result-oriented; that is, they try to act an emotion directly instead of reacting to the other actor and letting out whatever emotion comes. Too often acting students are taught to work from the literal meaning of the script. The Art of Not Knowing frees you from your self-imposed idea of what you *should* do. You may have decided from reading the script that you should be angry on a certain line. Now suppose you did not decide that, and, instead, you reacted with laughter purely from what the other actor did. That would be an honest spontaneous act, and the scene would become more interesting and believable. You might say that laughter at that point would be against the meaning of the scene and the intent of the character. But if your laughter comes from a genuine emotional response to the other actor and the circumstances, it is appropriate even though the scene may be no laughing matter.

Think of acting as steering a boat that's going down a wild river. The river is the set for the movie. The current of the river is the script, which, without your doing anything, always carries you to where it is going. An action adventure has rapids, rocks, snags, pirates. A comedy has lots of stupid obstacles, like a leak in the boat, falling overboard, and being chased by alligators. A love story has beautiful scenery and moonlit nights along with the river's regular obstacles. The director's ideas determine the size of the boat and how it is propelled—whether by oars, sail, or motor. He decides how you are dressed, whom you are with, the route you will follow, and all the river's obstacles. Your job is to steer down the river, engaging physically and emotionally with each obstacle as you come to it. The director guides you, but you are on your own. You have to make the decisions about how to steer around those obstacles and how to deal with the feelings that come up. The director makes the choices of where you will dock, on which side of the river to proceed, which tributaries to follow, when to stop, and when to start.

If you are locked into a fixed idea of how you are going to steer your course down the river, even before you have faced any obstacles, you lose your intuitive advantage. You have to deal with each sandbar, each submerged log, each snag when you come to it. If you fight the flow of the river by logically planning how you are going to deal with obstacles you have not yet faced, you may find yourself stranded on a sandbar with no one, including the director, knowing where you are or how to rescue you.

Great actors diligently study and understand their scripts. Yet in TV interviews and their personal statements, film actors like Tom Hanks and Gene Hackman tell us they learn their lines by rote and do their performances only when they are on camera. They prepare, all right, but they don't prepare their actual performances. They know that as they proceed down river, their feelings need to be intuitive when they come to each obstacle. Steven Spielberg has said, as did Bernardo Bertolucci, Alfred Hitchcock, and other directors, that he does not rehearse his actors for performance.

Great actors sometimes spend months getting ready to play a role. But understanding a script, its characters, and the given circumstances is one thing, and performing the scene is another. In my workshop and in this book, my goal is to teach you to learn how to relate and act intuitively, but I also teach that there are other things to do and know. I don't want you to think that all you have to do is get off the airplane, read a feature script once that night, and go on the set the next morning ready to give a great performance. There's more to it than that.

Your on-camera performance is the end result. Good directors don't want to set limits on what you might come up with. They won't tell you how to read lines, or what to feel, but they do give you help, guidance, and support. When the camera rolls, the director expects you to bring more to the scene than merely what the script says, something great that comes from your emotional relationship with the other actors and the scene's given circumstances. That is your job.

Summary

1. The director is responsible for ideas.
2. The actor is responsible for emotions and responses.
3. Pre-production means that before the actor is even cast, the director has worked for many months on script requirements and interpretation.
4. The director uses ideas to guide actors.
5. Good actors make things happen.
6. The director uses blocking to elicit responses.
7. The director does his scene preparation.
8. Physical movement can influence emotion.
9. The Art of Not Knowing helps your emotional responses.

Actor Practice

Watch the opening invasion scene of the movie *Saving Private Ryan*. Think of the preparation it took to capture that scene. How could you possibly conceive of what the director wants you to do? The situation is as close to reality as possible. The only thing missing is live ammunition. All you can do is show up on time, get into costume, climb into the landing boat, and do what the director tells you. To make your performance real, practice the Art of Acceptance and accept the imaginary circumstances.

Here's an exercise to show how physical action and position can change the performance. Two actors. One actor says a nondescript line such as, "I like your clothes," and the partner answers with the same line, "I like your clothes." Do this while both of you are in different physical positions.

1. One actor rolling on the floor.
2. Both actors rolling on the floor.
3. One actor sits on the other actor's lap. Then reverse positions.
4. One actor kneels and one stands. Reverse positions.
5. Both kneel.
6. The actors hold hands.
7. The actors give each other a hug.

Notice how the feeling of the line changes when it is spoken during different actions or from various positions.

Choose an emotionally descriptive line like "I love you," "I hate you," "You scared me," or "That is so sad." These are on-the-nose lines describing feelings. Change your physical positions and notice how the emotional meaning of the line changes.

9

The Art of Acceptance

For Hecuba!
What's Hecuba to him, or he to Hecuba
That he should weep for her! What would he do
Had he the motive and the cue for passion
That I have! He would drown the stage with tears,
And cleave the general ear with horrid speech . . .

Hamlet, *Act II, Sc2*

Hamlet asks how an actor can cry for an imaginary character in a play when he, Hamlet, with all his motive and passion, cannot cry for his dead father. "What's Hecuba to him or he to Hecuba / That he should weep for her?" Metaphorically, great actors accept Hecuba's importance to them and convince their audiences that their emotions and the circumstances are real. Learning to accept the character and the circumstances is one of the most important steps toward great acting.

Acceptance

Acceptance of the imaginary situation *as if* it were real allows you to be emotionally effective. Acting on film is not reality but a composite of imaginary circumstances and relationships. If someone holds a gun on you, you will have an emotional experience depending on your knowing that the gun is either loaded or unloaded. When you know the gun is loaded, your experience will be different from when you know it is unloaded. This is where you need the ability to accept the unloaded gun *as if* it were loaded. To put yourself mentally in that circumstance, suspend your judgment and disregard anything that is contradictory to the realness of the situation. Acting is make-believe, and your ability to accept imaginary circumstances determines the truth of your performance. This is the Art of Acceptance in film acting.

Two of my students—Bob, who is tall and easy-going, and Michelle, who has long black hair and startling blue eyes—do the following scene that forces them both to accept new circumstances.

```
                    BOB
          . . . Michelle, are you all
          right?

                    MICHELLE
          I'm pregnant.

(Embarrassed, she laughs and puts her hands over her face.
Bob's smile carries into the next line.)

                    BOB
          You're sure? Those drugstore
          tests aren't always . . .

(She avoids making eye contact with him.)

                    MICHELLE
          I saw a doctor. I'm sure.

                    BOB
          It's up to you. What do you
          want?

                    MICHELLE
          What about Med. School?

                    BOB
          Forget Med. School. It's your
          decision.

                    MICHELLE
          I want you to finish Med.
          School. I didn't plan this.

                    BOB
          I know.

                    MICHELLE
          I want the baby. I was so
          afraid to tell you . . . I
          love you. I don't want this to
          come between us.
```

JEREMIAH: **Michelle what is Bob feeling?**

> MICHELLE
> (to Jeremiah)
>> He's angry. He's going to have
>> to give up Medical School
>> because I'm pregnant.

JEREMIAH: **Forget all that. Look at Bob's face. What is he feeling?**

> MICHELLE
> (to Jeremiah)
>> He has a slight smile.

JEREMIAH: **Do you see any anger?**

> MICHELLE
> (to Jeremiah)
>> No. Not really.

JEREMIAH: **Good. What else do you see?**

> MICHELLE
> (to Jeremiah)
>> He's loving?

JEREMIAH: **Good! Just accept the fact that he's your husband and he loves you. Give each other a hug.**

> (They give each other a hug.)

JEREMIAH: **Now do the scene.**

> BOB
> You're sure? Those drugstore
> tests aren't always . . .

> MICHELLE
> I saw a doctor. I'm sure.

> BOB
> What do you want to do?

> MICHELLE
> What about Med. School?

```
                    BOB
              (His eyes fill with love.)
         Forget Med. School. It's your
         decision.

(Michelle starts to cry.)

                  MICHELLE
         I want you to finish Med.
         School. I didn't plan this.



(Bob gives her a hug.)

                    BOB
         I know.

                  MICHELLE
         I want the baby. I was so
         afraid to tell you . . . I
         love you. I don't want this to
         come between us. . . .
```

JEREMIAH: (to the class) **Michelle had to accept the fact that Bob loves her. She didn't accept it at first because her logic tried to tell her that a guy would be angry at delaying Med. School. Then her imagination took over and she accepted the situation. The concept of being pregnant became authentic and overwhelmed her. Acceptance allows her genuine feelings to be expressed within the imaginary circumstances.**

Play the Game

Children like to play. A mother tries to feed her child who presses his lips together and refuses to open his mouth. So she raises the spoon higher and makes the sound of an airplane and zigzags the spoon in front of his face. As she approaches his mouth, the child opens and lets the spoon enter. Children are willing to accept everything as a game. It is fun.

Play Like a Child

Children continually play games in which they accept all sorts of imaginary circumstances. I remember riding a broom and making believe it was a horse. I knew that it wasn't really a horse, but that didn't stop me. When I finished riding, I tied my imaginary horse to the banister. Children mimic adult behavior, such as sitting in an empty box pretending it is a car. They learn through playful imitation and imagination. They suspend judgment and act as if imagined things were real—this is the key to practicing the Art of Acceptance. Good actors accept everything and enjoy playing the games.

As we grow older, we become more socially aware and realize that riding a broom or driving an imaginary car is not something that our peers ordinarily accept. We eventually stop playing "make-believe," and our outward fantasy lives come to a halt. We become more pragmatic. Our imaginative skills dwindle. We save our fantasies for our inward, private life, and we turn into a respectable member of society. If by some chance we have avoided this path to respectability, we might have the good fortune to become actors. Approach acting as a child. Stop judging the propriety of things and entice yourself into accepting the moment-to-moment reality of imaginary circumstances.

In the movie *Basketball Diaries*, Leonardo DiCaprio turns in a brilliant performance of a drug addict who needs a fix. Lorraine Bracco is outstanding as his mother. The emotions in this scene are so intense that if they were not real to the actors, the scene would quickly turn into laughable melodrama. To be real to the audience, both actors have to accept the circumstances completely. Jim, played by DiCaprio, knocks on his mother's (Bracco) apartment door.

```
(She looks through the peephole, sees her son, then puts the
chain on the door before she unlocks it.)

                    DICAPRIO
       Mom! Mom are you in there? Is
       that you? Mom! Mom!

                    BRACCO
       Yeah.

(Bracco stands to the side of the door so her son can't see
her. It is too painful for her to look at him.)

                    DICAPRIO
       Hi! Hi Mom! Hi! Listen, I need
       you to help me out. All right.
       I need you to give me some
       money . . .

(He spits on the hall floor.)

                    BRACCO
       . . . I can't help you.
```

                    DICAPRIO
          Okay, listen. What you got to
          do is give me some money, Mom.

                    BRACCO
          Jim, I can't do that.

                    DICAPRIO
          Why not? Mom, you know I'm not
          going to do a thing with it. I
          just. I need to go out of town
          for a little while. I got in
          some trouble . . . So you got
          to give me some money. Mom,
          will you hold my hand?

                    BRACCO
          Yeah, . . . I'll hold your
          hand.

(He reaches through the door held by the chain. And Bracco
holds his hand. She looks at it. He is breaking her heart.
She is in a great deal of pain.)

                    DICAPRIO
          Mom can you give me some
          money? Mom can you give me
          some money please? Mom please.
          Don't fuck around. Mom give me
          some fuckin' money please.
          What are you doing? I'm your
          son.

                    BRACCO
          I don't have it.

(She tries to push the door shut.)

                    DICAPRIO
          Mom don't fuck around.

(She shuts the door.)

                    DICAPRIO
          Come on let me in the fuckin'
          door.

(He bangs on the door.)

>   DICAPRIO
>   Ahrrr . . . Oh fuck.

(He starts to cry.)

>   DICAPRIO
>   Let me in. I need some money,
>   I need some money real bad. Oh
>   fuck Oh . . .

(Bracco picks up the phone.)

>   BRACCO
>   Officer, someone is breaking
>   into my apartment. They have a
>   knife.

(She reaches into her purse and pulls out a ten-dollar bill.
She is contemplating giving it to DiCaprio.)

>   DICAPRIO
>   Oh Oh . . . You don't know
>   what you're fucking doing to
>   me. I'm in pain. How can you
>   do that to your son. You
>   Bitch! You fuckin' Bitch!!!

(He pounds on the wall. Screaming in pain. He cries.)

>   DICAPRIO
>   I won't do anything. I'll be a
>   good boy Mom. I'll be good if
>   you let me in . . .

DiCaprio has accepted the fact that his character needs a fix and is in pain. To play the game, he has to start the scene in real agony. His mother, played by Bracco, knows she can't give him money because he will blow it on dope. This is a scene that has all the makings of a cornball, melodramatic stinker. He asks his mother to hold his hand. He becomes childlike. He gets angry, begs, cries, even punches the door, and curses his mother. She goes through a different flood of emotions: fear, love, and tears. His pleading almost forces her into giving him money, but when he gets angry and calls her a bitch she changes her mind and calls the police. Actors in scenes like this often go over the top, but here the full acceptance of the circumstances by the two actors makes them both real and the scene authentic. The director Martin Ritt once said, in reference to an actor's performance that went over the top, "You don't have to tone anything down that is real."

Trust the Roller Coaster

Trust is the self-confidence to surrender control. When you get on a roller coaster you trust that you will not be killed, but that does not stop you from being scared. In fact, you want to be scared, or you would not have gotten on in the first place. You are thrown from side to side, hung upside down, dropped several hundred feet in an instant, and every so often you experience the fear that you could be killed. In reality, you know that there is no reason to be scared, but your subconscious overrides your logical brain and you experience fear because your logical mind cannot control those momentary glimpses at death. By accepting the imaginary circumstances and the fear, you are able to hang on and enjoy the ride.

More on Trust

Daniel Goldman, in his book *Emotional Intelligence*, talks about what he calls emotional hijacking, when you let your emotions override your good sense—for example, if you were to punch your teacher for giving you a B instead of an A. In acting, don't let yourself have out-of-control experiences. Besides your emotions, nothing is real. If dramas were real, the actor playing Othello would actually kill the actress playing Desdemona. In the 1947 film *A Double Life*, Ronald Coleman plays a famous actor who lets the role of Othello take over both his onstage and offstage lives. He crosses the line between imagination and reality and is stopped at the last minute from actually killing Desdemona onstage.

Your conscious mind knows the outcome of a story's plot, but your subconscious mind experiences it only moment by moment; so give your subconscious mind freedom to experience emotions. Your conscious mind stays out of the way, but it sets boundaries for keeping things safe. Trust allows you to have emotional experiences with safety. In my studio, I want actors to have life-heightened, subconscious, imaginative experiences. This means that you can touch anyone in a loving way. You can hug, kiss, hold hands, stroke them; but you can never cross the line between imagination and reality to be violent, push, slap, punch, or take any action that is not planned and agreed on ahead of time. Violence causes loss of trust between you and your fellow actors. They will think you are out of control and unprofessional. Always respect your fellow actors.

Having Fun

If you love being a show-off—pretending, playing, doing childish things, taking off your emotional underwear in front of the world—then acting is the profession for you. Great actors find enjoyment in everything that challenges them mentally, physically, or emotionally. Katharine Hepburn said she loved being in Africa while making *The African Queen,* even though the living conditions were terrible and dangerous. She found it stimulating. Acting is for creative, off-the-wall, interesting, physiologically sound nutcases who have never grown up. To be an actor, it is helpful if you are able to make an idiot of yourself in public without worrying about it. If you can't fail, you can never reach brilliance. Sir Laurence Olivier said that acting is "not an occupation for adults." Have fun.

Danny is an eighteen-year-old beginning actor. He is doing a scene with Michelle, a twenty-one-year-old college student. His youth makes him slightly uncomfortable working with a woman a few years older than he is, and his nervousness keeps him from accepting her as a love interest. This makes the Relating Exercise look stilted and unbelievable.

> MICHELLE
> Oh, Hi! You're in Mr. Murray's
> class?

> DANNY
> Yeah.

> MICHELLE
> You're the student that got
> the 98 on the test, aren't
> you?

(Danny is nervous. Michelle reaches over and tries to hold his hand. Danny uncomfortably ignores her touch.)

> DANNY
> It was an easy test.

JEREMIAH: **What did she just do, Danny?**

> DANNY
> (to Jeremiah)
> She's freaking me out. She
> grabbed my hand.

JEREMIAH: **Do you find her attractive?**

>   DANNY
> (to Jeremiah)
>   Yeah. I'll say.

JEREMIAH: **Then accept the fact that she is holding your hand.**

>   DANNY
> (to Jeremiah)
>   But this is class, and outside
>   she would never even talk to
>   me.

(Jeremiah stands and goes behind Danny's back. He signals Michelle to give Danny a kiss.)

>   MICHELLE
>   (to Danny)
>   Everyone says you're a genius.

(Michelle kisses Danny.)

>   DANNY
>   Like Ted Kaczynski.

(Danny pulls away. He's afraid of Michelle.)

>   MICHELLE
>   (laughs)
>   Are you?

(Michelle kisses him again. Danny giggles.)

>   DANNY
>   I hope not.

JEREMIAH: **Danny, kiss her back.**

>   MICHELLE
>   No. I mean a genius.

(Danny gives her a peck on the lips.)

JEREMIAH: **What was that?**

(Danny looks at Jeremiah. He tries again. Michelle gives him
a kiss. Finally he surrenders and accepts that she is kissing him. He starts enjoying what Michelle is doing.)

>   DANNY
>   What is your major?

>   MICHELLE
>   Bio. I'm thinking about being
>   a vet.

(Danny kisses Michelle. Michelle responds.)

>   DANNY
>   That's harder than getting
>   into medical school.

JEREMIAH: **Danny, see how natural that last line was.** (to the class) **Finally, Danny accepted that she took him seriously and that she kissed him.** (to Danny) **You started to play the game when you kissed her back. Did you have fun?**

>   DANNY
>   (nervously giggles)
>   She kissed me.

JEREMIAH: **Did you have fun?**

>   DANNY
>   Yes. I guess I did. Can we do
>   it again?

(The class laughs.)

I let both actors do the scene over. They now have an emotional connection that is stronger the second time.

JEREMIAH: (to Danny) **I know you were frightened at first, but when you accepted that Michelle liked you, your fear dissipated. You started to enjoy her. Danny, when you surrendered and had fun with Michelle, you became intimate— you shared feelings—we believed you, and we enjoyed your performance.** (to the class) **The Five Arts are connected in such a way that when you follow one, the others automatically fall in place. Concentration, Not Knowing, Giving and Receiving, Acceptance, and Relating. They are all interrelated. Break one and you probably lose the others.**

Sets and Locations Are Real

In *Hamlet*, Horatio describes exactly where and what the audience should visualize through the imagery of language:

Horatio:
But look, the morn, in russet mantle clad,
Walks o'er the dew of yon high eastward hill

Hamlet, *Act I, Sc1*

Through language Horatio evokes imaginative images that tell the audience the place, the time, and the weather conditions of the scene. This is a convention of theater. In film, the set and the location are almost always realistic. The camera can photograph the actual dew lifting off yon high eastward hill. You don't need imagination to create the setting, but you do have to accept the situation as if it were real. On film you have to react to this eerie place and give us insight into what you have just experienced.

Unlike the stage, reality on film is essential for believability. Everything has to look real. The set is often the actual location, and the props, costumes, and actors are as close as possible to those of real life. You merely have to accept yourself and your surroundings, relate to the other actor, and say your dialogue. The director and camera operator will take care of the rest.

In *The Films of John Huston*, John McCarty writes that Bogart's shivers on screen in *The African Queen* when he is reacting to the clinging bloodsuckers are as real as are the leeches, which Huston imported and placed on the actor's skin to give the scene an extra dimension of toughness and truth. After Bogart won that year's Best Actor Academy Award, Huston told him, "It's like I said, kid. Real leeches pay off."

Sometimes the actual air temperature and the look of the set may be incompatible, and you may need a lot of imaginative acting to make the scene believable. You might shoot a desert scene in winter's freezing weather, but the movie requires you to act as if it were hot. To give the appearance of heat, even though you are freezing, the makeup department may help a little by spraying water on your face to look like sweat. In any case, you have to accept the fact that you are sweltering. The audience's imagination supplies the missing element—heat. Temperature and climate can require imaginative acceptance when you are in the movies.

Summary

Accepting the imaginary character and the situation as if they were real allows you to be emotionally effective on film. Here's how to develop the Art of Acceptance.

1. Play the game. Acting is a game; be willing to participate.
2. Play like a child. Learn to play without adult inhibitions. Stop judging.
3. Trust.
   a. You are safe physically and emotionally.
   b. Don't be afraid to make an idiot of yourself.
   c. Respect your fellow actor.
4. Surrender the "I"—I can't, I won't, etcetera. Just do it!
5. Have fun. Great actors enjoy acting.

Actor Practice

Playing imaginative games develops you inner child because such games force you to participate. Enjoy it.

1. Sit in a chair. Accept that it is an airplane, racecar, racehorse, quarter horse, a jumper, a space capsule, or whatever. In your mind, actually fly the airplane, drive the car, ride the horse. Whatever you imagine, accept its reality.
2. Go to a park with a group of actors. Play hide and seek, ride a scooter, roller-blade, climb a tree, cross a creek by stepping on the stones. Run across the creek and get your feet wet. Play on the seesaw.
3. Each actor/actress needs a toy truck or car. At the park find an area that consists of dirt with little or no grass. Now get down and play with the cars. Make car sounds—honking, starting and stopping, speeding up and turning, and whatever else you can do.
4. At an amusement park, ride the children's amusements. This takes guts. Recall how you felt as a child. Watch how children respond on the amusements. Imitate them at the workshop.
5. Go to a petting zoo and observe how children respond to the animals. Children are impulsive: if they are frightened, they scream, or when a billy goat tickles them by licking their hand, they giggle. Enter the petting area and let your impulses flow.

Go to a thrift store. Do one or more of the following exercises:

6. Each actor/actress buys a doll. Play house with the dolls. Keep away from any sexual overtones. You always have some wise guy who takes his Ken doll and puts the moves on Barbie. Stay away from that trap.
7. Buy some used clothing to create a character. Buy a cowboy hat, a plaid shirt, and a big belt buckle, and now you're a cowboy. Buy a pair of leotards and a tutu and you're a ballerina. Buy a tuxedo for the groom and a

gown for the prom night and you're a groom and bride. Buy a pair of boxing gloves and shorts and you're a prizefighter. Now read a scene in these costumes. See how they change the scene.

8. Buy oversized clothing that doesn't fit. Remember how big your mother's dress or father's coat and shoes were? Deck yourself out in oversized clothing and play "as if" you are a child playing grownup.

Games lessen your inhibitions and help you develop your sense of acceptance of the imaginary character and circumstances.

9. View the following movies:

Basketball Diaries. Watch how Leonardo DiCaprio does the scene with his mother. Notice how his real feelings make his extreme performance real.

A Double Life. Watch how Ronald Coleman as *Othello* accepts his character and the circumstances of the play to the point where he crosses the line between imagination and reality.

10

The Art of Giving and Receiving

If you and I are in a scene, I don't have an emotional reaction unless it is provoked by something you do. So it's give and take, an aerial act between two actors.

Kathy Bates

Giving and Receiving

You are giving when you experience any emotion on a visible level. This affects the other actor, who then has the responsibility to be aware—to be receiving—and to deal with what you are feeling. Giving and Receiving are intertwined and inseparable. If you are angry and you direct that anger to your fellow actor, you are giving. It means having an emotional experience and sharing it with the other actor. You give her your emotion, which she receives. It stimulates her and helps her create an emotional response to you. As you receive her responses, you in turn respond according to how her responses have affected you. This continuing interchange becomes what scientists call a feedback loop. Richard Brestoff calls it the "most precious exchange" in acting. It is what Kathy Bates means when she says she doesn't have an emotional reaction unless it is provoked by the other actor: "it's give and take, an aerial act between two actors." It is what happens in every great performance.

Give your entire emotional experience to the other actor and then respond to his feedback. A giving actor, one that other actors often refer to as generous, gives you his emotion. He looks you in the face, looks into your eyes, maybe touches you. Your responsibility is to concentrate, receive his emotion, and respond by giving your own resulting emotion back. Through practicing the Art of Giving and Receiving, a good actor becomes an exceptional actor. This may sound simplistic since we all know that people don't talk to each other without having a back-and-forth exchange. True, but in a good movie scene, the dialogue is subordinate to the emotions. People go to a movie not to listen to its words but to see what is going on with the emotions of its characters. In close-up, you can see an actor's emotions and their effect on another actor. The story of a dramatic movie scene is told not in words but in the subtext, which can only be told with the emotions. The Art of Giving and Receiving is the tool of subtext.

Hap, an experienced actor but new to my workshop, is doing a scene from *Demo* by Barbara Bowen with Bernice. In the first reading of their scene, Bernice is superficial and uninteresting, and both actors are passive without really participating. Both give nothing and receive nothing. In the script, Bernice's husband had died and her baby was born with a severe brain malady. She is giving no emotion to Hap, and she is not open to receiving any. I have to jumpstart them into giving and receiving, so I ask them to redo the scene and tell Hap to get angry. Though anger is not necessarily appropriate for this scene, I need something to jolt them into giving and receiving and to get them out of their passivity.

```
                          HAP
(to Jeremiah)
                   But this is a loving scene.
                   Her husband has died. I
                   wouldn't get angry with her.
```

JEREMIAH: **I know it is a loving scene, but try to forget your ideas. Think of this as an exercise in giving.**

```
                          HAP
(to Jeremiah)
                   But she is so sweet, how can I
                   yell at her?
```

JEREMIAH: **Simple. Raise your voice.**

```
(Even though she had told him that his girlfriend was cheat-
ing, Hap has a lot of resistance to yelling. He doesn't
understand Giving and Receiving.)

                       BERNICE
             Are you busy?

                          HAP
                      (yelling)
                   Bernice. What are you doing
                   here?

                       BERNICE
             I stopped by to see Shelly.
```

```
                    HAP
        She's at lunch.
```

(Jeremiah interrupts.)

JEREMIAH: **Louder, Hap. Say it again louder.**

```
                    HAP
              (yelling)
        She's at lunch!


                   BERNICE
              (yelling back)
        Honestly, I stopped by to see
        you! You look great!
```

(Hap is still not feeling anything.)

```
                    HAP
        I should look exhausted. Being
        promoted was the worst thing
        that ever happened to me.
        Almost.
```

(Jeremiah interrupts.)

JEREMIAH: **Say it again. This time I want you to give it everything you've got. Take the roof off. I want 'em to hear you outside on Hollywood Boulevard.**

```
                    HAP
              (really yells)
        I should look exhausted! Being
        promoted was the worst thing
        that ever happened to me!
        Almost!
```

JEREMIAH: **Hap, again, louder, scream at the top or your lungs.**

(Hap is not yet really angry. He is yelling more loudly, but he's not angry.)

```
                    HAP
        I should look exhausted!!
        BEING PROMOTED WAS THE WORST
        THING THAT EVER HAPPENED TO
        ME!! ALMOST!!
```

JEREMIAH: **Angrier, Hap. Do it again.**

> (Finally, Hap becomes angry at me. At last, he is giving
> something that is real. He is frustrated and angry at me,
> but he releases it through the dialogue.)

                    HAP
              (really angry)
         I SHOULD LOOK EXHAUSTED! BEING
         PROMOTED WAS THE WORST THING
         THAT EVER HAPPENED TO ME!
         ALMOST!

(She responds with sadness. Hap continues to yell.)

                    BERNICE
         I've missed you.

                    HAP
              (yelling)
         I HEARD YOU HAD A BABY. CON-
         GRATULATIONS. WHERE IS SHE?

                    BERNICE
         With my mother.

                    HAP
         I HEARD ABOUT LEN'S DEATH.

(Hap is still yelling. Bernice breaks down and cries.
Bernice is immediately affected by Hap's real anger.
Finally, he has her attention.)

                    BERNICE
              (crying)
         I've been avoiding you. I feel
         like a jerk.

(Jeremiah interrupts.)

JEREMIAH: **Hap, what's she feeling?**

                    HAP
(to Jeremiah)
              She doesn't like me yelling at
              her.

JEREMIAH: **No. That's what you think she's thinking. What is she feeling?**

```
                          HAP
      (to Jeremiah)
                    She's crying.
```

JEREMIAH: **Then give your attention to her crying and receive her tears. In the workshop or in the real world, whenever your partner's emotions change, forget my directions and respond to the changes.**

```
      (From this point on, they are giving and receiving. They
      become real, honest, and believable.)

                        BERNICE
                       (crying)
                  I can't blame you.

      (Hap reaches over and lovingly holds her hand.)

                          HAP
                  I'm not blaming you either.

                        BERNICE
                  After all, I was the messen-
                  ger.

                          HAP
                  You were a friend. No one else
                  would tell me Susan was play-
                  ing around. But that's old
                  news.

      (Now they are giving. Both are affected by what they receive
      from the other.)

                        BERNICE
                    (tears in her eyes)
                  I wanted to go out with you,
                  but I thought you'd feel it
                  was a cheap trick.

                          HAP
                  I always knew how you felt.
                  But I couldn't handle a
                  divorce, not then.

      (Bernice's tears turn to love.)
```

<pre>
                    BERNICE
        I thought I wanted to be mar-
        ried. I never loved Lenny, but
        he was a good husband. Someone
        to have a baby with. God got
        even. The doctors say my baby
        will only live a few months.
        She's got water on the brain.
</pre>

(Hap melts. He gives her a hug.)

JEREMIAH: **Hap, your anger led Bernice to her tears. Your emotional commitment forced her to stop thinking and accept the imaginary situation. Giving in acting doesn't mean that you have to be kind and loving. Giving means to experience and impart emotions. When you yelled at Bernice you were giving. She wouldn't have reached this level of performance if you weren't willing to give. Your response to her after she cried was incredible.** (to the class) **Actually, doing this scene for a film would not normally call for anger and shouting, but both of them would have to participate with as much energy and involvement as Hap did with his anger and Bernice with her tears. I had them do the scene this way to get them to experience the level of giving and receiving they need in acting. The final part of the scene where they started giving and receiving was moving and believable. I made Hap yell to carry both of them beyond their nonparticipation. In the real world of film acting, you have to be in the giving-and-receiving mode and ready to go the instant the director says "action." I won't be there to nag you into it. Start by concentrating on the other actor.**

A Scene Is an Ecosystem

In a sense, you can compare an acted scene to the ecosystem of a coral reef with its teeming life. The reef is a continuum of birth, growth, giving, receiving, and dependency. If you kill one part of an ecosystem, the whole system suffers and may even die. When humans almost killed off the sea otters, which eat sea urchins, the sea urchin population flourished and is now killing the coral reefs. Think of your scene as a tiny ecosystem that is kept alive and fascinating by your energy, participation, and give-and-take. If one actor stops giving or receiving, the scene dies.

Chewing Gum Is Lethal

An essential aspect of the Art of Giving and Receiving is not expecting anything in return and then being totally involved with whatever is given to you. Having no expectations is related to the Art of Not Knowing. Give of yourself unconditionally. If you expect or anticipate a response from another actor, you will be disappointed. Respond to what you receive. True giving and receiving means to detach yourself from the aspect of "I"—what "I" want.

On the stage, "upstaging" is a form of not giving and not receiving where an actor, dominated by his self-absorbed "I," tries to attract audience attention to himself when it belongs on someone else. An example is the upstage actor who, while there is action and dialogue going on downstage, mimes getting rid of a piece of chewing gum stuck to his fingers. Instead of receiving what is going on in the scene and giving back his attention and feelings, the upstaging actor lets his ego dictate his actions. He gets the attention of the audience all right, but he kills the scene by being a selfish actor.

Upstaging, Film Style

The chewing-gum bit would be almost impossible for a film actor to do. It would be eliminated in the scene setup or on a second take and would never get to the screen. But you can easily become the upstaging actor in a film by not giving and receiving. The film version of upstaging occurs if you do not listen, do not see, do not respond to what is said and done, and do not accept the responsibility of being a dedicated participant—any one of these is an excellent way to kill the scene and make yourself look bad.

Whatever you give to another actor has to come from your willingness to be generous. Giving creates a heightened state of emotional interaction, and when you give, you generate an energy in your partner. The more you give, the more your partner receives and gives back, the more interesting the scene becomes, and the more interesting you become. I don't think you will ever see a good scene in which only one actor gives a great performance. Great performances are accompanied by other great performances, which are in part the result of the Art of Giving and Receiving.

An audience is a gathering of passive observers. If you are not giving and receiving when you act, you too become a passive observer, and you might as well be sitting out there with the audience. Good acting is active, engaging, and participating. Often someone will say, when watching children playing, "I wish I had their energy," referring to the unending enthusiasm of children as they give everything of themselves to the moment. When you are active instead of passive, you are giving feedback to your partner through your emotions and actions. The act of giving releases your emotional power and forces you to receive what is given back to you. That is film acting.

Giving, Receiving, and Subtext

The following scene is from the film *The Pledge*, with Jack Nicholson and Robin Wright Penn. Look at this film and study the scene. It is an example of a profound moment of giving and receiving, and you can learn a lot from it. It is a brilliant collaboration between Nicholson, Wright Penn, director Sean Penn, and the film editor. There are only six words of dialogue in the scene. The giving and receiving of emotions creates the subtext that tells everything.

```
(Robin Wright Penn has just watched Jack Nicholson reading a
bed-time story to her character's daughter. She goes to her
room. Nicholson, walking towards his room, hears Penn cry-
ing. He knocks, finally he opens the door. Penn sits looking
in the mirror crying.)

                      NICHOLSON
            Lori?

(Nicholson walks over to her and puts his hand on her shoul-
der. Penn kisses his hand.)

                      NICHOLSON
                  (concerned)
            Lori. Are you all right?

(She strokes his face. Nicholson tries to avoid eye contact
but can't help responding to her touch. Nicholson is bewil-
dered. Tears flow down her face. Again she strokes his face.
He is fearful and withdraws.)

(CLOSE-UP on Penn. We see love in her eyes.)

(CLOSE-UP on Nicholson as he drops his head. She strokes his
chest and face.)

(CLOSE-UP on Penn. She kisses Nicholson. Nicholson responds.
Both pull back and look at each other.)

(CLOSE-UP on Penn's hand as she takes his. She smiles at
Nicholson who responds to her advance. He kisses her.)
```

This is the Art of Giving and Receiving. Both actors share their entire emotional experiences with each other and with the audience. The result is a brilliant scene.

Accepting Responsibility

Responsibility distinguishes children from adults. The adult is responsible for the needs of the child. As an actor you have a responsibility for the needs of your fellow actors. When you make yourself responsible, you put yourself into a giving state. If other actors are sad, happy, loving, angry, or fearful, accept what is there and deal with the emotion. A good actor meets the needs of her fellow actor's emotional experience.

The actors in the next scene are Lynn, a beautiful twenty-eight-year-old woman with black hair and green eyes, and David, who is twenty-one, blond, and a surfer. Neither has much acting experience, but they are not beginners. Lynn does not yet understand that it is her responsibility to take what she gets from David and to bring her emotions actively to the scene.

>   LYNN
> I do like it here. I love the
> servants. And their customs.

(Lynn laughs, but it's not a comfortable laugh. She seems nervous. That is her fear.)

>   DAVID
> They are natives, not ser-
> vants.

>   LYNN
> What is the difference?

>   DAVID
> They don't get paid.

>   LYNN
> You mean they do it for free?

>   DAVID
> Well, not exactly.

(Jeremiah interrupts.)

JEREMIAH: **Lynn, what is David feeling?**

>   LYNN
> (to Jeremiah)
>   He's loving.

JEREMIAH: **Look more closely.**

                              LYNN
(to Jeremiah)
                    I see that he is loving. He
                    could be happy. He has a
                    smile.

JEREMIAH: **That's right, but there is something else. Do you see any fear?**

(Lynn looks closely, then takes off her glasses and looks
again.)

                              LYNN
(to Jeremiah)
                    Maybe, I guess he could be
                    fearful.

JEREMIAH: **When you started the scene, you subconsciously picked up his fear
without knowing it.**

                              LYNN
(to Jeremiah)
                    Isn't that what I should be
                    doing? Responding to his emo-
                    tion?

JEREMIAH: **Not until you know what it is. Then you accept responsibility for
his emotional state. You really weren't aware of his fear. What does he need? If
he were three years old and frightened, what would you do?**

                              LYNN
(to Jeremiah)
                    Three years old and fright-
                    ened. I'd spank him and put
                    him in the closet.

(The workshop laughs.)

                              LYNN
(to Jeremiah)
                    Sorry. I guess I would comfort
                    him.

JEREMIAH: **Why don't you give David a hug.**

The moment Lynn hugged David, she connected with his fear and both actors relaxed. She immediately became honest and intimate. This intimacy permeated the scene. Even though she is quite a bit older than David, we believe that they could have been lovers. It was a great piece of work after she accepted responsibility for his fear.

Receiving at the Same Level

When you are Receiving, you need to respond on a level that is equal to or greater than the emotion you have received from the other actor. Both Giving and Receiving are of equal importance. When someone gives you emotional energy, receive her generosity. Accept more than just the emotions you want or think are proper, and receive all feedback from the other actor— voice, facial expression, body language, tension, relaxation, passivity, aggression. Responding immediately to an emotion allows you to go beyond logical thought and let out your impulses.

The Relating Exercise

I developed the Relating Exercise in Chapter 1 to teach you how to recognize another actor's emotion and, by responding to that emotion, how to use your energy in such a way that you become a better actor. The first step in the process is emotional copying. If you receive anger at seven on a scale of ten, then return your emotion at seven or more.

Returning emotional energy at or above the same intensity you receive it does not mean to breathe harder, wave your arms, make facial grimaces and gestures, or shout louder. It means receiving the energy given you and internally matching its intensity so that you become an equally participating partner in the scene. If the other actor yells at you, with strong emotional energy, that he loves you, you may reject the love or receive it; but either way, you have to reject or receive with the same or greater internal energy than given. If you respond with a lesser energy, you then become a nonparticipant, an uninteresting place holder, and the scene dies. Again, this doesn't mean that you should go through external antics to demonstrate that you are matching the energy level given to you. You merely have to receive what is given, take it seriously, and respond honestly.

Different Emotional Levels

Your response to the emotion you receive from your partner does not have to be that exact emotion. As long as your energy remains equal to or greater than the level received, your emotion may be different. If your partner is angry, your response could be laughter, fear, sadness, love, or any combination of emotions, including anger. This is a reciprocal event that comes from both giving and receiving. It does not come from some idea as to how you should or would respond.

Two actors in my workshop do a scene in which their mother has just died. Earl starts off by trying to fake sadness and Ozzie is reading his lines without participating until Earl's faking strikes him as funny. Usually I stop actors who start off with an idea instead of an emotion, but for some intuitive reason I let them continue.

```
                OZZIE
        How are you holding up?

                EARL
            (trying to be sad)
        Okay. You?

                OZZIE
        I'm still in shock.

                EARL
        Maryann took her to the doc-
        tor. They just told her she
        was fine. Keep taking the
        pills.

                OZZIE
        The heart medicine?

                EARL
        Yeah. She was putting on her
        coat and . . .

(Earl takes a long pause. He is trying to force his tears.
Still working from his idea.)

                EARL
        She said she felt funny. Those
        were her last words. She col-
        lapsed and was gone.

(Ozzie sees Earl trying to fake sadness and tears, and he
starts laughing.)
```

> OZZIE
> (laughing)
> You're sure the doctor had
> nothing to do with it. I mean,
> could he have caused it?

(Earl is still trying to fake his tears.)

> EARL
> She's had heart problems for
> years. She was dead before she
> hit the floor.

(Ozzie still laughing, mimics Earl's whining.)

> OZZIE
> (mocking Earl)
> Okay, Earl. We've got to get
> back tomorrow. We can't take
> off any more time.

(The class laughs.)

> OZZIE
> (mocking)
> I wanted to clear up the
> details before we go.

When Earl realizes that Ozzie is making fun of him, he stops trying to fake his tears. He gets angry.

> EARL
> (angry)
> What details? Now you're going
> to tell me you hate the casket?

> OZZIE
> No, hell, no. It's fine.

> EARL
> Good, because it was a pain in
> the ass. The home tried to
> soak us for mahogany with
> inlaid mother-of-pearl. They
> get you when you're vulnera-
> ble. Maryann's crying her eyes
> out and that bastard. . . .

(Ozzie really laughs when he hears "crying her eyes out." He finds it hysterical.)

> OZZIE
> (laughing)
> Earl . . .

(Earl responds to Ozzie's laughter by getting angrier.)

> EARL
> I told him pine. She wouldn't
> have wanted me to blow it all
> on a box.

> OZZIE
> (laughing)
> You're right. I would have
> done the same thing.

> EARL
> (angry)
> It wasn't easy providing for a
> wife and kids plus Mom.

> OZZIE
> (laughing)
> I helped, when I could.

> EARL
> (angry)
> I wasn't saying anything.

> OZZIE
> (laughing)
> But the house?

> EARL
> (angry)
> What about it?

> OZZIE
> (laughing)
> We were both . . . It's half
> mine.

```
                    EARL
               (still angry)
          You moved to Springfield and
          stuck it all on me. Well, now
          I'm stuck with the house.

(This stops Ozzie for a moment. He gets angry.)

                    OZZIE
               (irate)
          The hell you are.

                    EARL
          Take your best shot, brother.
          My name's on the deed.

(Both actors have peaked their anger at each other. On
Earl's last line, Ozzie looks like he's been hit in the
stomach. They sit there for a few seconds in shock at what
they did. Then they relax and laugh.)
```

JEREMIAH: **That was great. Thank you. When you two quit being fake and started responding to the laughter and the anger, you looked great.** (to the class) **See how exciting the scene was when they started giving and receiving?**

The class has questions.

```
                    MARIA
(to Jeremiah)
               I have a question. I liked
               what they did, but they
               weren't copying each other's
               emotions. One was sad, and one
               was laughing and then angry.
               This negates everything you
               said about receiving and
               relating to the other actor.
```

JEREMIAH: **You picked up on that? Good. You don't have to always give back the same emotion. If you did, every scene would be all laughing, all anger, all sadness, or all whatever, and that's pretty monotonous. You can control what you think, but you can't control what emotion you are going to experience. In everyday life, you don't always let other people see what emotions you are feeling, but you feel them just the same. In acting, you don't hide your emotion. What comes, comes, and you let everyone see it. That's what makes a scene interesting. You have to relate to an actor's emotion and respond with the emotion it brings up in you no matter what it is. But you don't have to respond with** the same emotion, only with the same intensity. Your scene is more fascinating when the emotional feedback is unexpected, like Ozzie's laughter when he saw Earl faking sadness.

```
                        KATHY
      (to Jeremiah)
                   Yes, but Ozzie never dealt
                   with Earl's sadness.
```

JEREMIAH: **That's because there was no sadness. Earl wasn't sad. He was trying to be sad—he was faking it. Ozzie laughed when he saw how ridiculous Earl looked, but he was still sad about his mother. His emotional response was appropriate to what he received.**

There Are No Officially Sanctioned Responses

In their scene, Earl and Ozzie were both sad that their mother died, but each responded appropriately to what the other gave him. You don't always express an emotion according to some stereotype. In real life, the pressure of society and your logic often make you hide what you feel. In acting, you don't have that pressure, and it is your job never to hide an emotion. There is no officially sanctioned visual reaction to any emotion you experience in life. Happy people sometimes cry, but they are still happy. Sometimes women cry when they are angry. Embarrassed people sometimes laugh, but they are still embarrassed. People in love sometimes get angry at each other, but they are still in love. Sometimes people laugh when devastated by a tragedy; they do not know why they have laughed, but they are still devastated. Couples about to get married sometimes fight angrily in the few minutes before the bride walks down the aisle, yet they are still in love. Any emotional response in acting is valid just so long as it's genuine. When Earl tried to be sad, he was faking and looked awful. But when he really got angry at Ozzie for mocking him, he looked real and was interesting. Then Ozzie responded to Earl's anger with his own anger. Both were sad about their mother, but they responded to what each was giving the other.

Acting on a creative level can evoke a lot of different responses that can surprise both you and the other actors. This is what Jack Nicholson was referring to in an interview when he said that unpredictability is the most arresting quality an actor can have. The Relating Exercise never demands or dictates a specific emotion, only that you respond with what you feel and that you stay on the same emotional level as that of the other actor.

The Art of Giving and Receiving provides you with a natural way of creating energy. Your talent expands on the emotional feedback you receive from the other actor. Your emotion escalates to a point where this emotion changes—either because your emotion has peaked, or because the other actor has changed. When an emotion escalates to its maximum point, it will automatically shift. Also, when the other actor changes, you automatically respond. In either case, when you reach this level of Giving and Receiving, the experience happens without conscious thought.

Your personality and talent, combined with the Art of Giving and Receiving, equal your film energy. The more you give, the more energy you get. It is a regenerative process that makes for a good scene while enhancing your performance.

Summary

Give your entire emotional experience to the other actor and respond to all feedback. No matter what emotion you feel, as long as it does not injure the other actor, share it and be willing to accept any feedback.

Actor Practice

1. When another actor is experiencing a feeling, look for physical ways to enhance that experience.
2. Use the magic "If." Ask yourself: If the other actor were two years old, how would I deal with his emotion? If he were afraid, sad, angry, loving, or laughing, what would I do?
3. You can talk to a two-year-old, but you will be more successful if you are physical. When you hold or touch children, you get their attention. If an actor is sad, hold him. Wipe his tears. Be loving. If he is loving, hold him. Kiss him. Touch and stroke him.
4. Physicality is the essence of film acting. Say "I love you" without touching your partner. Now do it again but this time stroke her face. Notice the difference. When you share your physicality, you bring credibility to your work.
5. Get angry in a scene with a partner. Now do the scene again, but this time both actors should poke each other.
6. Share your emotions. Great actors only have to look and they are affected by the other actor. They are aware of their partner's experience and allow it to affect them on both the conscious and subconscious levels.
7. Begin by seeing your partner's experience. Eventually it will affect you on an emotional level.
8. In real life, practice recognizing the emotional experiences of other people. This is important to you, because recognizing and identifying emotions in others is indispensable for an actor.

11

The Senses

What I tell actors is to look and trust the circumstances and the audience will get it. Not just pretend to look, but really look.

Sydney Pollack

See through Untainted Eyes

As Abdullah Idrissi says, "The seller of horses who seeks success wears dark glasses and loose robes to conceal what his eyes and body are saying." Since actors don't usually wear dark glasses and loose robes, you can easily see what they say with their eyes and bodies. See your fellow actors undistorted by preconceived ideas, because preconceptions turn your attention to yourself and prevent you from performing well. See everyone and everything as if for the first time, with enchantment and through untainted eyes.

In this next workshop scene, Angie, who is bright and attractive with short red hair, is in my workshop for the first time. She has played a small role in a feature film and has been in two TV commercials. In this scene, she is interviewing for a job as an airline pilot trainee. James, the man interviewing her, is tall, easy-going, and relaxed, but the script says he is bored and tired. Angie accepts this idea and doesn't see and hear that James's eyes, voice, and body are telling her something completely different.

```
(James is friendly and open.)

                    JAMES
          Hello. I'm James Wilson.

                    ANGIE
          I'm Angie Anders.

(Angie is wary.)
```

                    JAMES
        Please sit down.

                    ANGIE
        Thank you.

                    JAMES
        I see that you just graduated
        from college.

                    ANGIE
        Sarah Lawrence.

(James shows genuine, friendly interest.)

                    JAMES
        I'll be direct. Why do you
        think you'd make a good candi-
        date for commercial airline
        pilot?

                    ANGIE
        I love it. I've logged over
        1,000 hours. It's my dream to
        fly for a living.

                    JAMES
        Good. I see you're not mar-
        ried. Are you engaged?

(Angie is wary and a little angry.)

                    ANGIE
        Do I have a boyfriend? Yes.

                    JAMES
        Do you plan on getting mar-
        ried?

(Angie is unreceptive.)

                    ANGIE
        Not until I finish my train-
        ing. But I don't want children
        right away, if that's what
        you're hinting at.

JEREMIAH: **Angie, what is James feeling?**

```
                        ANGIE
    (to Jeremiah)
              He's bored because he's been
              doing this all day. And he's
              tired of interviewing people.
```

JEREMIAH: **Not even close.** (to the group) **Angie is projecting an idea from the script onto James rather than seeing his real feelings. Angie, look at him. Is he feeling sadness, happiness, anger, fear, love?**

```
                        ANGIE
    (to Jeremiah)
              He's smiling.
```

JEREMIAH: **Good, you see him. Now, respond to what you see.**

```
                        ANGIE
    (to Jeremiah)
              But the script says he's bored
              and tired of interviewing.
```

JEREMIAH: **That's an idea. I don't see a guy who's bored. Look at him. You didn't see or listen to what was right in front of you, so you dealt with him as if he were bored, and you gave a performance we didn't believe. I don't care what the script says, the only thing you have to deal with is James as he is at the moment. Now, do it again. Forget the ideas. Look at him. Deal with James as he is, not as you decided he would be.**

When Angie did the scene again, dealing with James's real feelings rather than with what she had decided they were, she gave us an interesting and believable performance. You cannot know what another human being is thinking, only what he is feeling. "Why" he feels as he does is not important. "Why" causes judgment. When you guess at or examine the reason behind an actor's emotion, you become involved in thinking, not seeing or relating. The other actor's reasons for being sad, angry, fearful, laughing, or loving have little or nothing to do with your response. His emotional state at the moment has everything to do with your response. You can see what another actor is feeling, but you're not a mind reader, and you can't know what he is thinking. Don't even try. Just look and listen, and your responses will be appropriate.

Eyes and facial expressions give you insight into emotions. Right at the beginning of a scene, I try to get you to visually identify what the other actor is feeling, without interference from personal judgment or script interpretation. Bad acting happens when you project your ideas onto the other actor.

An actor's eyes, facial expressions, and voice tell you the most about his emotions. His body language gives you a lot of information. What are his mannerisms? Everything he does is related in some way to his feelings. How does he touch himself? Is he tapping his finger, his foot? How does he cross his arms? Is his posture defensive or aggressive? How does he walk, talk, run, take a drink, eat, light a cigarette, read, write, open a door? His body language comes directly from his emotional state. But you have to see it.

Several popular books on "body language" try to show that a particular body state or movement indicates a specific mental, emotional, or psychological state. Avoid these "idea" books. They are superficial adulterations of the anthropologist Edward T. Hall's scientific study of nonverbal communication, and they can lead you into what Stanislavsky called mechanical acting. In your work, reading body language is much more than just your mechanically correlating a body position with a state of mind. It is seeing and hearing everything the other actor does and says, and being open to what he is feeling relative to you and to the given circumstances. Acting is not—and neither is life—a list in which you match one term against another to come up with the proper way to conduct yourself.

The Abilities

Seeing, listening, and touching stimulate intuitive responses when you take in what the other actor says and does. Although hearing, touching, smelling, and tasting tell you a lot about another person, your eyes reveal the most. You can grasp a huge amount of information in one glance. So don't cripple your keen visual sense by categorizing and stereotyping and deciding ahead of time how you are going to respond. See everything as a child does, with simplicity, and discover the world as it truly is, not as you expected it or planned it to be.

In the next scene, Ellen, an attractive, athletic girl with the self-assurance of a good athlete, plays an ice skating instructor who is giving skating lessons to John, a handsome and rugged novice skater.

```
                JOHN
     I heard that some girl got
     hurt today.


                ELLEN
     One of the beginners slipped
     and hit the back of her head.
     There was blood everywhere.
```

```
                    JOHN
          Is she all right?
```

(Ellen begins to cry. Her crying is real, and it catches us
by surprise because of her initial self-assurance.)

```
                    ELLEN
               (crying)
          We don't know yet. It was
          really bad. If she hadn't
          tensed up and gone with it,
          you know, relaxed, she
          wouldn't have gotten hurt,
          but she fought it. I was
          there when it happened.
```

(John doesn't know what to do. He looks at Jeremiah.)

JEREMIAH: **Stay in the scene, John. Don't look at me. Look at her.**

```
                    JOHN
(to Jeremiah)
          Why is she crying? I don't
          understand why she's crying.
```

JEREMIAH: **Why she's crying is not important. What's important is that she is
crying. Don't try to figure out why. Just see her tears and deal with that. Ellen,
your intuitive response was marvelous when you told him about the skater's
fall.**

```
                    ELLEN
(to Jeremiah)
          It wasn't the skater. My dog
          Kerrie died yesterday, and she
          keeps popping into my feel-
          ings. I'm sorry. I couldn't
          stop crying. I guess I
          shouldn't have come today.
```

JEREMIAH: **We're all sorry, Ellen. No, come to workshop. It's a safe place to let
out emotions.** (to the group) **Here in the workshop and on film, we wouldn't
know why Ellen is crying. We assume it's because of her empathy for the skater
who got hurt. But we don't know what she's thinking when she's crying. We can
see what she's feeling. She's sad. Deal with the sadness, John. Don't take yourself out of a scene by trying to figure out why she's sad.**

Don't take your gift of sight for granted. When you see clearly, your acting will become more intuitive. Remember, become enchanted with and enjoy the unique qualities every human being has to offer.

The Maestro's Ears

Great actors are sensitive to the slightest variation in the other actor's tone. Train yourself to hear every line as if you are hearing it for the very first time. The maestro of a symphony orchestra can detect a single incorrect note played in a hundred-piece orchestra. Develop your hearing so you can detect the emotional meaning—not rational meaning—behind every vocal intonation and nuance. How do you develop your hearing? By practicing the Art of Concentration, through focused concentration on the other actor. The other actor's tonal variations and his way of speaking reveal his emotional state. Using this information, your intuition will give you the right choices for your responses.

How to Listen

Why do we stop listening to our girlfriends, boyfriends, husbands, wives, parents, friends, children? Why do we constantly talk about our problems but feel that nobody is paying attention? Probably because they aren't. Everyone is too busy, overworked, and self-absorbed. Many of us have forgotten the art of listening. We are so assaulted by information, language, and advertisements that we tune out. We are not only oblivious to the meaning of the words, we are oblivious to the emotions behind them.

Hear everything. True listening improves your awareness. If you were to participate in a mixing session for a movie, you would see how many sounds go into a single scene, sounds you hear all the time but of which you're not consciously aware. It's not unusual for a scene to have twenty or more sound tracks, with a single different sound on each track—dialogue, footsteps, car alarms, clothing rustling, laughter, music, people talking, doors opening and closing, dogs barking, traffic noise, sounds of nature—all taking place at the same time. When all the sounds are mixed together at the proper volume, the result is plain old real-life sound. In an ordinary room, listen for the sounds that most people would never hear simply because they are not listening.

Shunryu Suzuki, a Zen master, gives perfect advice for actors: try to stop thinking when you listen to someone. Forget what you want to say, and just listen, because if you have an idea and are trying to respond to what someone says, you won't hear everything. Your understanding will be one-sided. When you listen, be completely involved. Usually when you listen to a person say something, you hear it as a kind of echo of yourself. You are actually listening to your own opinion. If the statement agrees with your opinion, you accept it. But if it does not, you will reject it, and you may not even really hear it. Do not be caught by this or by taking what the person says only as a statement without understanding the spirit behind the words.

Just listen. When you listen to the other actor, forget all your preconceived ideas and your subjective opinions. What is right and wrong is mostly irrelevant. The meaning of the words is never as important as the emotion behind them. Listen to how the other actor feels about what she says. Don't judge! Even when the literal meaning of the words contradicts her feelings, go with the feelings. Your experience will come from listening to her experience and seeing her emotions. You want your subconscious mind to assimilate this input and then react emotionally and intuitively.

In the following scene, Janet, tall and sun-tanned, is open and aware. Rob, a beginning actor, is pleasant and good-looking. He is seriously concerned with the directions in the script and what they tell him to do.

```
(Rob is uptight from the beginning. He is not listening to
Janet. He keeps his eyes on the page. He hears her words,
but only to listen for his cue line. He doesn't see her
face or respond to any changes in Janet's tone.)

                    JANET
                 (laughing)
            Do you ski?

                    ROB
                 (eyes on the page)
            I snow board.

                    JANET
            Are you married?

                    ROB
            Separated.

                    JANET
                 (smiling)
            You mean she is in the hotel
            room waiting for you.

(Rob's eyes still on the page. He never looks at her.)

                    ROB
            No. I mean like, I'm waiting
            for the divorce papers.
```

(Janet is intent on Rob. She is sensitive to what he says and how he says it. She is believable.)

> JANET
> How long were you married?

(Rob is still concentrating on the script.)

> ROB
> Two years. Until I discovered she was in love with the shop-ping channel and I was twenty-one thousand dollars in debt.

> JANET
> That's what I make a year.

(Rob is really stiff and proper.)

> ROB
> My accountant said it will take three years to pay it off. I have every penny accounted for. I lost 10 pounds so far.

(Janet laughs with real enjoyment.)

> JANET
> (laughing)
> Maybe I should try that diet.

JEREMIAH: **Rob, what did she just do?**

> ROB
> (to Jeremiah)
> Uh . . . What do you mean?

JEREMIAH: **I mean, she just did something. Do you know what she did?**

> ROB
> (to Jeremiah)
> She . . . I don't know.

JEREMIAH: **She laughed. You didn't hear her, and you didn't see her. You weren't doing a scene with her, you were doing a scene with the script. I want**

you to look at Janet when she's talking. Don't take your eyes off of her. Listen
to the sound of her voice. Try to imitate her tone of voice. If she laughs, I want
you to laugh. If she raises her voice, raise yours. If she gets angry, you get angry.
I want you to do everything exactly like she does. Look at your script only when
you need your next line.

I whisper in Janet's ear that I want her to yell on the first line, laugh on the
second, and be loving on the third. Then repeat that pattern until the end of the
scene. I ask for this to force Rob into concentrating on her. He has to concentrate on her in order to be able to mimic her. They continue.

```
                    JANET
              (really SHOUTING)
          DO YOU SKI?!
```

(Rob is surprised. He looks frightened. He looks at
Jeremiah.)

JEREMIAH: **Don't look at me. Look at her! You can't tell what she's doing when
you look at me. Imitate what she's doing. Janet, start it again.**

```
                    JANET
              (again, SHOUTING)
          DO YOU SKI?!
```

(This time he shouts his line at the same level as hers.)

```
                     ROB
                 (shouting)
          I SNOW BOARD!
```

(Now she changes and laughs as she gives her line.)

```
                    JANET
                 (laughing)
          Are you married?
```

(Rob, again surprised, laughs as he speaks. By now he is
watching her like a hawk so he won't miss what she's doing.)

```
                     ROB
                 (laughing)
          Separated.
```

(Then, as Jeremiah asked her, she becomes loving.)

```
                  JANET
              (loving)
          You mean she is in the hotel
          room waiting for you.


                  ROB
              (loving in return)
          No. I mean like, I'm waiting
          for the divorce papers.
```

(Rob is working hard to catch her every expression, attitude, and tone of voice. It makes him look believable even though he is shouting.)

```
                  JANET
              (yelling)
          HOW LONG WERE YOU MARRIED?!


                  ROB
              (shouting back)
          TWO YEARS! UNTIL I DISCOVERED
          SHE WAS IN LOVE WITH THE SHOP-
          PING CHANNEL AND I WAS TWENTY-
          ONE THOUSAND DOLLARS IN DEBT!
```

JEREMIAH: (to the group) **See how his performance immediately changed? I told him to mimic her exactly, so he had no choice. He had to concentrate on her.** (to Rob) **You concentrated on Janet, so you reacted to her, not the page. Even though you were shouting, we actually believed you. Did you feel the difference?**

```
                  ROB
      (to Jeremiah)
              It was scary.
```

JEREMIAH: **Sure it's scary. That's because you were alive. To mimic her exactly, you had to concentrate on her. You were forced to hear what she was doing—was she soft, loud, sad, fearful, intimate? Was she stuttering or stammering? Did she pause, giggle, laugh? You didn't have time to worry about keeping your eyes on the page. So you really concentrated on her. And you were scared because you didn't know what might happen. That's what life is—that's what acting is—you take everything as it comes and deal with it, and it's scary. If you act according to what she does, you're relating; if you don't, you're in your head. Stay out of your head, and react honestly to what you see and hear.**

The Sense of Touch

Touching is using some part of your body to contact, stimulate, reassure, or get a response from someone else. If you touch the other actor, the scene you are doing will be improved. You may touch another person in many ways—your hand on an arm, fingertips to the face, a pat on the back, a handshake, a kick under the table, a nudge with your shoulder, cheek to cheek, a hug, a shove, a slap, a kiss, holding a hand, using your body as a weapon, a caress, a blow with your fist, and so on. Every one of these concentrates your attention and says something. Touch is an important element of practicing the Art of Giving and Receiving.

The information of touch comes mainly from the hands. Everyone you meet shakes your hand or touches you in his own unique way that reveals something about himself. Is he afraid or confident? If it's a handshake, is it limp, calming, friendly, damp, strong, painful, clinging? If it's a touch on your arm, your body, your face, what does it tell you? Become aware of what a touch tells you.

Your touch makes an intimate connection between you and whom you touch, and conveys some part, or even all, of your emotional state. Your touch gives the moment its own reality and your acting becomes more grounded. Your touch also helps both you and the person touched to sense what the other is feeling. In my workshop, I use touch in these ways: to relax, to stimulate love, to provoke anger, and to stimulate laughter.

Touching to Relax

If you don't know how to control personal fear in a scene, it will show. Touching acts as an escape valve to alleviate fear. If your partner is frightened, touching him helps calm him down—and it helps you too. When you respond to an actor's touch, you automatically activate a process of giving and receiving. This next scene shows one way an actor can help another with a touch. Alvin, a beginning actor, is big and strong but tries to hide his intimidation at acting before a group. Casie is a pleasant young woman who has already played a role in a TV movie.

                    ALVIN
               (fearful)
          How are you?

                    CASIE
          I'm great.

(Alvin is stiff, and we can see that he is really scared.)

> ALVIN
> I'm going to get another soda.
> Would you like one?

> CASIE
> A Coke. Please.

(Jeremiah interrupts.)

JEREMIAH: **Casie, what is Alvin feeling?**

> CASIE
> (to Jeremiah)
> I think he's loving.

JEREMIAH: **I don't see love.**

> CASIE
> (to Jeremiah)
> Fear . . . Is he afraid?

JEREMIAH: **Yes, good! Now if Alvin were two years old, what would you do?**

> CASIE
> (to Jeremiah)
> I would talk to him softly.

JEREMIAH: **Two-year-olds aren't great at verbal communication. What else could you do?**

> CASIE
> (to Jeremiah)
> I'd probably give him a hug.

JEREMIAH: **So give him a hug. And take it from the top.**

> (From her chair, Casie leans
> over and gives Alvin a hug.
> Then they do the scene. Alvin
> has lost a lot of his fear.
> His performance is not great,
> but without his fear, he does
> better, and he's in a better
> space to learn.)

JEREMIAH: (to the group) **See that? When Casie gives Alvin a hug, he relaxes. The hug made her real to him. She's now a person, not a character in the script, and he can trust her. A hug is a strong way to connect emotionally with another person. See how Alvin's work immediately improved?**

Touching to Stimulate Love

In the film *A Map of the World*, Julianne Moore, who has recently lost a child in the film, is baby-sitting David Strathairn's children. The children are asleep and Straitharn and Moore are sitting on the floor.

```
(Moore was crying and has just woken up after napping on
Straitharn's lap. Both look in each other's eyes. Straitharn
strokes her face while straightening her hair. She places
her hand on his hand. He touches her face. Both hesitate.
They kiss. She caresses his hair. Finally, Moore, who is
also married, pulls back. She drops her eyes.)

                    MOORE
          That's all.

(Straitharn nods in agreement. Moore turns slightly and
rests her head against his head.)
```

Touching visually lets us know that both characters are lonely and attracted to each other. It allows the actors to express love and affection on screen without dialogue.

Emotions follow physical action. Touching, as in this scene, can stimulate genuine feelings and create intimacy—caring, concern, even love. A hand stroking a cheek, or a kiss, can look sexual without necessarily being sexual, because intimacy is not the same as sexuality. My workshop exercises are designed to achieve intimacy and stimulate genuine emotions. These emotions sometimes look sexual, but they are not.

Touching to Provoke Anger

As an actor, you need to be able to feel anger immediately and completely. Anger is a feeling that many women suppress, just as men traditionally suppress their tears. In my workshop, a quick way for my students to get in touch with anger is through physically poking and pushing. Objectionable physical contact forces you to deal with anger.

```
In the following workshop scene, Michael, who is six feet
four inches and weighs two hundred and fifty pounds, is a
```

former linebacker for the Dallas Cowboys; he has never acted before. In the scene, the two characters are in contention, so Michael starts out trying to be angry. He is tense from the nervousness of acting for the first time and from thinking he has to be angry. His voice becomes high and squeaky.

>   MICHAEL
>   (squeaky voice)
>   Happy Birthday Billy.

>   BILLY
>   What are you following me for?

>   MICHAEL
>   I wanted to know where you buy
>   your clothes.

(The workshop thinks it's funny that this big football player speaks in a squeaky, shaking voice.)

>   BILLY
>   Why don't you bother somebody
>   else?

>   MICHAEL
>   I like bothering you.

(Jeremiah interrupts.)

JEREMIAH: **Michael, we can see that you're nervous. What I want you to do is poke Billy's shoulder with your finger.** (Jeremiah holds up his index finger.) **And Billy, you poke him back.**

(They continue the scene.)

>   BILLY
>   What do you want?

(Michael pokes once, half-heartedly, and continues to be nervous and squeaky.)

>   MICHAEL
>   Money. It's payday.

(Jeremiah interrupts.)

JEREMIAH: **Come on! Poke each other. Keep poking and read your lines.**

> (Michael pokes Billy in the shoulder on each line. Billy pokes back. They continue poking, each getting a little more heated on each poke.)

>   BILLY
>   (poke!)
>   What?

>   MICHAEL
>   (poke!)
>   100 Ben Franks.

>   BILLY
>   (poke!)
>   You're out of your mind.

> (They progressively put more and more energy into poking each other. Their faces are flushed. Michael's voice becomes normal—normal angry. They finish the scene, flushed, excited, angry. They finally laugh.)

JEREMIAH: (to the group) **See, it takes about a page before Michael's voice drops; that's when he feels real anger and forgets about being nervous. From poking, Michael's concentration becomes focused, his emotions become honest. He gets angry—and believable.** (to Michael) **Michael that was excellent. No one would ever suspect this is your first workshop.** (to the group) **See how this simple physical action stimulated his anger?**

> **Caution:** Don't use physicality in the workshop, in an audition, in rehearsal, or on the set unless it is planned and you are given specific directions. Physicality can be, and often is, dangerous. Physical movement in a film is carefully planned and rehearsed to prevent both injury and lawsuits. Even actions that look simple—like slapping, or grabbing an actor's arm to turn him around—can, without careful planning, cause injury. Don't do anything physical without the knowledge of the film's stunt coordinator, whose job it is to insure that both routine and complex physicality is planned and properly done. A further caution: if you give the impression that you get physical without planning, you risk being labeled as unstable and dangerous—and therefore unemployable.

In my workshops, I use a certain amount of planned physicality to stimulate students into learning how anger develops. But eventually, you gain confidence in your ability to generate anger, and it will become instinctively available, without physical action.

Touching to Stimulate Laughter

Tickling can stimulate laughter. I sometimes use tickling, as in the following scene, to get an actor out of his head and into the experience.

```
                    BILLY
         You are a mean, rotten, con-
         temptible, vicious, despica-
         ble, and ill-tempered . . .
```

(Joan starts to smile but stifles it.)

```
                    BILLY
         person and on top of that you
         smell.
```

(She again stifles a smile.)

```
                    JOAN
         Is that a no?
```

```
                    BILLY
         I can't work with someone as
         spiteful as you.
```

(Jeremiah interrupts.)

JEREMIAH: **Joan, you started to smile. Did you think what Billy said was funny?**

```
                    JOAN
(to Jeremiah)
         Yes, but I don't think my
         character would laugh when
         someone is calling her names.
         It doesn't make sense.
```

JEREMIAH: **Instinctively, you had the impulse to smile. A big part of good acting is acknowledging your impulses. Any impulse is genuine feeling, so let it out. I want you to do the scene again. This time I want both of you to laugh. Laugh through the whole scene while you say your lines. If you can't really laugh, force your laughter.**

Joan tries to laugh as she does the scene again, but because she has a fixed idea about the scene, she can't let go. Finally, I whisper to one of the women in the workshop to kneel down behind Joan's chair and tickle her. She breaks into laughter. Then I have her go to the beginning of the scene and do it over. This time, she lets go of any ideas as to what her character would or would not do, and she laughs at what strikes her as funny.

JEREMIAH: **Tickling you forced you to let go of your ideas and participate with Billy in the scene. A director wouldn't do this when shooting a film, but here in the workshop, I do it to help you break through your preconceived idea. Your intuition was listening to him, and you had the impulse to laugh. But your logic stifled your impulse.**

```
                         JOAN
        (to Jeremiah)
                    But it was inappropriate for
                    the scene.
```

JEREMIAH: **That's a judgment. But acting is having experiences and then letting out your impulses. With impulses, acting has no right or wrong. Impulses make you interesting to an audience. When you do the scene, forget about judgment. When you look at your tape later, look at how interesting you are. On film, what you think is an inappropriate reaction, if it's honest, works better than anything you can plan. That's why engineers, scientists, and accountants rarely make good actors. Trust your instincts and impulses—they will make you a brilliant actor.**

Smell and Taste

In acting, we generally don't have the opportunities to experience smell and taste as we do the other senses. Odors do stimulate and can help you into a state of pleasure (perfume) or an unpleasant state (pungent odor). Odors strongly evoke memories. If you are sensitive to odors, you can color your performance by letting a scent affect you emotionally. One student, after a steamy scene, said that her partner's cologne reminded her of her ex-boyfriend. I think five of the actors in the workshop later bought that exact cologne.

Summary

1. Look at everything through child eyes, undistorted by preconceived ideas. The primary way to have experiences is through the sense of sight.

Look at the other actor. Is he laughing, sad, angry, fearful, or loving? When you can answer that, you are in the moment. Seeing with clarity is the key to the Art of Relating.

2. Don't let preconceived ideas or judgments prevent you from using your senses of sight, touch, hearing, and smell.
3. You can only see what someone is feeling. You cannot know what someone is thinking.
4. Seeing and hearing tell you the most about a person's emotional state.
    a. Look in your partners' eyes for their emotional state.
    b. Look at their body language.
    c. Listen to the tone and emotion behind the dialogue.
5. Life around us consists of sounds that we ordinarily tune out. Concentrated listening makes us aware of all these sounds.
6. Touching another actor helps to dispel fear, creates intimacy, and often makes a scene go better.
7. Emotions follow physical action.
8. Acting is having experiences, and then letting out impulses. Impulses make actors interesting to an audience.
9. Smell and taste are less important than the other senses, but they sometimes do indicate and stimulate emotions.

Actor Practice

1. Look at the model in a full-page magazine ad for thirty seconds. Try to recognize what he or she is feeling.
2. Close the magazine and write down a description of the model: what the model was wearing and everything that was in the picture, such as props, printing, and background.
3. When you watch movies, try to guess what each actor is feeling. This is relatively easy on the big screen, but not in real life or when you are acting. To be a great film actor, you have to develop the ability to see what the other actors feel.
4. To enhance your ability to listen, close your eyes and listen to the sounds around you. Then write a list of what you have heard. Do this every day for a week in the same location and see if you can increase the number of sounds you hear.
5. Before you start a scene, close your eyes, take a deep breath, and listen to the sounds of the workshop. Can you hear yourself breathe? Can you hear your partner breathe?
6. Listen to the change of tone in your partner's voice. Does he speak in a monotone? Does he emphasize certain words? Is he using his real voice?

7. Look at the tape of your scene and see if you are really listening to the other actor. When were you most interesting? When you were listening or talking? It should be both.

8. Touching relaxes you and connects you to the other actor. It can arouse love, provoke anger, and stimulate laughter.

   a. Watch how actors on screen use touch.

   b. Become aware of how people respond to your touch.

   c. Become aware of how you respond to a touch when someone shakes your hand, holds your hand, kisses you, hugs you, or touches you in any way.

12

Intimacy, Empathy, and Intuition

Like any artist, the actor has to be open to inspiration, intuition, and the unconscious. When you know what you are looking for, that's all you get. But when you're open to what's possible, you get something new. And that's creativity.

Alan Alda

You Are What You Are: The First Ingredient of Intimacy

Good actors come in all configurations—tall, short, fat, skinny, handsome, beautiful, homely, awkward, old, disfigured, handicapped, and funny looking. They know what they are, and they have accepted themselves. They have no need to keep secrets, and as a result they can share emotions and intimacy with other actors. To become a good actor, accept yourself. If you're fat, you're fat; if your nose is crooked, it's crooked; if your voice is squeaky, it's squeaky; if you're afraid, you're afraid. You are what you are. Accept what is and get on with turning yourself into a great actor.

In *Terms of Endearment*, Shirley MacLaine invites Jack Nicholson to her bedroom. They face each other on opposite sides of the bed. Shirley opens her negligée. Jack, cockily and without apology, unzips his sweatshirt and out pops his big belly. Jack lets Shirley know, like it or not, that this is who he is. Instead of sucking in his gut and hiding what could reduce his masculine image in front of this beautiful woman, he is being intimate by revealing a truth about himself. As a result, their relationship becomes more intimate.

Early in her career, Shelly Winters was typecast by the movie studios as a sex kitten. She finally escaped that trap, and today, she is a great actor who is overweight and not afraid to be what she is. In one movie scene, she dances gleefully on the bed with her skirt hiked up, showing her dimpled, pudgy legs. Both she and Nicholson unconditionally accept themselves, and like all great actors, they are not afraid of intimacy.

Intimacy: The Quality of Good Actors

Intimacy means sharing with someone your most private and personal feelings, and not hiding your inner character. People are usually truly intimate only with loved ones; but even then, almost all of our culture's marital disruptions can be traced to problems of intimacy. People hide personal thoughts and feelings for fear of being rejected or ridiculed, of losing status, of being humiliated, or of being demoted or fired. Actors, in their work, can't afford the luxury of keeping emotional secrets, because it is those secrets that are the core of great performances.

Being intimate also means being vulnerable and sharing your personal feelings. In true intimacy, regardless of the consequences, give and receive emotions without judgment and without interference from your ego. Be concerned only with your partner's needs, not your own; let your deepest feelings come to the surface, and you cannot fail to give a good performance.

Memory and Fear: The Enemies of Intimacy

Fear and emotional pain inhibit you. The loss of a job, the death of a loved one, betrayal of a friend or lover, and a bad performance are some of the traumas in life. Your memory of the emotional pain from any one of these can, if you let it, makes you unwilling to be vulnerable again. How many times have you heard someone say after a love affair has come apart, "I'll never trust a man again as long as I live"? Intimacy then becomes a dreaded place that prevents you from communicating your true feelings to someone else. But your fear is only a perception, not a reality. The enemy is the fear that comes from the history of your past. In your personal life, hide all the emotional secrets you want to; but in your acting life, never be afraid to reveal your secret self. Be vulnerable. In this scene, Ann, the person, lets a personal trauma affect Ann, the character.

```
(Ann, in real life, has just recently gone through a
divorce. She is doing a scene with Tom, who is flirting with
her. Ann ignores his flirting.)


                       TOM
          How was your lunch?

(Tom reaches over and touches her hand.)


                       ANN
                  (all business)
          Tell me about your meeting.
```

JEREMIAH: (interrupting) **Ann, why aren't you responding to Tom's touching your hand?**

```
                         ANN
(to Jeremiah)
             Because . . . that's exactly
             how men try to manipulate me.
             I won't play that game any
             more.
```

JEREMIAH: **That response comes from the pain of your past instead of from what Tom's giving you. When you do that, we don't believe you. How can you be creative when you apply a real-life judgment to the character you're playing? React to Tom, not to some logical generalization about men. Now do it again, and use it as a chance to experience your genuine feelings without the actual inhibitions you have in real life.**

```
(She continues.)

                         ANN
             Tell me about everything. I'm
             . . .

(Tom reaches over and takes her hand. She looks at him and
accepts his touch.)

                         ANN
                 (with true intimacy)
             I'm anxious to hear about what
             happened last night.
```

JEREMIAH: (to the class) **See that? She responded to Tom's advances within the circumstances of the scene, not from some judgment she made in her personal life. See what also happened? A new subtext came through. She says she wants to hear about his meeting, but the subtext tells us she also wants to hear about him. Ann, that was a great moment.**

Intimacy lets you express your emotion to the other person, and at the same time lets you be susceptible to the emotions of the other person. In film acting, you can't get along without intimacy. Intimacy is shared feelings, but it does not necessarily mean a loving or sentimental situation—the relationship between a prisoner and his torturer can be intimate.

Intimacy builds on itself. It allows your feelings to escalate to a conclusion, or be driven in another direction, as in the following scene from *A Bronx Tale*.

Robert De Niro plays a father who tries to instill honest values in his eight-year-old son (played by Francis Capra), who idolizes Sonny, a gangster played by Chazz Palminteri.

(De Niro has returned six hundred dollars that Palminteri had given to his son. He drags his son from the bar.)

                    CAPRA
          Where is my money?

                    DE NIRO
          I gave it back.

                    CAPRA
          How could you do that? That
          was my money.

                    DE NIRO
          That was bad money. I don't
          want you to have that money.

                    CAPRA
          I earned that money.

                    DE NIRO
          You stay away from him.

                    CAPRA
                (yells)
          PLEASE LISTEN TO ME!

(De Niro slaps Capra's face.)

                    DE NIRO
          You heard what I said, you
          stay away from him.

                    CAPRA
          Sonny is right. Mickey Mantle
          is a sucker.

                    DE NIRO
          He was wrong. It don't take a
          strong man to pull the trig-
          ger. Try getting up every
          morning and going to work day

```
                            after day for a living. The
                            working man is the tough guy.
                            Your father is a tough guy.

                                      CAPRA
                            Everybody loves him. You think
                            they love you on the bus?

                                      DE NIRO
                            It's not the same. People are
                            afraid of him. There's a dif-
                            ference.

                                      CAPRA
                                   (crying)
                            I don't understand.

                  (De Niro hugs Capra.)

                                      DE NIRO
                            You will after you get older.

                  (De Niro picks up Capra and carries him home.)

                                      FATHER
                            I'm sorry I hit you.
```

This scene contains both intimacy and empathy. The father gets angry. The son gets angry and yells at his father. This is intimacy and shared feelings. The father hits his son; later, when the son calms down, the father kisses him, showing his love for the boy. Again, intimacy and shared feelings. Then the father picks him up and is overwhelmed with sorrow for hitting his crying son. He shows his empathy by seeing the son's pain. The father says he's sorry and carries him home. This scene would be nothing without the empathy and intimacy.

Empathy

Empathy is seeing, recognizing, and sharing the emotion that another person is feeling—sadness, happiness, love, anger, fear. Empathy evokes the same feeling in you, and inspires your response. We are familiar with empathy in everyday life: parents share the happiness and misery of their children; we relate emotionally to a friend; we feel the pain of someone who is sick; we feel happiness at someone's success. Without empathy, relating emotionally to others becomes virtually impossible.

Great Actors and Empathy

Great film actors subconsciously have empathetic responses. They are capable of instantaneously feeling sadness, happiness, anger, fear, and love without the paralyzing logic of thought. They have conditioned themselves to accept the other actor and the imaginary circumstances (i.e., practicing the Art of Acceptance) and, as a result, are capable of experiencing strong emotions.

Empathy—feeling the other person's emotion—is the source of a good actor's experience. In my acting classes, I sometimes ask a beginning actor to sit facing an advanced actor and imitate exactly her partner's actions and emotions. I ask her to copy exactly in minute detail what the other person is doing—facial expressions, eye movements, words and speech patterns, body movements, even emotion. This exercise requires total and intense attention on the other actor. I use it to introduce students to concentrating on someone other than themselves. I want them to recognize and experience the other actor's feelings, because, as Alan Alda tells us, when you can recognize emotions and respond to them intuitively, you become creative. Rivet your attention on the other actor, empathize, and respond.

Intimacy and Empathy

Intimacy and empathy complement each other. Empathy means being emotionally involved in the other person's feelings. Intimacy is receiving those feelings and freely responding with an appropriate emotion, but not necessarily the same emotion. Say the other actor is sad. Your empathetic response will be to immediately experience his sadness. You might become sad, but not necessarily. Depending on the situation and the relationship, your stimulated response could be anger, happiness, love, or fear. To start the acting feedback loop, you first have to experience the other actor's emotion through empathy, and eventually the situation and circumstances will result in intimacy. Without conscious thought, you will experience emotions that are responses to, but different from, those of the other actor. This is what makes a scene and its characters interesting to an audience.

In the next scene, which is about dealing with anger, each actor responds with empathy to the other but without the same emotion. When you see that another actor is angry, you have to empathize with that anger. You do not necessarily have to become angry yourself, but you do have to be at the same emotional level.

SARA
I knew you'd pull this.

(John, irate, shouts at Sara. She is frightened and presses back in her chair.)

                    JOHN
               (shouting)
          FATE HAS A WAY OF LETTING THE
          TRUTH SLIP OUT!

                    SARA
               (trembling)
          I was going to tell you.
          Mark's new in town. He doesn't
          know anybody.

                    JOHN
               (yelling)
          EXCEPT HIS OLD GIRLFRIEND!

(Sara is shaking. John has an empathetic response to Sara's
trembling. He stops yelling. Then he reaches over and gently
takes her hand.)

                    JOHN
          How convenient.

                    SARA
          It wasn't like that . . .

(When John touches Sara's hand she feels love and starts to
cry.)

                    SARA
          I was just trying to be nice.

                    JOHN
               (lovingly)
          You're just spreading goodwill
          all over the place, huh?

                    SARA
               (crying)
          Are you going to pick on me
          all night . . .

(John lovingly smiles, forgiving Sara. She cries uncontrol-
lably.)

                    SARA
          . . . or do you really want to
          hear what happened?

```
                    JOHN
               (laughs)
          This better be good.


                    SARA
          He called me a month ago.


                    JOHN
          A month ago?


  (Sara gives John a hug, followed by a kiss.)


                    SARA
          I asked you what you'd think
          if one of your old flames
          moved here. You told me the
          past is the past.
```

Intimacy is receiving feelings and freely responding with an appropriate emotion, but not necessarily the same emotion. John is angry, Sara is frightened. John sees Sara trembling and responds with empathy by holding Sara's hand. Sara sees John's love and starts to cry. John laughs and forgives her. Sara hugs and kisses him. The feelings are appropriate, but the two are not experiencing the same emotions. The energy level is equal.

Scenes "Not Worthy" of an Actor

Occasionally when I make new assignments in class, an actor will refuse to do an assigned scene. "How can you expect me to do a scene like this? It's a nothing. It's a waste of my time!" But empathetic and intimate actors, in spite of inane words and improbable situations, can make a scene fascinating by their emotions and by the subtext they create. The scene below is one of those scenes that mediocre actors are contemptuous of as not having any "meat" in it. The writer knew what he was doing, because it becomes fascinating when it is played by good actors who relate and become intimate. The comments in parentheses are not script directions but what the actors actually did.

```
(Judy, an advanced student, has reached a level of total
intimacy. In this scene she plays a divorced woman who runs
into her ex-husband in a doctor's office. He is waiting for
his new wife, who is being examined in another room.)

                    JUDY
          It's your smell.
```

```
          JOHN
Nobody can crack my back the
way you used to.

          JUDY
One sniff.
```

The words say one thing, but what is going on emotionally between the two (the subtext) says something entirely different. This scene is not about odors or chiropractic maneuvers; it is about the feelings of this man and this woman. Their emotional exchange, not how they say the words, takes what appears to be boring, meaningless dialogue and makes it fascinating.

```
          JUDY
        (laughs)
It's your smell.

          JOHN
Nobody can crack my back the
way you used to.
```

(She cries through her laughter. They are both sad.)

```
          JUDY
One sniff.
```

(They hug each other. We see love in the eyes of both.)

JEREMIAH: **That was brilliant.** (to the class) **This scene works, but it has nothing to do with the words, which are pretty stupid. It works because of what's going on between these two people. This is an example of empathy and intimacy. The sadness allows us to see that they still love each other. This is empathy. The laugher lets us see that she loves him, misses him, and forgives him. The hug tells us both have regrets and are sorry. That's acting, that's acting on an intuitive level. Judy, did you have any idea this would happen?**

```
              JUDY
     (to Jeremiah)
          Surprised the hell out of me.
          (laughs)
```

JEREMIAH: **Thank you. That was exciting.**

This all happens in three silly lines, but the class loved it. We identified with and understood her feelings for him. A performance this good and this interesting cannot be made by logical "choices." A good prescription for disaster in preparing for a scene like this is to plan how to say each line so that it has meaning; to rationally mark the beats; to logically decide what "choices" you are going to make; and so on. This guarantees that the crew will either fall sleep or bust out laughing. A scene like this works when you relate to the other actor and are open to impulses from your intuition.

Physical Actions

In my class exercises, I ask my students to do certain physical actions that stimulate intimacy and empathy. But be careful. In an actual movie shoot, you should only do these things if they are true impulses, or if the director asks you to.

Touching: Stroking an actor's face or hair, holding hands, etc. In a scene when you touch the other actor, the scene always goes better. You cease to be isolated, and intimacy follows.

Kissing: One actor kisses the other after every line. Eventually, the kissing becomes so inane and meaningless that the actors surrender to what is really happening in the scene, and they begin to experience intimacy.

Hugging: Another version of touching.

Shouting: Shouting the lines then hugging each other releases inhibitions.

Laughing: Laughing the lines is physically freeing. Laugh on each line, then shout each line, then finally talk normally—all of which lead to greater intimacy.

All of these actions help reduce tension and stimulate empathy and intimacy. It's okay to touch, kiss, and hug in a rehearsal or on the set as long as your partner is responsive to your impulses. Yelling just before the actual take is an effective way to bring your feelings to the surface, particularly tears; but you might come off as looking pretty silly if you start yelling just before the director calls "action." Don't do anything radical without discussing it with the director. Some actors, during a shoot, manage to find an isolated spot for shouting. But the best way to forget logic and get into an empathetic state is by concentrating not on yourself but on the other actor.

When you are in an empathetic state, you can never really be sure how other people are seeing you. But don't let that bother you. Just respond to what you get from the other actor and let your behavior fall where it may, because that, says Alan Alda, is when acting becomes creative.

Intuition: Your Sixth Sense

Intuition is all your knowledge, dexterity, and skill stored in your unconscious. It is your quick and ready insight, aware of everything you know. If you don't muck it up with logic, it will tell you the right thing to do and say. Intuition has access to everything you have ever learned and experienced. Through impulses, it tells you what to do in any situation. It uses your subconscious experience and knowledge to give you the correct acting choices you never knew you had. The trick is to be open to impulses, and act on them. Through listening to their impulses, artists get their inspiration, scientists make breakthroughs, musicians hear unheard melodies, mystics acquire vision, and actors give brilliant performances.

The development of the logical left brain has created a loss for all of us. The change from a hunter-gatherer culture way of life to a civilized one has submerged our ability to fully use intuition under a flood of logic and reason. For prehistoric peoples, intuition was necessary just to stay alive. But since we have turned into high-tech-super-computer-hot-shots, our daily survival rarely depends on listening to our intuition. Generally, our modern logic-driven society distrusts intuition. Fortunately, we haven't completely lost our ability to use it. It has become dormant, and we only need to wake it up.

To revive your intuitive awareness, be alive to the moment. Be open and aware of your five senses—seeing, hearing, touching, tasting, and smelling. Be open and let your intuition block the logical part of your brain. Years ago I was working on a ranch in Australia with an Aborigine station hand. I was a "jackaroo" (cowboy) herding cattle. We were never out of sight of each other, but every couple of days he would say, "Yank, go 'round that hill and bring back the two yearlings and the calf stuck in the gully." Or he would send me across the river, or over two hills, or up some canyon. And the cattle were always where he said they would be. All the time I rode with him he always knew where strayed cattle were. I asked him once how he knew. He said he didn't know, he just knew. I don't think he had ever heard the word *intuition*, but that's what it was. Stored in his subconscious was this vast knowledge of both cattle behavior and the country, and when a problem came up, he didn't have to think about it—his intuition instantly gave him the answer. Your intuition can do the same for you by giving you the right choices.

Intuition Applied to Acting

Ava, a new student, has never acted before. This is her second class.

```
                      AVA
          Who do you admire?
```

PAUL
I admire you.

(Ava breaks down and cries.)

PAUL (CONT'D)
You look like an angel on top
of a Christmas tree.

AVA
(weeping)
My Daddy always called me his
little angel.

PAUL
He must have loved you.

AVA
He never said it.

PAUL
Dads are frightened by little
girls, because they are so
soft and cuddly. I know he
loved you. I love you.

(Scene ends, then Ava turns to me.)

AVA
(to Jeremiah)
I don't know why I was crying.

JEREMIAH: **Your tears were perfect. That blows me away. This is your second class. WOW! . . . Ava . . . Trust your talent. Accept it. It is always correct.** (to the class) **That's her intuition, that special place inside of her that knows, even though the actress doesn't logically know. During the scene she thinks, why is this happening?** (to Ava) **Ava, that thought, "why was I crying?" is your inexperience and your logic trying to make sense out of a creative situation.** (to class) **Ava's intuition overrode the thought process and allowed her impulses to let her experience the other actor.**

The dialogue in the above scene is difficult to make believable. Ava's emotional insight made it look easy. Subconsciously, even though she is a model who doesn't believe she is beautiful, she is touched deeply when he calls her an angel. She responds, out of love and appreciation, with sadness. Before she did the scene, Ava read it only once. She logically did not understand how this material would affect her, but her intuition knew what the material meant. She was open to her intuition, which overpowered her logic, and she cried.

Everyone has intuition and has listened to it at one time or another. A simple glance from a loved one tells you, without your having to think, that something is wrong. This instant awareness comes to you as a gut feeling—intuition again. When you act on your impulses, you are listening to your intuition. Women, because they are more emotionally open and less wedded to logic, are far more intuitive than men, which may explain why there are more great women actors than great men actors.

The Creative Inner Child

In the book *I'm Okay, You're Okay*, Eric Berne says that in each of us there is a parent, an adult, and a child. The **parent** part is the voice of authority—parent, teacher, boss—who lives by rules. "Don't!" "Shouldn't!" "Wouldn't!" "Can't!" "Should!" "Must!" This is the judgmental part of the personality. The **adult** is the logical part of the inner self that exercises good judgment and maintains harmony between the child and the parent. The **child** is the emotional part of you that often behaves like a three-year-old and acts irrationally without thinking about consequences. This child part is going to make you a great actor. To be creative, your child needs freedom from the limitations placed on it by your logical inner parent.

Your intuition, or your "gut feeling," is sometimes called "the little professor" because it remembers every experience you have had and everything you have ever read. Learn to trust the "little professor" because he will give you the right answers. Everyone has experienced doing something or making a decision that turned out badly, and then later saying, "I knew I shouldn't have done it. I should have listened to my gut." That gut feeling is your intuition, the little professor, talking to you; and in acting, it is a hell of a lot smarter than your logical brain. Listen to it!

There is a scene in *Roman Holiday* in which Audrey Hepburn is lying to Gregory Peck about not being a countess, and he is lying to her about not being a reporter. They are standing by a statue of a creature with a large mouth. Local legend says that if you are telling a lie and put your hand in the statue's mouth, it will take your hand off. Peck slowly sticks his hand in the mouth and then, as if it is being pulled, shoves the rest of his arm farther into the mouth. Hepburn intuitively screams, grabs his arm, and tries to pull it out. She becomes hysterical. Peck pulls out his arm with a missing hand, which, of course, is covered by his sleeve. Hepburn responds with fear and shock. Peck pops his hand out and they both laugh. Hepburn's childlike instincts responded appropriately for the situation and made it a delightful and believable scene. She did not know ahead of time that Peck was going to put his hand in the statue's mouth. It was planned by director Billy Wilder and Peck without Hepburn knowing anything about it.

How to Stimulate Your Inner Child

Your creative child needs approval. How do you give your inner child the approval it wants? By acting as quickly as you can on everything that comes into your head, the kinds of desires and thoughts you may have stifled for years. Acting on them is the approval that your creative child seeks. When you do act, your inner child then knows you're ready to play. Listen to your inner child's voice. Listen to the messages sent by every thought, desire, or whim relative to your partner. "His collar is crooked"—so straighten it. "He is frightened"—so hold his hand "She is yelling at me"—so deal with her anger. "He's talking nonsense"—so laugh at him. These messages may be almost indistinguishable at first, but the more attentive you are, the louder they get. These thoughts and desires will eventually tap into your intuition and turn into impulses. When your inner child knows you are paying attention, the impulses will flow. It is like a rambunctious three-year-old waking up after a nap. Be prepared. Remember, your inner child has probably been ignored for years and will act out by doing things you have been too embarrassed or inhibited to do. Now you must approve them by acting on them. Enjoy this, because not only is it fun, it is one of the sources of great acting.

In *Five Easy Pieces*, Jack Nicholson feels that his girlfriend, played by Karen Black, is an embarrassment, and he doesn't want to take her home to meet his dying father. In this scene, Nicholson finds Black lying in bed, depressed and crying.

NICHOLSON
I have to go home to see my
father. He is sick.

(starts to pack his bags)

NICHOLSON
. . . Come on DiPesto, I told
you it would never work out to
anything, didn't I? I'll send
you some money, that's all I
can do. I'll try to call you
from up there. . . . Bye Ray.

(Nicholson exits to his car.)

Jack gets in his car. He is embarrassed to take a woman like Karen, whom he sees as a bimbo, home to meet his folks. In the car, he has the impulse and takes out his anger and frustration on the steering wheel, the ceiling of the car, the window, punching everything that is within reach. Nicholson lets himself go all the way, and we believe him. He trusts his creative impulses and goes absolutely berserk! This is the childlike total abandonment we strive for as actors. The director may or may not have told him he wanted some kind of frustration, but either way, a response like Nicholson's is intuitive, not logical. If it were to come from a logical decision, it would most likely look fake, and we would not believe him. Wild actions look believable only when they come from real feelings.

Who Says You Can't Act Like a Child

. . . and get away with it? Jim Carrey, a bright, talented comic actor, is a present-day Jerry Lewis. Others, like Robin Williams, Mike Myers, Adam Sandler, Pauly Shore, all have great appeal because they let themselves act like emotionally uncontrolled children. Watch these actors closely, because everything they do, including their serious moments, comes from impulse, not planning. Their actions are comic. But you don't necessarily have to be a flamboyant comic to let your inner child work. All impulses—normal, tragic, or comic—are instructions from your intuition and the mainstay of a good actor.

Serious Actors Act on Childish Impulses

In the following scene from *Terms of Endearment*, Debra Winger has just been told by her doctor that she is dying. She realizes that her children will grow up without a mother. Shirley MacLaine plays Debra's mother.

```
Nurses station at night.

                    MACLAINE
          Excuse me. Is it after
          ten . . . Give my daughter the
          pain shot . . . please.


                    NURSE #1
          Mrs. Greenwood, I was going to
          . . .


                    MACLAINE
          Oh good, go ahead.


                    NURSE #1
          In just a few minutes.
```

> MACLAINE
> Please, it's after ten. It's
> after ten . . .

(MacLaine moves to another nurse.)

> MACLAINE
> I don't see why she has to
> have the pain.

> NURSE #2
> Ma'am, it's not my patient.

(MacLaine points to her watch.)

> MACLAINE
> (agitated)
> It's time for her shot . . .

(She hurriedly moves around the nurses station to another
nurse.)

> MACLAINE
> You understand. Do something.

(MacLaine moving quickly, raising her voice.)

> MACLAINE
> (screaming)
> All she has to do is hold on
> til ten. And . . . It's past
> ten
>
> She's . . . MY DAUGHTER IS IN
> PAIN.

(MacLaine, frustrated, bangs her fist on the nurses station.)

> MACLAINE
> (hysterical)
> GIVE MY DAUGHTER THE SHOT.

(MacLaine, almost running, enters the nurses station.)

> MACLAINE
> (screaming hysterically)
> YOU UNDERSTAND ME!

(MacLaine flails her arms and stomps her feet. She reaches
the pinnacle of her anger, and out of control, she screams.)

                    MACLAINE
        GIVE MY DAUGHTER A SHOT!

(The nurse exits to give MacLaine's daughter a shot.
MacLaine calms down immediately and tries to regain her com-
posure. "Like nothing happened.")

                    MACLAINE
                (dignified)
            Thank you very much. Thank
            you.

This last shift in the action changes the pace and attitude of the scene and gives us a moment of comedic relief. In this scene Shirley MacLaine acts like a spoiled child throwing a temper tantrum. She is a serious actress who has the ability to use childlike impulses to heighten her character's intensity and to provide comic relief.

Rekindle your relationship with your creative child by cajoling it into participation. To encourage your child's cooperation, stop judging. You stifle your inner child whenever you think, "I can't do that," "It's improper," "What will the other actors think of me," or "That's too embarrassing," or "That's stupid." The child has to feel important; your adult-parent must no longer discourage it. When was the last time you played with dolls or got on a broom and rode it around a room pretending it was a horse? (I once saw Robin Williams do this on a talk show on national television.) When was the last time you finger-painted? When was the last time you ran under a hose? There is a TV commercial where a businessman sees children sliding on a plastic sheet sprayed with water. He follows his impulse and dives to slide on the wet plastic in his suit and tie. It's something we would all like to do, but logic opens its big mouth and says, "Don't do that! You know better. You'll look ridiculous, and besides, you'll get your suit wet and people will think you're unstable."

Play like a child and become excited by life and its childish aspects. Watch children. Adults have turned learning into work, but children learn by playing. Good actors spend a lot of their time observing people in all sorts of activities from all walks of life, including children. Watch how their impulses guide them in reaction to what is happening at the moment.

Words That Prevent Good Acting

Stop using the words "should," "shouldn't," and "can't" because they inhibit you. They are words that come from fear. Use positive action words that encourage—I can, I will, I am going to succeed. Remember, the glass is not half-empty, it's half-full. Be positive. Change your perception. Enjoy your mistakes. Enjoy your successes. This will help you learn to love and respect your inner child.

Why can you cry in a movie theater but not in acting class? In the safety of the dark theater, your emotions flow freely; but when you start to act in front of other people, your adult-parent enters the picture with its impeccable logic. Your child withdraws to its hiding place and relinquishes control to the left brain (adult-parent). Your creative child, if you've got the sense to let it, listens to your intuition and ignores your adult-parent.

Act on an impulse immediately. We are so used to squashing impulses that we generally believe the word "impulse" to mean something bad or unwanted; so we tend to ignore not only the impulse but its existence. A hard thing for beginners to grasp is what an impulse is. Bill, an actor who is a handsome mature man in his seventies, has just finished a scene and turns to me:

JEREMIAH: **You looked as if something were bothering you on your last line. What was it?**

BILL

(to Jeremiah)
        I was repressing a terrible
        impulse to scratch my ear.

JEREMIAH: **Why didn't you?**

BILL

(to Jeremiah)
        I thought it would be
        improper.

JEREMIAH: **Bill, remember there is no "right" way to do a scene. You can't judge your impulses if you expect to become impulsive. It is the child part of you that wants to scratch your ear. If you act on that impulse the next time it happens your response will become more spontaneous. This is what I meant by "getting in touch with your child." It simply means acting on desires you might consider stupid.** (to the class) **Can anyone give me an example of impulses?** (no one answers) **Can't think of any. Okay, how about a kiss, a hug, a laugh, a wink—are they impulses?**

JOHN

(to Jeremiah)
        A kiss is definitely an
        impulse.

JEREMIAH: **Yes, if it's related to your partner. Any physical desire that you have that's related to your partner can be an impulse. Act on it immediately and without judgment. Thoughts and impulses are connected and interrelated. If you sit on an impulse it becomes a thought. If you immediately act on a thought, without time to judge, it becomes an impulse. The difference is only the length of time that separates them. The trick is to become so aware of the other actor that you respond in the shortest possible time. If I see my partner wants to kiss me and I decide to wait for a more comfortable moment, it's a thought. If I act immediately and kiss her, it's an impulse.**

Don't make any judgments, and don't do any prolonged thinking—which is any thinking that takes more than a microsecond. Your impulses may not always be right at first, because you may be still holding on to a tiny bit of inhibition or a minute sense of what is "proper." But impulses will keep coming if you respond to them. Eventually, without thinking about it, you will intuitively make decisions that are correct for the circumstance you are in. Intuition is your natural gift. Sometimes it will tell you to do some pretty crazy things, but pay attention; do what it tells you, as long as that is not destructive or hurtful to your fellow actor. Don't be afraid to take chances or make mistakes. When your intuition is confident that your judgment has ceased to function, it will respond freely, and your performance will be creative.

Act, Don't Think

When you respond to the other actor and are in the moment, you cannot separate thought, experience, and intuition. Use everything; do not stop the flow regardless of where it comes from. By the time you think, "Oh, that came from my partner," "That came from the script," or "That came from a past experience when I was three years old," the moment has been lost. When you say, "My character wouldn't do that," your logical mind locks out all spontaneity and impulse. Everything we think or feel happens for a reason. Do not judge. Just act.

You can develop a split-second sensibility that allows you to decide immediately whether or not to follow an impulse. It doesn't make any difference what triggers an impulse—the other actor, a thought, a feeling, an action, or an accident. Quiet the incessant internal rap in your brain and let your impulses move you.

Summary

1. Intimacy is sharing your personal feelings and personal thoughts with another actor without judgment.

2. Empathy is the ability to experience another person's feelings.
3. Reawaken your creative inner child and learn to trust it.
4. Trust and act on all your impulses. Don't judge.

Actor Practice

Trust your impulses.

1. Sit facing your acting partner. Don't plan. Don't force. Allow yourself to do nothing. Just wait for an impulse. The impulse might be to smile or a desire to touch a your partner's hand or scratch your nose. The purpose of this exercise is to respond immediately to every legitimate urge. The faster your response, the shorter your judgment time and the more impulsive your actions.

   Remember that a *legitimate* thought or action does not harm another person, but a slap or touching another in a private area does.
2. When you are with your boyfriend or girlfriend, ask him or her to do the above exercise with you. See what happens. This is a great way to develop a deeper level of trust and intimacy.
3. Light a candle, sit in a comfortable position, and watch the flame. Try to block out all thought. This is an impossibility; thoughts constantly come into your mind. If you are aware of your thoughts it will be easier for you to act on them and turn them into impulses.
4. Listen to your inner voice, "the little professor." Next time you have a bad feeling about anything, stop and respond appropriately to the impulse. Your gut instinct can be your best friend.
5. In class, don't be afraid to make an idiot of yourself. Remember Jim Carrey as Fire Marshall Bill. He was hilarious, but if he had ever considered how stupid he looked or acted he never would have created that character. But he pushed himself as far as he could, unconcerned about how anybody would judge him. Nor did he judge himself. He just did it. Do it. Most of all, enjoy it.

13

The Audition

Auditioning is part of the actor's job.

Ed Harris

Getting Ready to Audition

There is no getting around auditioning. Maybe some big-time stars don't have to audition for a role, but most actors do—even well-known, successful ones. Auditioning is showing casting directors, producers, and directors what you look like and how you act. It is getting up in front of people and convincing them by your persona and your performance that you are the one they have to have in their movie or TV show. It is up to you. No one has any reason or obligation to "give you a chance," and you have to knock 'em dead on the first try or it's all over—for that time, at least. If you have trouble being instantly brilliant, keep on studying and auditioning for films and plays, and one day you will do it.

When you audition for film or TV, your first session and perhaps two or three callbacks will be for the casting director. After the casting director selects you, she will take you to read for the director and producer. When you prepare for these beginning sessions for a casting director, you will do better if you prepare the same way as you would for a stage play. What I teach about the Art of Relating in film acting works best when you finally get to read for the director, who knows, or should know, how to recognize a film performance. There are some casting directors in film who truly understand film acting, but most of them do not; so to look good in an initial audition usually requires a broader, or more theatrical, performance than is appropriate for film. Stage experience shows you the way to prepare for auditions. In this chapter I will discuss some of the elements of theater acting that will be useful for you to consider.

Before you ever get to read a line in an audition, you have been preselected for your physical type. Casting for movies and TV is "typecasting." This means that the casting director first evaluates you according to your type, or your "persona," which is your visible outer personality that other people see. Later she will ask you to audition to see how you can act. For most film roles, directors cast actors who have already shown they can play the type of part for which they are being considered. Almost all actors are typecast, and each star is a special type that producers can depend on—or think they can—to make financially successful movies. Casting stars according to type takes some of the risk out of producing, because the stars have already demonstrated that their films make money. There are plenty of good actors who can do star roles; but since money shouts louder than aesthetics, producers are more interested in actors who have already shown that they can attract audiences. Typecasting is a visual shorthand, a way of quickly conveying to a film audience the information as to who a character is.

Film stars have their own personas. We know who Robert De Niro is whether he is the boxer in *Raging Bull*, the bounty hunter in *Midnight Run*, or the chief petty officer in *Men of Honor*. He is the tough blue-collar worker who always fights the odds. Meg Ryan is cute, sweet, funny, and lovable. Demi Moore is sexy and strong. Julia Roberts is the outsider who gains strength and confidence and has the smarts to become an insider. Russell Crowe is the handsome hard-fighting hero with a temper. Al Pacino is the tough little Italian guy who does the right thing. Brad Pitt is Mr. Goodlooks. Tom Hanks is today's Jimmy Stewart, the good, decent average man. F. Murray Abraham is the dark, intellectual villain who will never be a handsome leading man. Nor will the handsome leading man play the villain. Film actors fill the roles that call for their types.

Casting for Type

Let's say you want to cast a New York cab driver who argues with the star about the fare. If you cast a beautiful blonde dressed like a cheerleader, you are setting up the audience to expect something that is not in the story. When she never appears again, or her looks and dress have nothing to do with the story, the audience is confused and wonders why, and it becomes a glitch in the movie's coherence. Unless your story, for a reason, calls for a blonde dressed as a cheerleader to be the cab driver, you would not cast her type. You need an actor whose persona says to the audience, "I am a New York taxi driver."

In the film *The Out-of-Towners*, Jack Lemmon's character is late and needs to catch a train. He has only a $20 bill, and the cab driver doesn't have change. Lemmon says, "I'll send you the money." The cab driver says, "Give me your address and I'll send *you* the money." The director needed a cab driver who was strong and would not be pushed around. Jack gives him the money. De Niro would be great—as he once demonstrated—and so would F. Murray Abraham. But a young blonde woman, or a Mr. Milquetoast type? Not for this scene.

Every year, the *Hollywood Reporter* publishes a list of the top one hundred actors who bring in the most money to the box office. It rates actors like Tom Cruise, Arnold Schwarzenegger, Bruce Willis, Denzel Washington, Tom Hanks, Julia Roberts, Helen Hunt, and other stars according to how much money their movies made. The biggest moneymakers are those who will most likely be typecast for the following year's mega movies in pretty much the same kind of roles they have done in the past.

Film and Stage Casting

For stage actors the physical type does not have to be as strictly delimited as for film actors, whose types have to be recognizable early in the film. In a stage play, everything is told in words. Speech onstage is constant, giving the actors plenty of time and opportunity to present their characters and relationships. In film, actors speak less than a tenth of the words they would speak in a stage play. To understand what the movie is about, the film audience relies on seeing your emotions in close-up and on already knowing what type of character you are. In a stage play, you might not actually experience the emotion the scene calls for, yet the scene can work since your dialogue makes explicit what you are feeling. If you do not experience an emotion in a film close-up, the scene dies because your lines in a movie do not explain what is going on inside you.

Head Shots

Your first introduction to a casting director is through your photo. Make your head shots look like you really are. Don't have head shots made that reflect your own idealized image of yourself as more glamorous and more attractive than you really are. Use head shots that show you as you. No director or casting director is going to hire a glamorized image in a photograph. They want to hire what you really are, and they can only see this in a picture that shows what you really look like. Directors and casting directors do not want to see head shots that don't look like you, and if they do, they sometimes get very upset about it—which translates into your not getting hired.

The film or TV casting director is faced with the problem of making her initial selection from head shots. If your picture is the type they are looking for, you will be called in for an audition. In the back room of a casting director's office, you can see the huge problem casting directors face. There can be thousands of head shots in stacks literally covering desks, tables, and floor. The casting director and her assistants look at each head shot for maybe one or two seconds, sometimes less, to make first selections of actors according to type.

Sometimes they riffle through a stack of head shots like a pack of cards, and if your head shot catches the casting director's eye, she will pull it out of the stack and look at it. She may call you in for an audition to see if you really look like your picture, how well you can act, and how you come across. Working in a film or TV show starts with this kind of typecasting. If your type is not what they are looking for, your head shot goes into the basket.

Auditioning

For the stage, serious actors can usually audition for any part they wish regardless of what type they are. For film casting, if the casting director thinks your "look" is not right, you do not get to audition. This is unfortunate, because the type of actor that many producers and bad directors envision for a role is often so specific that a casting session can amount to no more than looking for an actor who fits into their rigid mold. Matching an actor this way to a set concept of type is bad casting. What Alan Alda said with reference to acting applies to casting, too: if you know what you want, that's all you get. Producers and directors who are open and receptive are sometimes happily surprised to find actors who, at first look, do not exactly fit the type but are perfect for the role. For *The Graduate*, the producers originally wanted a blond, football-hero type for the role of Benjamin. Fortunately, someone who knew what he was doing, probably director Mike Nichols, insisted on casting Dustin Hoffman. Robin Williams was a successful, outrageous comedian who was put in serious roles (*Dead Poets' Society, Awakenings*) and surprised everyone. Williams fits at least two stereotypes—the wild comic and the serious, sensitive human being.

Directors

Auditioning is more like acting on the stage than acting in a film, because you have to do more than you do in film, and you do it before a live audience. Happily, there are a few good casting directors and a fair number of film directors ranging from competent to great who know what to look for when they are casting. Sadly, most casting directors and most film directors know little about what good acting is. Everyone wants to be a director. It's a prestigious position. You get to tell others what to do, you get to make creative decisions, and your name is big in the credits. It looks easy, but only because the good directors know what they are doing and have worked themselves to the bone to make it look easy. The result is that many incompetents somehow manage to cast and direct a lot of mediocre movies.

Auditioning before mediocre directors and mediocre casting directors is frustrating because they don't understand what the camera does and do not know what a good film performance is. They don't recognize when you are relating to another actor at an experiential level with no theatrics. Michael Caine once referred to a film director calling for a retake of Caine's performance; the director said that what he wanted wasn't in Caine's take. Caine told the director that he may not have recognized the performance, but that what he wanted was on the film—and he was right. With an actor of lesser stature than Michael Caine, that director might have made many takes of the scene without recognizing what he wanted, until the actor, finally in desperation, overacted and made it obvious.

Ideal Audition

In an ideal audition for a dramatic scene, you and another actor perform for the casting director. This way both of you can relate and work from each other's emotions. But customarily, you do a film audition reading with the casting assistant, who will rarely relate to you. Happily, you may sometimes be auditioned by one of the few really good casting directors who will themselves read the scene and interact with you. Later, in callbacks, you may be called in to audition with other actors for the director to see if the two of you and your chemistry are compatible. But in the beginning, you will probably read with the casting assistant while being evaluated by the casting director, and sometimes the director. You can't do what you do in my Relating Exercise in every audition, because all auditions are different. Some are based on relating, but some are based on more overt actions. If the casting director is not one of the best, you need other tools to complement what I teach in class to give a successful audition.

Film Audition

Prepare for a film audition as you would prepare for a stage role. Study the character. Determine what you think the audition script means, and then plan your choices and your reactions. Acting in plays makes your auditioning skills better. Michael Shurtleff, in his book *Audition*, outlines what he calls "The Twelve Guideposts" of auditioning.[1] He formulated these for theater actors, but you should read them.

Auditioning for film is not the same as actually acting for film. For one thing, you are not doing a scene with another actor but with a casting assistant. You can, of course, relate and respond in the way you actually feel about the assistant's disinterested reading or her attempt to "act." You might respond with anger, frustration, tears, or laughter—anything that you really experience as a result of dealing with this particular person. Often, this is a way to get

---

[1]Shurtleff, M., *Audition*, New York: Bantam, 1980.

through an audition with a good performance when the other person gives you nothing but what she is, a casting assistant with her eyes stuck on the page and her emotions out to lunch.

There is a danger when you respond with honest emotion to what you receive emotionally (zero) from a casting assistant. As fascinating and honest as you may be, your emotional responses may not appear to the casting director to support the words and intention of the scene. Only the few good directors and the few good casting directors would see that you were doing a great job by relating with what you had to work with. The mediocre directors will only see, for example, that you have laughed when they think you should have been sad, or angry, or whatever seems to be required according to what they think is the literal meaning of the script.

Acting in Plays

What I teach applies to acting in film, but, as I have said, you often need something more because auditioning is much like stage acting. Acting in plays allows you to learn how to make dramatic choices and recreate moments night after night. It shows you how to move on stage and make it look natural. It gives you the technique and confidence you will need when you audition. Knowing how to prepare for a stage performance is essential for auditioning, especially for a film audition, because you may have to do your preparation in the few minutes between first seeing your sides and going in to the audition studio. Say you are auditioning for a role in which your character is stressed out because you think somebody is trying to kill you. Actually, you are being followed but can't prove it, and nobody believes you—not the cops, your friends, or your psychiatrist. You have to come into the audition and start on a believable, stressed-out emotional level. Michael Shurtleff says that something always precedes what you are doing. He calls this "the moment before," and writes, "You have to do a number on yourself; you have to talk to yourself, flay yourself into feeling, so that you are aching to get on the stage and start to fight."[2] If you don't start off instantly with believable emotion, your audition is done for.

Approaches to Acting

Let's look at three approaches to acting. The first is the technical approach, which relies on rehearsal and performance, with attention to external character development rather than the internal or emotional. Sir Laurence

---

[2]Shurtleff, p. 68.

Olivier was the master of technical acting and developed a role from the outside in by working from the physical characteristics, the costume, the makeup, the walk, and the voice, and by rehearsing until the external technique disappeared into the character.

The internal-motivation approach comes from Stanislavsky's system, where you find your character by completely accepting the given circumstances and making everything real (what we have been calling the Art of Acceptance). You invest yourself emotionally into the situation, and a genuine character evolves. You seek to find physiological motivation behind your actions to drive your character. The internal-motivation approach does not include Stanislavsky's emotional memory, where you consciously recall an old experience to recreate its emotion in the present. Stanislavsky discarded the emotion memory theory as his teaching, acting, and directing matured.

The third approach is Sanford Meisner's teaching that the logic of the script should not control your experience. He started beginning students with what he called "the word repetition game," in which two actors face each other, and without trying to be logical, each repeats exactly what the other actor says. Meisner's repeat exercise ignores the dialogue and reaches your feelings through improvisation, forcing you to relate to the other actor without preplanned reactions. My approach is essentially Meisner's, except that I start actors right out with scripted dialogue, because in both auditions and acting, you have to say exact script lines at the same time that you are feeling and relating, so you might as well learn to do that from the beginning. As you study with improv material, relating eventually becomes natural to you; but later, when you have to speak lines from a script, it is too easy to fall into the trap of analyzing the material and thereby losing that marvelous moment-to-moment quality of Meisner's repeat exercise. Meisner was brilliant in understanding that an actor should place his concentration on the other actor, and that the actor's response to dialogue should come from his or her partner's actual feeling, rather than from what the dialogue means literally.

Technical acting deals with external characterization. Stanislavsky dealt with internal feelings and motivation. And Meisner dealt with responding to the other actor. My approach deals with experiencing your personal emotional power through your relationship with the other actors. I don't work with improvisation because I believe writing, especially great writing, is the basis of good dramatic acting, and the actor eventually has to learn how to say the lines as they are written regardless of how he or she is feeling.

On stage, any one of these approaches can cross over into one or both of the other two. Use anything that works. Good actors are good actors and have the ability to relate and feel emotions from moment to moment. They combine both external characterization and internal feelings into a performance, which is what you must do when you audition.

Stage Acting

Stage acting is fundamental to all acting and provides the experience in voice, movement, and character development that every actor needs. While you are waiting to be cast in a film, act in as many stage plays as you can. It used to be that there was enough professional theater production for an actor to earn a living and at the same time learn the craft of acting by working almost constantly on the stage in all kinds of roles. There is still a lot of theater, but most of it is in amateur community groups and in colleges and universities. In some cities like Seattle, Minneapolis, and New York, there are several professional theaters, but in most places they are rare. There are about two thousand or more theaters, professional and amateur, in the United States. But today it is almost impossible for a beginner to learn acting by being employed as an actor. Universities and colleges maintain stage acting programs, and almost any one of these is a good place to start. Today, many of our successful actors and directors are graduates of university drama schools.

University and college drama schools do not provide training in film acting, although they think they do when they teach some of the mechanics of working in front of the camera—hitting your marks and the like. I have spent most of my career searching for the most effective way to teach film acting, and I am both entertained and horrified at some of the convoluted theories of acting that don't do anything but confuse. One teacher has a brain dominance theory based on a fifty-question test. Under each answer is a color, and the test determines which color dominates your brain. If you have too much red you are supposed to work on improving the yellow or blue or green to balance out your acting ability. Another teacher claims the actor must develop what Stanislavsky calls "public solitude," resulting in one actor masturbating in front of the workshop to demonstrate that he could concentrate in front of an audience as if he were alone. Useful, perhaps, for some unsavory movies, but I don't think it would be very helpful in an audition. Another teacher claims you should do character research and live like the character. If you play a prostitute, actually pick up johns and experience what a prostitute experiences. This is taking preparation too far. Another approach is to use abandonment exercises where the actors scream and contort physically just before a scene to free up their emotions. Try this in an audition or before the opening of play? I don't think so.

One professional director, instead of rehearsing, actually mounted a play by spending many days talking about the biographies and motivations of the characters. The week before the play was to open, the director asked each actor to bring in an example of the most disgusting thing imaginable. One bright actor brought in a small phallic object. Looking at it, he told the director, "The most disgusting thing I can think of is we open in a week." This actor knew that nothing replaces solid directing, blocking, and rehearsing. There are tons of theories, and in some situations some odd ideas may work. But nothing is as valuable as rehearsal.

Biographies

Biographies are imagined past histories about your character. Who is this character? Where was she born? Where did she go to school? Who were her mother and father? What were her life experiences? Who were her friends? Some biographies can be based on information in the script, but most usually come from the actor's imagination. You can spend hours writing and pondering a character's past, but the effectiveness of biographies is questionable. You are better off rehearsing the scene than thinking about some manufactured imaginative history. Find answers during the rehearsal process through your relationship with your own life, with the other characters, and with the given circumstances. Imagination can be useful to create an event that helps you jump-start an emotionally heightened scene, but biographies keep your acting intellectual and logical, and limit your spontaneous emotional responses. Biographies put you, and especially a beginning actor, into your head and keep you thinking rather than acting and reacting. It might work for a few parts like roles that require a complete character transformation, but the time could be better used for memorizing and rehearsing. The reactions you need in a scene are your own, not those of some hypothetical character.

Physical and Emotional Aspects of Characterization

Observation and imitation are the foundation for characterization. To play an old man or woman, look at old people—how they stand, walk, talk, and react. Notice how aware old people are about every physical action and about how their bodies don't function properly anymore. They are afraid of falling. Notice how difficult it is for them to stand. Do they use a cane or a walker? Do they walk or shuffle? In your quest to be a great actor, make these same kinds of observations about every type of person you can—bartenders, generals, doctors, crooks, junkies, teachers, everyone. After observation comes imitation and rehearsal. Learning a physical mannerism is like learning magic: first you observe how the trick works, then you practice until you perfect it, and finally you perform.

Building and playing stage characters is a great way to enhance your physical stage presence, which can put you in a commanding position when you walk into an audition. Your ability to use your body is important. Learn a body-control activity and make it a part of your training: fencing, karate, tennis, biking, water skiing, swimming, scuba diving, or whatever it is that gives you training for control of your body. Physical activity is a great way to improve your coordination and flexibility and to give you confidence and control on the stage.

Acting on the stage is built on developing and understanding characters, and it gives you confidence in handling yourself for auditions, both stage and film. All characters need both a physical and emotional life. For some, you can emphasize the emotional aspects; for other characters you need greater physical characterization. The emotional life would be emphasized if you were doing a character from *Twelve Angry Men*, in which twelve jurors are arguing about a murder case. A physical characterization would be appropriate for Shakespeare's King Richard, a hunchback with a crippled arm, in *Richard III*. In one Royal Shakespeare Company production of the play, the actor playing Richard had such physical control that he actually put a glove on his hand with the same hand. It took several minutes, but it was brilliant. The physicalization this actor brought to the character was highly effective.

When you act in a stage play, your craft and talent count much more that your looks or type, and you can usually play a greater age range on stage than on film. You can use makeup to better advantage, and you have the time to experiment with physical traits, quirks, or mannerisms. You can try a more exaggerated limp or change in voice to make your character come alive. Rehearsing for the stage, you have the time to find out if being a larger villain, hero, or buffoon helps or hurts your role. Plays allow you to develop and discover characterizations. Characterization for the stage offers excitement and adventure, and prepares you for auditions.

Your Objective

In Stanislavsky's search for how actors could be consistent night after night, he came up with the "objective"—what does your character want? What are his needs or desires? In life we act because we expect results. You want a drink of water. You get out of the chair, go to the refrigerator, pour a glass of water, and drink. The act of walking to the refrigerator and pouring the glass of water carries out your objective: to drink. What you want drives you in your scene. Before you walk into an audition, decide what your objective is.

Logical or preplanned choices help you reach your objective. Your choices can be intuitive or logical. Intuitive choices happen at the moment and cannot be planned. Logical choices are your preplanned ideas of what you are going to do in the scene. Well-trained actors are able to make logical choices look spontaneous. Use choices to heighten moments and to give you depth, so you can arrive at your objective. Since you repeat the same scene night after night on stage, you need choices for your performance to remain consistent. Otherwise the play's action develops haphazardly.

Dramatic Choices

Make dramatic choices. Stella Adler told me of the time Marlon Brando was doing a scene in which he was arm wrestling with another actor; the loser would be bitten by a scorpion. The other actor's dramatic choice was, "I want to kill him." Brando's choice was, "I don't want to kill him but I have to." Look for the humanity in your choices. Humanity draws the audience to a performance.

In the audition, logical choices are necessary because you only have one chance. You have to be prepared, just as you have to be when going out on stage for a performance. Know what you are going to do. If you make a strong choice, you will look prepared and professional.

Jeopardy

Identify the jeopardy in every scene you do. Jeopardy is what is personally at stake for the character. Why does a character put himself at risk? He either places himself in jeopardy or is placed in jeopardy by the circumstances. The more of a life and death struggle there is the better. Actors make the strongest choices when in jeopardy. In Arthur Miller's *Death of a Salesman,* Willy Loman has based his whole self-image on his job and on his ability to be a likable salesman. As he gets old enough to retire, he realizes he has no savings and no friends except for Charley, his next door neighbor. Selling becomes harder and harder. His old customers are all retired. He has destroyed his relationship with his son, Biff, who found him having an affair. Every event puts Willy in greater and greater jeopardy until he is fired from his job. Willy is in a life or death situation. He rationalizes his suicide, believing he is sacrificing his life for his family. Find the jeopardy.

Conflict

Conflict is a choice the author makes for his characters, so understand what it is. It creates drama and propels the story. There is conflict, for example, when a woman is trying to make a choice between two men. The young wife in Paddy Chayefsky's play *Middle of the Night* has to make a decision between her young husband and an older man. Which one does she love? Who is the right one for her? Who does she feel better with? Who can take care of her children? Who is morally upright? A writer sets up choices that create conflict for a character, and the actor uses that conflict as motivation. The resolution of the conflict is what fascinates audiences.

The screenwriting teacher Robert McKee reminds his students and readers that there are three kinds of conflict: man against man, man against nature, and man against himself. Internal conflict, or man against himself, is the hardest to show but it is the stuff that makes great drama. In *Death of a Salesman*, the conflict is Willy Loman against himself. In *Moby Dick*, Captain Ahab's conflict is not with nature in the form of the great white whale, but with himself. Be sure you know what the conflict is in your play, because it gives you direction.

Ideas

When you act in film, ideas limit your creativity because an idea usually has only a single direction and often locks you into a single destination. Yet actors repeatedly fall into the trap of getting a great idea that they think is the only way to do a scene. In the scene we discussed in Chapter 1, "The Exercise," the actor playing the highway patrolman gives a terrible performance because he is stuck with the idea that he has to "act" like a cop. When he finally gets that idea out of his head, he gives a good performance. Don't decide that there is a certain way to do a scene.

Emotional Intention

Even though ideas restrict your performance, there are situations that require you to start with an idea. Recall the situation I referred to earlier, for example, about auditioning for a scene in which your character is being followed and threatened by someone yet no one believes your character. Both the script and the casting director want you to start the scene in a highly emotional state. If you don't start off instantly with believable emotion, your audition is done for.

What is the feeling you must start with—happiness, sadness, anger, fear, love? Say the scene requires you to start off in a high state of anger. This is an idea and also your emotional intention. This is what the director, the script, and the casting director call for, so that's what you have to do. As Shurtleff said, do whatever it takes to flay yourself into the feeling before you go into the scene. But be ready to instantly abandon this first emotional intention of anger, because once your idea has helped you jump-start the scene, your feelings from then on have to come from your reaction to the other actor. No more ideas, only honest feelings. You think your girlfriend has cheated on you. So your emotional intention, or idea, is to start the scene being angry with her. Your anger on the first line causes her to cry, and from here on you have to respond to her tears, and your anger has to change. You could get sad and comfort her. You could get angrier, even enraged, or you could laugh. But what you do has to come from your response to what she is feeling and doing. After that first idea of anger, you must then respond to her for the rest of the scene according to how she and the circumstances emotionally affect you.

In class we did the following scene twice. First with one set of two actors, and then with another set of two different actors. Neither couple saw the scene acted by the other couple until afterward on videotape, so the second couple was not influenced by what the first two did. I told each actor to be angry at some time during the scene, and to use the other actor to affect the anger. The scene involved a husband and wife, Al and Rosemary, who had gone to a car dealer to buy a new pickup truck. After the deal had been arrived at and the papers had been filled out, Al changed his mind. They discuss it in the car on the way home.

Couple #1 started out angry and stayed angry throughout the scene with no variety. They started with the idea of anger, but paid no attention to their own feelings or to any changes in the responses of the other. As a result, the scene and the performances had no depth and soon became annoying. Couple #2, on the other hand, begin the scene talking calmly and naturally until something Al does makes Rosemary angry:

```
(Al and Rosemary are coming home from shopping for a new
car. Al had called off the sale after the contract papers
had been all filled out and ready for signatures.)

(They start off talking naturally and calmly.)

                    AL
          It's not my fault.

                    ROSEMARY
          I'm not the one who wasted
          that poor man's time. We
          should have discussed it
          before he did all that work.

                    AL
          I just had a gut feeling. And
          every time I go against that
          feeling, something happens.

                    ROSEMARY
          You embarrassed me.

(Al gives a condescending smile. This makes Rosemary angry.)

                    ROSEMARY
             (angry, raising her voice)
          I thought you wanted that
          truck. I can't believe you let
```

him fill out all the paperwork
. . . He must have thought we
were idiots.

(Al responds to Rosemary's anger. The scene builds
naturally.)

                    AL
               (angry)
          We start off with twenty-three
          thousand dollars, and with tax
          and license it goes to twenty-
          nine seven! Twenty-nine seven!

                    ROSEMARY
               (angry)
          Why didn't you discuss this
          before? Not when he had every-
          thing ready to sign.

                    AL
               (angry)
          Before? I thought I still
          wanted it.

                    ROSEMARY
               (angry)
          Do you have any idea how
          humiliated you made me feel?

(Al sees that she really was humiliated. He is sorry.)

                    AL
               (apologetic)
          Okay . . . I shopped for the
          best price. But I got scared.
          I'm thinking, fifteen miles to
          the gallon? And that pickup
          was a lot bigger than I
          thought at first.

               (laughs)
          Damn, I mean it'd be a bear to
          park.

(She responds to his humor.)

                              ROSEMARY
                         (laughs)
                    Well, we could have talked,
                    but you and your communica-
                    tion.

(Lovingly, Al reaches over and touches Rosemary's hair.)

                              AL
                         (loving)
                    Well, do you think I should
                    have signed all the papers and
                    drove the truck home, and then
                    told you I had second
                    thoughts?

                              ROSEMARY
                         (forgiving)
                    Do you know how embarrassed I
                    felt?

                              AL
                    I'm sorry. I just felt buyer's
                    remorse.

(Rosemary leans over and kisses him on the cheek.)

JEREMIAH: (to the class) It is obvious which couple used the idea. With an emotional intention, or idea, you know that you are going to get angry, but you don't know where or when. An idea like this allows your emotions to be stimulated naturally.

                              LUCY
(to Jeremiah)
                    But could your emotions go in
                    a different direction than
                    your original emotional inten-
                    tion? What if Rosemary cried?
                    Does Al have to stay angry?

JEREMIAH: Of course not. As long as he is relating to her, Al can have any number of experiences. The emotional intention is only an assumption to get you started. We are assuming that we are going to respond in a certain way, but your emotions are not predictable. The variations in human emotions are the essence of art.

Imagination

Your imagination lets you dream, fantasize, and create. Sometimes your imagination diminishes as you get older, mostly because you don't use it as much. A developed imagination is the most important element you have as an actor. Through your imagination, like a child, you can accept and play with unreal circumstances, characters, sets, and props as if they were real. Imagination can be stronger then real experience. Imagination allows you to enter a scene emotionally full. Use your imagination to create a present moment that stimulates your emotions. Then relate immediately to the other actor.

If you have to stimulate the feeling of love, imagine being with Julia Roberts or Brad Pitt. If you have to be frightened by the sight of an accident, you could think of something horrific. I saw a man with elephantiasis, whose legs were horribly disfigured from the kneecap down. They were five times the normal size and the skin was broken, showing tissue and peeled skin. When I imagine that sight, I cringe. If you need to be angry you might carry a rubber ball in your packet and squeeze it with intensity. Imagine that you are squeezing the neck of someone who is trying to kill you. Use your imagination to stimulate your emotions and jump-start a specific feeling before you go into the scene. But don't let it go further than that. Relate to the other actor as soon as you get a response.

Subtext

You have been given the following film scene to audition for, and the casting director is having you read with another actor who is also auditioning. Read it and see if you can figure out how to proceed. Remember, when you go into the casting director's office, you have to start off in an emotional state that is believable, and you have only one chance. You don't have to be terrified, or deadly calm, or anything as specific as that. You just have to be in a state that is believable and will allow you to relate to the other actor.

EXT. NEW YORK CITY. NIGHT.

(John and Beth, both strangers, are in an elevator. It stops between floors. The lights go out. After a few moments, the light goes back on but the elevator is still stuck.)

                              BETH
          Oh no . . . Don't tell me.

                    JOHN
A rolling blackout.

                    BETH
Great . . . I'm late for an
appointment on the other side
of town.

                    JOHN
You can use my cell.

                    BETH
Thanks, but I've tried them in
elevators before . . . No
reception.

                    JOHN
It should be over soon. Good
thing I'm not claustrophobic.

(looks at Beth)

                    BETH
Neither am I, but I always
have this fear that the elevator is falling.

                    JOHN
Don't worry. They build in all
sorts of safety precautions.

                    BETH
How long do you think we'll be
stuck?

                    JOHN
No idea. I'm John.

                    BETH
Beth . . . You work for Golden
State Equities don't you?

                    JOHN
Yes I do.

                          BETH
          They occupy the entire twenty-
          eighth floor. You dress like a
          lawyer, but my guess is that
          you're a CPA.

                          JOHN
          And do you tell fortunes?

                          BETH
          No. I work for a living.

Both actors playing this scene have to know what emotion they are going to feel when the lights go out. That's what you have to prepare for. After that first emotion, you have to relate to the other actor and play the rest of the scene according to what you get from each other. The dialogue is perfectly understandable, so neither of you has to emphasize it or try to explain it for the audience. Your job is to give the dialogue a subtext and make the relationship between the two of you fascinating. This is what is going to get you the job.

The subtext is the hidden meaning behind the dialogue. It represents the thought process underlying complex feelings that motivate what a character says. It is based on what your thoughts and emotions are revealing about what your character really means or wants. It enriches your character's relationship with the other actors. Subtext stimulates emotions and helps the dialogue flow more naturally. In the scene version below, some possible subtexts are in parentheses after each of the actors' lines.

EXT. NEW YORK CITY. NIGHT.

                          BETH
          Oh no . . . Don't tell me.
          **(What in the world. Not
          again.)**

                          JOHN
          A rolling blackout.
          (A good-looking woman.)

                          BETH
          Great . . . I'm late for an
          appointment on the other side
          of town.
          **(This guy always dresses
          nice.)**

                    JOHN
You can use my cell.
(Wow!)

                    BETH
Thanks, but I've tried them in
elevators before . . . No
reception.
**(Just keep looking at me, like
that . . . I love it.)**

                    JOHN
It should be over soon. Good
thing I'm not claustrophobic.
(Maybe I can get her number.)

                    BETH
Neither am I, but
(I hope he comes on to me.)
I always have this fear that
the elevator is falling.
(I'll stroke his ego.)

                    JOHN
Don't worry. They build in all
sorts of safety precautions.
(I'll make her feel safe.)

                    BETH
How long do you think we'll be
stuck?
**(He's cute, and he's flirting
with me.)**

These subtexts show what the actor is really feeling and thinking while saying the script lines, and they come from each actor intently concentrating and listening to the other. They are not the only possible subtexts for this scene. The possibilities are many. They depend on how the actors relate, the requirements of the script, and the director's wishes.

Types of Actors

Good actors come in all configurations—tall, short, fat, skinny, homely, handsome, beautiful, awkward, old, disfigured, handicapped, and funny looking. Good actors know what they are, and have accepted themselves. To become a good auditioner and a good actor, first accept yourself. If you're fat, you're fat. If your nose is big, it's big. If your voice is squeaky, it's squeaky. If you're klutzy, you're klutzy. Accept what you are and get on with learning to be a great actor. Don't fool yourself. If you are not beautiful or handsome or appallingly charismatic, don't delude yourself that you are. Only a few actors make it to stardom, but there is lots of room in movies and TV for every type of person there is. Be honest. How you come across to others, especially to casting directors, determines what type of character you are going to be cast for. The image of your type is not necessarily linked with what your life has been. One of my students looks nothing like a cowboy even though he grew up on a cattle ranch in Montana and worked cattle most of his life. Another student, who is a brilliant actor, is a university professor, but he is never cast as a professor in TV commercials because he doesn't "look" like a professor. Examine your perception of yourself and how you appear to others. This is a neat trick, because ego and wishful thinking make it hard for us to see ourselves realistically. It takes courage. But if you wanna be an actor, you gotta do it. The Scottish poet Robert Burns articulated the problem in his poem *To a Louse*:

> *Oh wad some power the giftie gie us*
> *To see oursels as others see us!*

Seeing yourself as others see you, Burns says, frees you from a lot of mistakes and stupid ideas. Good actors may be celebrity-driven and self-involved, but they know what their personas are and what they look like to other people. As a result, they know which roles to accept or reject.

The story is told that Julia Roberts was originally offered the role of a highly successful but selfish actress in *American Sweethearts*. But Roberts turned down the part in favor of the role as the actress's sister, who, in the script, has devoted her life to seeing to all the needs of her famous movie star sister. In the role, Roberts finally sees that she has subordinated her own life to her sister's, but she frees herself and ends up with the leading man. Roberts is perfect for the part of the sacrificing sister who wises up. It is clear that the role was the right one for her. She knows who she is and what kind of role she should play. She knows her type better than the producers who hired her—all they knew was that if Julia Roberts were in their film, it would make money. She made them even more money by knowing what kinds of roles she should and should not play.

The Message You Send

How are you perceived? What message do you send? What do casting directors think when they see you? Do they see what you really are? Do they see the superstar who, in your dream time, breaks the bank at Las Vegas, tolerates all the beautiful people clamoring for your sexual favors, owns thirty-bedroom homes in New York and Malibu along with a garage full of foreign cars? Who stars in the most successful movie of all time and, after winning the Oscar, delivers the most moving acceptance speech in the history of the Academy Awards? And all you need for this fantasy to happen is for producers and directors to come to their senses and cast you in leading roles. Is this how you see yourself, yet you are not getting cast in the big roles? Is this what casting directors see? If not, then you have to figure out what they do see; for when you do, you move closer to becoming an actor instead of a "wannabe." It's okay to want all those things (and you might even get them someday), because the desire and the dreaming may force you into seeing the reality of yourself. You may become a great star, but doing so starts with knowing what and who you are. Your face, your physical configuration, and your body language tell a certain story. You need to know what that story is.

Summary

Auditioning for film has an affinity to stage acting. On stage you do one complete, continuous performance each night. If you make a mistake, you can't go back and do it again. Similarly, in an audition, you have only one guaranteed reading. On stage you use your environment. In the audition you use the auditioning room. On stage you have a partner. In the audition you read with the casting director, but almost everything else is like the stage. On stage, brilliant actors are the ones who are prepared. In the audition, be prepared, know your emotional intention, and decide on what to achieve in the scene. Part of being prepared is learning how to incorporate ideas and use intention. On stage you have the whole play. In the audition you only have the sides. On stage you have time for preparation. In the audition you have limited time because you are given the sides maybe a day or two in advance—and sometimes only a few minutes ahead of time.

You are expected to give a brilliant performance without any rehearsal or partner or props. Impossible? No! Difficult? Yes! Remember, someone will get the part. It should be you.

Actor Practice

1. You won't get cast on every audition no matter how good you are. It's a matter of numbers. If you go out on enough auditions, you will eventually be cast.
2. When other actors get called for auditions, ask them for a copy of their sides. This will allow you to study and practice sight reading on a variety of actual audition materials.

3. No matter what you plan or rehearse before the audition, remember the Art of Relating. When something unexpected happens, adjust to the experience. Do not hold fast to your ideas.
4. Keep a record of each audition:
   a. The casting agent
   b. Date
   c. Scene or material
   d. Did the casting agent relate to you or not?
   e. What did you do right in the audition?
   f. What did you do wrong?
   g. How can you improve?

14

More on the Audition

You've got one of two things to do in that audition: get the job or be remembered.

Richard Dreyfuss

The Casting Director

Who are casting directors? There are no specific qualifications. I know a casting director who is a film producer and a writer. Some casting directors are ex-actors. Some start as secretaries or mail clerks with little or no experience in theater or film. Many are bright college graduates with degrees in theater. Casting can be an end in itself or a way toward directing, writing, or producing. A casting director should be able to distinguish between good and bad acting. As basic as that might seem, it may come to you as a shock that many casting directors and film directors cannot distinguish between a good and a bad performance. Casting directors come from diverse backgrounds, but all of them have one thing in common—they hope that when you come through the door you are the one they are looking for. They want to give you the job.

Some casting directors are good actors and will relate to you in your reading. Some are great observers but lousy actors and will read with you in monotone, eyes never lifting from the page. Some hire readers, but most have a casting assistant read with you, allowing them to observe. Some will dislike your performance and others will love it. Some will direct you through every line. Some will be abrupt, some gentle. Some will order you around and others will mother you. Some are having a good day, others a bad day. No matter what they do, you have to get past your ego and give them one hundred percent. Don't judge them. Be grateful and cordial. After all, you are the guest, and your purpose is not to prove anything but to get the job and be remembered.

The Job

If you want to work in film you have to audition. You will spend most of your time auditioning and a little bit of time working. Doing the Relating Exercise regularly (see Chapter 1) gives you an edge in auditions because my process teaches you to be truthful as well as professional. In this chapter, I try to make you aware of both the benefits and limitations of the Art of Relating when you go for an audition. In the workshop, the Exercise teaches you the fundamental skills you need to become a good film actor. Reading the material once stimulates your intuition. Quickly memorizing your lines excites your emotions, but doesn't give you time to become paralyzed by thinking about the literal meaning. And sight reading gives you the freedom to concentrate on and relate to the other actor. But auditions are different. The first audition and callbacks for a role are conducted by casting directors for whom you have to give a performance that is more theatrical than you would normally do for a film, even though the audition is for a film. After you pass the first audition and a callback or two for the casting director, you will most likely be given an audition with the director, who will, we hope, be looking for pure film acting; that is, she will watch you to see if you are relating to the other actor and working from your feelings rather than from your preconceived ideas.

Film acting is an art. And like all artists, actors learn by imitation, discovery, and application. To master your art, you particularly need application, which is acting in films. A successful audition for a casting director gives you that opportunity.

Acting Is a Business

Acting is a business that depends on actors, preferably the most talented, who are right for the part. The people who cast actors have their own criteria. Most casting directors understand creativity but that's not what they want; they are looking for a solid performance. The good casting directors know from the moment you say your first line whether or not you can act and whether or not you're what the director wants.

Roughly 10 percent of the actors get 90 percent of the jobs. Your livelihood depends on your understanding and perfecting the audition process. It is a skill that working actors have mastered. Clay, a student of mine and a well-known commercial actor, had worked out an effective audition procedure. I went with him once on a commercial interview. (I find it interesting that actors in Hollywood uniformly refer to auditions as "interviews.") When we arrived, Clay signed the sheet and then introduced himself to each woman in the waiting room who was there for the audition. He then selected the one he thought he would like to read with and talked to her. They stayed together until the casting assistant called for two actors to read. They went into the audition studio together, and both were hired. While the other actors were absorbed in themselves and working on their lines, he established a rapport with one actor and positioned the two of them so that they would be selected to go in together. He knew it was most important to establish a connection with the actress ahead of time so they would be able to relate and act like a couple.

An audition is a combination of the Exercise, working for the camera, and a stage performance. Casting agents need to be sure you are professional. Some will give you adjustments to see if you can take directions. Other casting directors will expect you to deliver exactly what they have visualized ahead of time. Auditioning is a complex skill. If we could map out the exact route to a performance, anybody could do it, but there is no exact route. You have to figure out how to combine your persona and your acting skill to make yourself desirable to a casting director.

Expect Change

Skillful auditioners have several tools. Through practice they learn which ones to use and when. The one tool you will always need is relating, because it is the foundation of all acting. But auditioning based only on relating will not always give you the required results. Results are necessary. In the audition, you have only one chance. Without preparation, the chances are that you will not give your best performance. My student Michelle asked about this during class.

```
                    MICHELLE
        Jeremiah—then how does this
        jive with what you said
        earlier about not preparing?
        Remember Alicia who didn't
        prepare and got the job.
```

JEREMIAH: **Michelle, that's an insightful question.** (to the class) **You remember Alicia, who had just taken her dog to the vet and didn't have time to prepare but got the job anyway. Customarily, when she auditioned, the ideas in the material and preparation seemed more important to her than relating. This time, she didn't have time to prepare her ideas, so she was forced to relate to the casting director. Since she didn't have time to develop a character, she was forced to play herself, and so her real personality came through.**

Her ideas had always inhibited her emotionally and made her choices look planned rather than spontaneous. In this instance, she gave an emotionally honest performance partly because of the personal trauma with the dog and partly because of the unexpected positive response from the casting director. Alicia is

a good stage actress, and when she was not trying to act—this is important, Michelle, and I think it answers your question—all her knowledge and previous training subconsciously came into play. Which is what I'm trying to teach you, to be yourself without trying to act. So in the audition, Alicia was emotionally honest, and her personality was displayed in a way that excited the casting agent and the director.

To expedite your understanding of the Arts of Concentration and Relating, I purposely stay away from ideas until the Arts become second nature. Then ideas, emotional intentions, or necessary script direction will allow you to give a more compelling performance in the audition. But the Art of Relating should always take precedence over any idea. In the movie *I Am Sam*, Sean Penn, playing the mentally challenged Sam Dawson, is in court when the judge orders that custody of his small daughter, Lucy, be taken from him. Penn, working from a characterization of a retarded person, allows the judge's comments to sink in before he relates his emotional experience back to the judge. Penn, a marvelous actor, relates through the character. There are ideas and a logical element in his performance, but his emotional quality and his relating are so strong that we never see the ideas or the thought.

Keep in mind, talent alone will not guarantee you the job. No single acting process will work for every audition. No performance is totally dependent on acting alone. You are not going be hired if you fall in the "too" area: too tall, too short, too young, too old, too handsome, too beautiful, too ugly, too fat, too skinny. Many things you have no control over can exclude you from the job. One of my students, a fine, handsome actor, was called in for an audition in a feature film starring Gregory Peck. When my student walked into the audition studio, he knew instantly he would not get cast. On the wall was a long black horizontal line that represented the star's height. He did not even get to read for the part because he was two inches taller than that line on the wall. Directors don't normally cast actors who are taller than the star. You may not get cast in a part for reasons that have nothing to do with you as an actor. All sorts of unrelated stuff have to come together for you to get work. So don't become discouraged.

Credits

Most professional actors have a videotape of film scenes they have acted in with recognized actors in a legitimate show. By legitimate I mean a produced film intended seriously for release, not a scene shot for you as a demo tape by a photographer. The judgment of your performance often depends on the professional production value of your demo tape, which may be unfair, but it's true. Scenes in a tape show the director your work and how you look and handle yourself on film. If you don't have a professional tape, you are an unknown commodity. The casting director and director are taking a chance.

Personal Tapes

A videotape is something every working actor needs. Start building a tape: act in student films, independent movies, projects with your friends, anything to get film and experience. Make a short film. Get a digital camera and do a scene with a fellow actor. These give you experience. But unless your acting is brilliant, don't show anything to anybody in the profession. Heed this admonition carefully because it is a human trait to be fascinated by ourselves. When you see yourself on tape, it is almost impossible to be objective—in fact, you will probably be fascinated regardless of how bad or good your performance. Few will give you an honest evaluation of your acting. Your friends won't, your mother won't, casual acquaintances won't, and strangers don't care. The only critics of your acting whom you can believe are the director, the film's editor, an audience, your acting teacher, or sometimes a professional critic. To show anyone taped scenes in which you are less than brilliant marks you as an amateur.

The casting director's job is get someone who can fill a role. A good picture and résumé get you in the door. If you are an unknown, casting directors may have doubts about your ability. Remember, their jobs are on the line. They cannot risk being embarrassed in front of a director or producer. A good tape is an asset that gives a producer the confidence to hire you.

As unfair as it might seem, when you show a demo tape of yourself to casting directors, directors, or producers, you are most often judged by the professional quality of the tape rather than by the brilliance of your performance. Unfortunately, your performance in a demo tape carries the burden of amateur and inept production. Film is a function of money. The more money, the better the quality; and it is almost impossible for professionals to see beyond poor technical quality. When they look at your tape, they are thrown off when it is not the quality of an A-level movie or primetime television.

Why Actors Don't Get Cast

Actors fail to get hired because they do not audition well. They get nervous. They don't understand the audition process. They don't know how to prepare. They don't know how to make choices. They don't know how to listen. They don't take directions. They can't sight read. They don't know the TV show they are auditioning for. They don't know if it's a comedy or a drama. They haven't read the stage directions. Some don't even know how to act.

Enjoy the process of meeting the casting director and the experience of reading. Be grateful that you have the opportunity to audition. Be positive. Moe, a student in my advanced workshop, let out the frustration and pessimism that invade every actor once in a while:

```
                         MOE
(to Jeremiah)
            I hate this town. It's not
            like New York, where the cast-
            ing directors respect actors.
            I get callbacks, but I never
            get the job. Hollywood doesn't
            respect talent.
```

JEREMIAH: **Stop the negativity, Moe. You're blaming your failure on the casting director rather than taking responsibility and realizing it's a different medium. You're talented, we can see that, but your acting is too broad for film.**

Every time Moe did a workshop scene, I had to remind him continually to look at his partner and respond without a lot of physicality. He was usually all over the place, nodding his head, indicating his meaning by significant looks and gestures. He moved his head so much the camera operator had trouble keeping him in the frame. In every session we worked to get him to relate to the other actor and not to worry about physically indicating his every meaning. It was a struggle for him to relate to the other actor and enjoy what he was doing.

In his complaints, Moe was expressing his disenchantment with Hollywood. He was getting callbacks but not bookings. He had a great character face. He was also impressed by his own acting ability, but apparently nobody else was. Remember, it's not the casting agents' or the producers' fault when you don't get cast. You are responsible for adjusting to what they want if you want to work. You usually get callbacks because you look right for the part. After that, it's up to you to turn in a performance that knocks 'em out of their socks.

Once Moe realized his acting had to change, his attitude got better. One night in the workshop I was able to announce:

JEREMIAH: **Class, Moe just booked a movie.**

```
                         MOE
(to Jeremiah)
            . . . it's because, you know,
            it's the first interview that
            I had fun.
```

JEREMIAH: **If we love what we do it will permeate our work and everybody around us. When acting becomes enjoyable, your creative potential is released effortlessly. Your personality and talent begin to work for you.**

Audition Pressure

In the audition you are under tremendous pressure. Every potential job has value. "If I'm cast, I can pay the rent . . . get a new car . . . earn seventy-five hundred bucks a week for twelve weeks . . . *eat*," and the reasons go on and on. This is why you study, act in showcases, and hustle to get an interview. Students often say to me, "This is my big chance." No it is not! It is one of the many opportunities you will run into over your career as an actor. Professional actors know that the audition is part of the job, only you don't get paid. The pressure on you in any audition can be overwhelming. The competition is stiff. What do you do?

You have your sides but you probably have not been given the entire script. Do you read it once, as we do in the workshop, and wing it? Do you rehearse? Do you memorize it and fake that you are reading it? How do you study for the part? Do you develop a character? Do you make specific choices? Do you give a film performance? Do you give a stage performance? Do you get coached? What approach will work best for this particular audition? You have plenty of options, but what's the answer? Experience is the answer. From each audition you will eventually learn how to produce results.

The Differences between the Relating Exercise and the Audition

You cannot always approach the audition as you would the Relating Exercise, which teaches you how to acknowledge experiences, how to trust your intuition, and how to become adept at relating to another actor. The audition demands immediate, predetermined results. In the Exercise you have the advantage of relating with another actor. In the audition you are reading to a casting director, not an actor, and there is no guarantee that she will relate to you. However, you must relate to her. In rehearsals for a stage play, you learn how to relate to another actor, go for your objective, and use your predetermined choices. Similarly, for an audition, you can perform to better advantage by analyzing the scene, deciding on what you are going to do, and making your choices ahead of time.

                              HARRY
              This seems to contradict what
              you have said previously about
              not preparing.

JEREMIAH: **In the audition the actor is at a distinct disadvantage because you don't know what is expected or what will happen. Will the casting director relate to you? You are only going to have one chance (one reading) to show them that you are professional. If you don't have an idea or an emotional objective you will be leaving your reading up to chance. If you have mastered the Arts of film acting, then when you read the audition material once you will know how or when it will affect you. If the casting director relates to you and you connect with the material emotionally, then all you have to do is relate. Preparation carries you through when nothing happens. It keeps you from looking amateurish. It helps beginning actors who are just starting to audition and develop confidence and trust their ability to Relate, Not Know, and Concentrate. As these abilities increase, you will use ideas and emotional commitment less and less.**

The Art of Not Knowing

Once you make a decision as to how you will do a certain role, then you *know*. This knowing is an idea that will not let you do a good job in a film scene. The Exercise is designed for you to learn how to discover the "moment" through the dialogue and with the other character. The Art of Not Knowing works for film, especially for multiple takes where you have to be fresh with moment-by-moment discovery on each take. It is essential for a beginning actor to learn to relate. On stage you have the rehearsals and the time to develop a character and incorporate it into a spontaneous performance. But in the audition you need immediate results. Know what you intend to do with the scene before you walk into the casting office.

Predetermined Emotional Response

At times in an audition you will need a specific emotion. He is loving, she laughs, he cries, she is angry. In comedy, generally, the emotion will be incorporated into the dialogue. In drama, it may be in the description of the action or in parentheses that describe your character's emotional state. As an actor you are required to provide the necessary emotion. In the auditions for a movie directed by William Shatner, Jerry, an actor, had not read the screen directions. When the casting director reads the line, "Stop crying, we'll get out of here," Jerry realized too late that he should have been crying. He should have been prepared with that predetermined response, but he wasn't and he lost the job.

Here's how to arrive at a predetermined emotional response.

```
                        KIMYA
(to Jeremiah)
             What if you need to cry? What
             do you do?
```

JEREMIAH: **Easy, cry.** (to the class) **Tears come easily to some actors, who can cry on cue. It sometime helps them get the job. Actors who have trouble crying on cue can often get honest tears without planning when they rely on the situation, the material, and on relating to the other actor. Some actors can accept the imaginary circumstances and cry real tears through being in the moment. But unless you're confident working this way, don't count on it. You can use emotional memory, but I don't recommend it because when you try to recall an emotion from the past, it most often puts you back in your head where there are no emotions. Use your imagination to stimulate sadness, and allow that to affect your character. Use your personal life if you are in pain. Practice crying when you sight read. Emotions are like a muscle that needs exercise to work properly. Good actors can touch any emotion whenever they want. Stage training is valuable because you are forced to stimulate specific emotions night after night. But on stage if you don't bring up the real emotion, you may be able to fake it believably. On film, you cannot—it has to be real. However you manage to do it, learn to bring up your emotions. Learn not just to act as if you are feeling an emotion, but to really bring that emotion up. The best way to do this is to fully Concentrate your attention outside yourself; Accept the circumstances; forget ideas (Not Knowing); and be emotionally and mentally receptive to what others are feeling (Giving and Receiving). Don't "try" to feel emotion; let it come to you as a result of accepting what you see and hear.**

You have to prepare for an audition because you have only one shot. The first time is often the last time. Make strong emotional choices. Catherine Wilshire, a producer and casting agent, once said, "Try to make three emotional changes in a reading. Casting directors are looking for your range."

Personality

The Relating Exercise develops personality. In the audition they are looking for *you*, not a character. In the film, they will put you in the appropriate costume, but they are hiring you.

The "Where"

In an audition, you have no control over your surroundings, and nothing can be moved. Establishing the "where" may be necessary in some auditions. You should know where the scene you are in takes place. If you are on a golf course, you can audition standing. If you are in a wheelchair, sit. If you are in a hospital bed, sit, don't lie down.

>   ELTON
> (to Jeremiah)
>   Well, it's not a stage play
>   and we have no set, so how do
>   you play the environment? You
>   have no idea what furniture
>   you will find in the audition
>   room.

JEREMIAH: **Don't try to create the "where." If it's a scene where you are having dinner with your girlfriend, the "where" rarely has an effect on your performance. The casting director doesn't care about the setting. She's looking for your emotional choices, not the environment. But know where you are, know the physical location of the scene.**

>   ELTON
> (to Jeremiah)
>   Do you pantomime that you're
>   on a golf course? Or do you
>   bring in a golf club?

JEREMIAH: **Neither. Stay away from props.**

>   ELTON
> (to Jeremiah)
>   But without props my acting
>   seems dishonest. I can't work
>   miming things.

JEREMIAH: **Don't mime. Look her in the eye and say the dialogue.**

Blocking and Props

Acting on stage is a great way to learn how to move and handle props. On stage this is called blocking. On film it's called hitting your mark. A mark is usually a piece of tape on the floor to show you where to stand or stop. In an audition, if the casting director should want you to sit, she will offer you a chair. She may ask you to sit or stand, whichever is the most comfortable for you. Keep movement to a minimum, and don't touch the casting director or her assistant. Wendy, a casting director visiting my workshop, explained how she and other casting directors feel about actors kissing or touching them.

> WENDY
> My assistant was reading with the actor, when he gives her a kiss. It wasn't just a peck, he was using his tongue. We were embarrassed for her, watching and wondering what this poor girl was going to do.

> ALLEN
> What happened to the actor?

> WENDY
> Nobody even watched him because they were so embar-rassed for her . . . He sure didn't get a callback. I'll never call him in again.

Sides

The sides are the pages of the script containing the scene you are to audition. Sometimes casting directors give you your sides a few days ahead of time; sometimes you won't get them until you arrive for the audition. Screen directions often specify action and movement, but don't try to follow them real-istically. In one audition, the actor was playing the part of a reporter doing an interview. He was so involved in trying to mime the taking of notes in an imag-inary notebook that he barely saw the other actor. About a third of the way through the scene, the casting director thanked him and called for the next cou-ple to come in.

Fear

Fear is a big problem and can cause you to give a mediocre per-formance. Learn to relax. On a morning talk show, Anjelica Huston remarked that Jack Nicholson was a very relaxed actor. If he makes a mistake, she said, he bounces right back and does it again. Jack accepts that he will make mistakes—he doesn't worry about them—and this alleviates his fear.

                              MARK
(to Jeremiah)
                    That's great, but how do you
                    relax?

JEREMIAH: **Concentrate. Concentrate on the reader. See and listen to her. Once you start, the fear should dissipate into energy. Concentration on someone else is one source of relaxation.**

Relaxing

Every acting program recognizes the importance of relaxing. Stanislavsky says that knowing how to relax is essential to becoming a good actor, and he goes into detail telling you how to do it. Read what he said in *An Actor Prepares,* and learn to relax. There are books on relaxing. Yoga relaxes you, and so does meditation. You have to teach yourself how to relax, particularly in film where the camera picks up the slightest bit of tension or nervousness that you may have. If you are not physically and mentally relaxed, you cannot look good in a film scene. So learn.

Another way to relax is this: It may seem impossible, but treat the audition as if it doesn't count. Don't go in with any expectations. Ryan, one of my students, was offered a one-year contract with the *Power Rangers.* He said that it was the *Power Rangers,* and he didn't care. "I mean, I did the best job I could, but I wasn't worried about getting the job. I think that was why I got it." Enjoy the audition and don't give a damn! Don't let 'em see you sweat.

Benefit of the Relating Exercise in Audition

The audition is similar to an opening night in Carnegie Hall without any formal rehearsal. But no matter how prepared you are, you don't have a clue as to how the casting director will respond. You have no way of knowing exactly what she wants. Skilled actors make strong choices. Remember, there is only one of you in the whole world. You are unique. That's what makes you marketable above all else. You! The Exercise trains you to make immediate adjustments by responding to what you are given. It develops your emotional power and your self-confidence. Once mastered it improves the possibility of your getting a job.

Skills for the Audition

There are many skills that are useful for auditions. First of all, read film scripts. Scripts are visual, not verbal. The best way to understand dramatic structure is to read scripts. Read at least a script a week. Is it dramatic or comic? Is it a romantic comedy, black comedy, horror movie, or thriller? Cultivate the ability to distinguish between daytime TV (soaps), primetime TV, and situation comedies. With experience, you can even tell the difference by the style of typing and the thickness of the script.

Read scripts, and also read novels that are being produced as movies. Visualize how you would act the scenes. Then see the movie. How did they turn this material from a concept into a film? Once you have seen the movie and know what has happened, reread the material. Watch for emotional intention and changes. In auditioning, you will need to know your character's emotional intention and when it changes.

When you read scripts for auditions, examine them scene by scene, and for each character write down the following:

1. What is the conflict and what causes it?
2. What is the emotional intention and when does it change?

When you are preparing to audition, remember that your choices have to be active and "actable." Make strong choices. You cannot act being bored, so it is not an actable choice. Wanting to be somewhere else is not actable. But you can act the choice, "Silently, he boils with rage." Rage (anger) is actable.

And be sure to read all screen directions. Dialogue often requires an understanding of the screen directions to work. Read every line on the pages you have been given, even if they do not pertain to your character, for they will often give you clues. Screenplays are very specific, and screen directions often help you understand the dialogue. You need to be aware of this to make emotional choices for the character. Casting director Wendy Gigler said, "You would be surprised how many actors don't read the screen directions." Not doing so makes an actor look unprofessional.

I was coaching a student for a movie. The second line was, "Don't you ever knock?" When James said those lines they didn't make sense. He hadn't read the screen directions and didn't know what he was supposed to be doing.

```
(James, relaxed, lies on his bed as he inhales some of
Humbolt's finest. Three copies of Penthouse magazine rest
on his chest. He shuts his eyes. He is in a state of
euphoria.)

                        JAMES
           This is as good as it gets.

(Juanita, a Hispanic maid, 38, gorgeous, enters.)
```

```
                        JAMES
                   (joke, casual)
              Christ! Don't you ever knock?
```

JEREMIAH: **Screen directions can illuminate the text. After James reads the screen directions and finds that he is smoking pot and is startled by the maid, he understands what the scene is about. So this time, when Juanita enters, James tries to hide the joint and fans the smoke. When he says the lines, they make sense.**

```
    (James imaginatively inhales a joint.)

                        JAMES
              This is as good as it gets.
```

JEREMIAH: **Then he reacts to Juanita's entering.**

```
                        JAMES
                     (panicked)
              Christ! Don't you ever knock?
```

JEREMIAH: **It's a very simple idea, reading the screen directions, and you wonder sometimes why an actor would not do that. Understanding the screen directions brought this dialogue to life. James looked professional.**

```
                        JOHN
    (to Jeremiah)
              What do I do when the casting
              director doesn't react or
              relate to me?
```

JEREMIAH: **The casting director's job is to see if you can act. She's not trying to be an actor, and she doesn't see her job as requiring her to relate to you. This means that you've got to be prepared and know your emotional intention in the scene.**

```
                        JOHN
    (to Jeremiah)
              This negates everything we are
              learning here.
```

JEREMIAH: **Good point. First of all, I am not teaching auditioning. I am teaching film acting and how to relate. Even if the casting director doesn't relate to you, you relate to her. That is the only way you can make your performance believable.**

> JOHN
> (to Jeremiah)
>> But if she not giving you any-
>> thing . . . How can you possi-
>> bly relate?

JEREMIAH: **Listen and be present. That's what this process is about. Training yourself to experience true emotions.**

> JOHN
> (to Jeremiah)
>> I don't see how you can give a
>> good performance when you have
>> nobody to act with.

JEREMIAH: **What happens on the set, when you do your close-ups with the script supervisor because the star has gone home? When the camera rolls it stimulates your adrenaline. You have to imagine that someone is there. See that person's face in your imagination. Really see it and talk to it. Your subconscious knows what to feel, look at, listen to, and trust. Some of the stars are generous enough to stay around until you finish your close-ups. When you are acting in a film, no matter how big a star you become, please don't be a jerk by leaving and forcing another actor to do close-ups with the script supervisor.**

> MICHAEL
> (to Jeremiah)
>> But how is that possible with
>> no one to relate with?

JEREMIAH: **Imagination. The magic *if*. You have to learn to do it. The Relating Exercise develops your intuition. When you accept the given circumstances, concentrate on the reader, and use your imagination, you can experience real emotions.**

I once was sitting in the waiting room of a casting studio when an actor walked out of the casting director's office. He was angry and indignant. He said she asked him to cold-read a scene on the spot instead of the one he had studied. He showed me three pages of dialogue. Even though this happens a lot, he was caught unprepared to do a cold reading. If you have learned to sight read and relate, you won't have trouble when this happens to you.

> THERESA
> (to Jeremiah)
>> I was cast in a series because
>> of sight reading. They were

```
considering six women for the
same part. On the last callback
they gave each of us a script
we hadn't seen before and asked
us to read it on the spot. I
love sight reading, I knew
exactly what to do. I was
hired.
```

JEREMIAH: I was cast in my first major film because I could sight read. It was a monologue three pages long. Apparently nobody else could work off the page, which means relating to the other actor while you are reading new material. A good sight reader can read material he has never seen before and look like he has it memorized.

Commitment

You can't tell what casting directors want, so make your choices and commit. If you are right for the role, the casting director might give you an adjustment. Once you finish, thank them and leave.

```
                    KUNI
(to Jeremiah)
          What if my choices are wrong?
```

JEREMIAH: Right or wrong, commit to your choices. The casting director can see your quality. Bob McDonald, who cast *Runaway Train*, said that John D. Ryan read for the director, Andrei Konchalovsky, who immediately wanted him for the part. Bob asked if he had liked his choices. The director said they were all wrong, even though they were strong. The director saw John D. Ryan's personality and knew he was right for the part. Your choices may not be what the director had in mind. You can't outguess the director anyway, so don't even try.

```
                    PATCH
(to Jeremiah)
          I went on a reading. The cast-
          ing director put me on tape,
          and when I was finished she
          said, "That was brilliant."
```

JEREMIAH: **Good for you.**

```
                    PATCH
(to Jeremiah)
                I had a great time. I felt
                elated. But I never got a
                callback.
```

JEREMIAH: **That happens all the time. Casting directors often really like what you do, but for no fault of your own, they can't cast you. Patch, the main point is that you felt good about the work. The audition has to be your payoff. The bonus is that she made you feel good.**

Take Direction

If the casting director is gracious enough to give you information, take it. Use it. Don't argue or debate about how you see the character. Mark Tillman, a casting director, says, "Remain flexible and open to feedback even after the scene. If you are given directions, do not presume that you know more than the one giving them to you. Character and circumstances may change without your knowing it." If you can take directions, it's a plus. It gives the director confidence that you will be able to respond to his vision.

If the casting director redirects you, make sure that you do it differently. Remember, once you do a scene, especially one that you have prepared for, you have a pattern. You need to push your emotions and physicality beyond what you have planned to break away from your previous pattern. You have to do more than you might think to demonstrate your directability.

If you wing it by simply relying on your vast talent and flexibility, it is too easy to fall on your face. Approach a scene in a professional manner. Remember, the audition is a cross between doing a stage play and a film. If you were acting in a stage play, you would rehearse many times before being presented to an audience. But in an audition you don't have time for rehearsals, and if you did, you wouldn't know what to rehearse. So I am giving you an approach that is simple and effective. As you develop your skill in auditioning, your subconscious mind will play a bigger part in this process

Preparation for Audition

Read the sides and understand all screen directions.

Underline all your character's action. This helps you connect the action in the script with your character's dialogue.

Determine if your material is comedic or dramatic. (The following tips are for dramatic auditions. Comedy auditions are explained in Chapter 15.)

Know the show. If you are reading for a TV sitcom or TV movie, make yourself familiar with the program.

Know where to start. This is an audition, and the casting director is interested in results.

Know what emotion your character is experiencing when the scene begins.

Know where the emotional changes in the scene occur. If the core emotion is anger, start with a different emotion—laughter, love, or fear.

Know where the anger will peak. If you know you are going to end with anger, start with a different emotion to give your performance color. You may object that this is result acting. You would be right, and you wouldn't prepare this way for acting in an actual film. But auditioning for film is a strange kind of animal, and the casting director has to "see something." This does not mean that you have to overact and indicate, but it does mean that you have to come in with something. There are a few casting directors who can recognize a good film performance; but most of them cannot. In the casting office, you are recorded on tape. If the scene is with another actor, the camera operator frames you in a home-movie two-shot. If you do the scene as you would for a director in an actual film, the full effect of your emotional relationship will be lost. Your best performances in a film are staged in close-up when you are feeling and relating. In an audition, you try to give the casting director a little more theatricality so she can see something she recognizes.

If you know you're going to start with a certain emotion, find a place for the opposite emotion in the script. If you start off angry, express love if you can towards the end.

Know the conflict in the scene. When and where does the conflict take place?

Get coaching, especially if it is a big part. The competition is fierce, and without help you might miss a moment or even overlook your objective in the scene. It is hard for actors to direct themselves.

Dress for the character. Wardrobe helps indicate the character. If your character is in the army, you might wear a brown shirt and pants. If your character is a waitress, you might wear your hair in a bun and a simple dress. If your character is a golfer, wear a golf shirt. If your character is a female executive, you might wear a business suit. Don't come in full costume, but do give a hint of the character.

The Audition

Be prompt. Always be on time or call if you are going to be late. Try to get to the audition an hour ahead of time. This gives you time to get focused.

Be friendly. Be thankful you have the chance to read.

Memorize your first line of dialogue. Make eye contact. Wait until the casting director looks at you before you start. If she doesn't look at you, wait until she glances up, then start.

Commit to your choices. Make strong emotional choices. Your choices may all be wrong, but don't worry about it. Commit! The casting director is looking for your personality. Are you professional? Did you display your emotional range?

Accept the imaginary character and the situation. This will fill you up emotionally.

Take control of the room. Don't be timid. This is your time. You have one shot. Walk in and be confident. Enjoy the audition.

Cheerfully take direction.

When the audition is over, thank the casting directors and leave. Don't stand around waiting for them to ask you to leave.

As Mark Tillman says, "After the audition, let it go, forget about it." You did your best and you have no control over whom they will hire. The audition is part of the job.

Remember, the audition and the Exercise are two separate aspects of film acting. You need results in the audition to get hired. Once you've been cast and are on the set, do the Exercise.

If you have mastered sight reading, the casting agent or director can quickly determine that your film personality is right for the role, that you can take direction, and that you can relate. They want to know that you are a professional who can handle the job. Remember this: developing your talent depends on sight reading more than anything else I teach.

As an actor you will have personal thoughts about the scene when you are acting. Accept them as the character's thoughts. You may think, "The scene is too slow. I am not relating." Use it! Turn those thoughts into those of the character: "I should go faster," then go faster. Concentrate on the casting director's response to limit your random thoughts. Accept everything as if it were happening now. Right now. Share your feelings, be generous. Give everything to the casting director—every bit of love, anger, sadness, happiness, or fear.

Audition Don'ts

Don't ask to do it a second time. You have one chance. I've heard many casting directors say that second readings seldom improve your chances.

Don't use a highlighter to underline your dialogue or mark you sides. What happens if you forget your highlighter or the casting director gives you different sides?

Don't be argumentative. Never debate about how you see the character, especially with the director. She is telling you how she prefers the character to act. She is not interested in your comments, but in getting her vision on screen. Be quiet, listen, and give her what she wants. Disagreement and argument are red flags for the casting director. The last thing a director wants on the set is trouble.

Don't ad-lib, and don't add dialogue unless the director, produce, writer, or casting director gives you permission. Some actors think they are talented writers. Forget about it. You are an actor. Period! Do what is written. In TV, the writer is often the producer and sometimes gets unreasonably testy even when you mistakenly add a word or leave one out. He doesn't want his sacred dialogue touched.

Never touch the casting director or her assistant. They are not actors, so give them space. If you touch the casting director it makes him or her a participant, not an observer.

Don't judge or make negative comments about your acting, during or after the scene. One casting director said, "It is the fastest way to lose a job." Stop judging yourself. You did your best. The moment you make a self-deprecating comment, you scare the casting director, the director, and the producer. They are never a hundred percent sure about whom they cast. If you make negative comments about yourself, they can easily see you as a miscast actor who can ruin their movie. They want their actors to look secure and professional, which reassures them that they have cast the right person.

Commercial Improvisation

TV commercials depend on typecasting and are more about a look than acting. The ad agencies, who pay for commercials, have a distinct image of what they want. For many commercial auditions, the casting director will ask you to improvise a specific response or a look. Getting the job can depend on your dramatic or comic ability. Commercial auditions are a great experience because you have one shot, it's extremely competitive, and you have to do it right the first time. A casting director may audition fifty or a hundred actors for a single spot.

```
(Room with a casting director, who is behind a video camera
pointed at the actor.)
```

```
            CASTING DIRECTOR
I'm going to shine this light
on the ceiling. I want you to
follow the light with your
eyes. When I stop moving the
light, the sky is completely
covered with owls. I want you
to be shocked when you see the
owls, but don't drop your
mouth to indicate shock. The
director wants it subtle.
Slate your name and agency and
begin when I start to move the
light.
```

That's an actual commercial interview. What do they want, or what are they looking for? They probably don't know either. Listen, concentrate, and have fun.

Comedic Improvisation

Second City, the Chicago improv group, specializes in comedy sketches. Improvisation is also used by stand-up comedians, *Saturday Night Live*, *In Living Color*, and *Whose Line Is It Anyway?* Improvisation takes years of study and performing. It is bigger than life—and usually outrageous. The actors make a situation funny with only a premise. The really great improvisational comedians like Robin Williams, Jim Carrey, or Eddie Murphy have brilliant minds and natural comedic timing. They are also fine actors.

Dramatic Improvisation

Richard DeLancy, the casting director for the TV series *Unsolved Mysteries*, uses improvisation to determine the actor's level of proficiency. He supplies the scenarios and pairs the actors. He visited my workshop and talked about improvisation. First, he said, understand the premise of the improv. Every point that the casting director makes must be taken into account. Don't go off on a tangent and miss the story. Know "who" you are! Know "where" you are! This is one time you do need to create the environment.

Discuss with your partner your character's name. What does your character do for a living? What is your marital status? What is your relationship with your partner? Lovers, coworkers, friend of husband or wife, mother-daughter, father-son? Know your relationship.

Establish the conflict. What keeps these people apart? What are they fighting over? Both should be trying to achieve different things.

DeLancy told the workshop that listening is an art that allows you to experience the other actor. In one of his improvs, an actor was accusing another actor of having an affair with her husband. She kept talking the whole time, nonstop. The other actor couldn't get a word in, although she tried. Finally, she broke down in tears. She had listened and experienced.

Don't talk directly about the premise, DeLancy told my students. One improv was about a white woman and an African American woman who discover that they are half-sisters through their father, who is dying of cancer. Richard told the white actor that her premise was that she is prejudiced. To show her prejudice, she used obscene language. DeLancy told her the audition was for a primetime show, so no foul language. The actor then played it by never interacting with the other actress to show the prejudice indirectly through the relationship.

Finally, be sure not to miss the premise. DeLancy told a story of two actors completely missing the premise given to them. He gave an actor and an actress the premise that they are in love. She is married and has a three-year-old by her husband, and she is also pregnant with her lover's child. She was given specific instructions that she could not tell her lover that she is carrying his child. For his premise he was told that he knows that she is pregnant but isn't sure that it is his baby. But the actors never completed their objective, because during the scene he went off on the tangent that her husband was a wife beater. The premise of the improv was about the man finding his child, who was born twenty years earlier. The core emotion was two people who are in love. DeLancy said he never believed he loved her for one moment.

Summary

To prepare for a scripted audition:

1. Read the sides and all stage directions.
2. Underline all your character's actions and physical movements.
3. Is it a comedy or a drama?
4. Know the show.
5. What is the character's emotional state before the scene starts? (Sadness, happiness, fear, anger, love?)
   a. When does it change? Try to use two to three different emotions in the audition.
   b. Know where to start emotionally.
6. Know the conflict.
7. Know where and when the scene takes place.

8. Get coaching.
9. Dress for the part.

In the actual audition:

1. Be prompt.
2. Be friendly.
3. Memorize your first line of dialogue.
4. Commit to your emotional choices.
5. Accept the imaginary character and the situation.
6. Take control of the room.
7. Take direction.
8. Leave immediately.

Audition don'ts:

1. Don't ask to do it a second time.
2. Don't use a highlighter.
3. Don't be argumentative.
4. Don't ad-lib.
5. Never touch a casting director.
6. Don't make personal comments about your work.

Improvisational summary:

1. Listening is necessary for improv.
2. Establish the facts about your relationship and the other character.
3. If it is a primetime show don't use profanity.
4. Be aware of your blocking. Make sure the casting director can see you.
5. To take back control of the scene, stop talking!
6. Don't give away the premise.
7. Create a beginning, middle, and end.

Actor Practice

Many skills are useful when auditioning. Unfortunately, some only come from the actual audition experience. One is scene study and script analysis. Another is doing plays with a live audience. Practice your sight reading. Listen to the casting director and make adjustments. Other practice activities include:

1. Read a book that will be made into a movie and select the character that you think you would play.
   a. Find a scene with your character and script out the dialogue, act out the character.

    b. If you really feel you are right for the part write to the casting agent and ask for a reading.

    c. View the movie after it is made.

2. Any time you can get sides, work on them.

    a. How you would do this part in an audition?

    b. Try rehearsing when you are alone.

3. Improvisation.

    a. Play little improvisational games. Have a phone conversation with an imagined character, like the president of the United States, your boss, your girlfriend, a member of your family. Before you start, think of a line to begin and a line to end. Give yourself a minute for the exercise.

    b. Play an imaginary game of ping-pong. Make sure you visualize the table at a certain height and length. Know where the net is. Have another actor play with you.

    c. Read Viola Spolin's *Improvisation for the Theater.*

    d. Start or join an improvisational group. To develop your improvisational skills you need practice.

15

The Comedy Audition

An old actor is lying on his death bed. Another actor says, "I guess it's hard dying!" The dying actor answers weakly, "Not as hard as comedy."

Edmund Gwenn

Comedy is like skydiving. You fling yourself out there all alone into free fall, and you hope you said the right thing just before you jumped, because only laughter can open your parachute. Comedy ends in either laughter or death.

In a drama, relating to the other actor creates an unspoken subtext that is what you really feel and mean regardless of what the dialogue says. Subtext rides beneath the dialogue. In contrast, comedy is stated overtly and rides on the surface of the dialogue along with the actions and reactions of the characters. Comedy's important elements are the dialogue and what goes on in addition to it. I call this the "supratext," which is the character's responses and business that are added to what is said. The character, the objective, and the dialogue all combine to drive the humor. In comedy, the emotional experience is already built into the script, and we are interested not in the subtext but in the speech and actions of the supratext.

Comedy and Exposition

Comedy is a forgiving craft in that it allows you to take liberties with plot and structure that you couldn't get away with in a drama. The audience wants to laugh, so it usually participates willingly and accepts the impossible and the improbable without a second thought. Comedy is also terribly unforgiving because it has to be funny. But even a serious story can have witty or humorous dialogue, particularly when exposition has to be worked in. The film *A Few Good Men* is a melodramatic story in which Tom Cruise plays a naval lieutenant, a hot defense attorney, who defends two enlisted Marines in a

court-martial from being unjustly accused of a crime. Demi Moore plays a lieutenant commander who is overseeing the case. The careers of both Cruise and
the two Marines are at stake. The humor and the wit in the script's dialogue
soften the melodrama and add amusement. The following scene contains exposition, which is difficult to inject into a film. The writer, through a series of
jokes, artfully gets across what the audience needs to know without being dull
and intrusive. The jokes are not knee-slappers or roll-on-the floor jokes, but
they take the scene out of being ho-hum exposition. Cruise is dressed in sweats
and is batting baseballs out into the field.

(EXT. BASEBALL FIELD - DAY. Demi Moore approaches Tom
Cruise.)

                    MOORE
        I wonder why two guys are
        locked up while their lawyer
        is hitting balls.

                    CRUISE
        I need the practice.

                    MOORE
        Lieutenant, would you be
        insulted if I recommended to
        your supervisor that he assign
        a different counsel?

                    CRUISE
        Why? You don't even know me.
        Ordinarily it takes someone
        hours to realize I'm not fit
        to handle a defense.

                    MOORE
        You're wrong, I do know you.
        Daniel Alister Caffey, born
        June 8, 1964 . . . I would not
        be doing my job if I allowed
        Dawson and Downey to serve any
        more time in prison than
        absolutely necessary because
        their attorney has predeter-
        mined to proceed on the path
        of least resistance.

                    CRUISE
Wow, I'm sexually aroused,
Commander.

          MOORE
I don't think your clients
murdered anyone.

          CRUISE
Doctor's report said that "in
Santiago there was asphyxiation, acute lactic acidosis,
and the nature of the acidosis
suggested poisoning." I don't
know what that means but it
sounds pretty bad.

          MOORE
Santiago died at one A.M. and
at three, the Doctor still
wasn't able to determine the
cause of death. Two hours
later he said "It was poison."

          CRUISE
Oh, now I see what you're saying. It had to be Professor
Plum, in the library, with a
candlestick.

          MOORE
I'm going to talk to your
supervisor.

          CRUISE
Okay. Go straight up
Pennsylvania Ave. to the big
white house with the pillars.

Consider what we learned about the Lieutenant. He is arrogant, intellectually superior, hates authority, has influential connections, and knows how to use his verbal machete. We also learned about the case, and we saw the beginnings of the relationship between these two characters. This is well-written material that would otherwise be routine without the comedy. In the following breakdown of the same scene, I have indicated each setup, joke, and punch line. These are the three necessary elements for comedy.

         MOORE

SETUP: I wonder why two guys are locked up

JOKE: while their lawyer is hitting balls.

         CRUISE

PUNCH LINE: I need the practice.

         MOORE

SETUP: Lieutenant, would you be insulted if I recommended to your supervisor that he assign a different counsel?

         CRUISE

Why? **JOKE:** You don't even know me. Ordinarily it takes someone hours to realize

PUNCH LINE: I'm not fit to handle the defense.

         MOORE

SETUP: You're wrong, I do know you. . . . because their attorney has predetermined to proceed on the path of least resistance.

         CRUISE

JOKE: Wow,

PUNCH LINE: I'm sexually aroused, Commander.

   . . .

         MOORE

SETUP: I don't think your clients murdered anyone.

         CRUISE

JOKE: Doctor's report said that "in Santiago there was

asphyxiation, acute lactic
acidosis, and the nature of
the acidosis suggested
poisoning."

PUNCH LINE: I don't know what
that means but it sounds
pretty bad.

                MOORE
SETUP: Santiago died at one
A.M. and at three, the Doctor
still wasn't able to determine
the cause of death. Two hours
later he said "It was poison."

              CRUISE
JOKE: Oh, now I see what
you're saying.

PUNCH LINE: It had to be
Professor Plum, in the
library, with a candlestick.

                MOORE
SETUP: I'm going to talk to
your supervisor.

              CRUISE
JOKE: Okay. Go straight up
Pennsylvania Ave.

PUNCH LINE: to the big white
house with the pillars.

Look for the humor and the jokes in the scenes you act in. Then relate to the other actor. Jerry Seinfeld said in a TV interview that every joke has three parts: a setup, the joke, and the punch line. There are no absolute rules for comedy. But there are reasons why we laugh. Comedy may seem random, but good standup comedians know that it is not random, and they work endlessly, writing jokes and structuring routines to make them hilarious.

Melvin Helitzer, in his book, *Comedy Writing Secrets,* uses what he calls the "PAP" test, a progression that constitutes a good joke. *P* stands for *Preparation,* or the setup, which explains the situation to the audience. *A* stands for *Anticipation,* or the joke, which leads the audience in a direction it can follow. The final *P* stands for *Punch line*, which is a change from the anticipated direction that makes the audience laugh.[1]

The film *A Few Good Men* is about a murder trial. Moore, in her Preparation, explains the situation.

```
                MOORE
    I don't think your clients
    murdered anyone.
```

Next, Anticipation, or the joke, leads the audience in a direction that it can follow but will in all probability be reversed.

```
                CRUISE
    Doctors report said that in
    Santiago there was asphyxia-
    tion, acute lactic acidosis,
    and the nature of the acidosis
    suggested poisoning.
```

The Punch line, or payoff, comes from "punching" the line by saying it louder. You want the audience to pay particular attention to this part. Comedians don't always punch the line and use instead a slight pause or a facial reaction. It is the story payoff that gets the laugh. Once you know the punch lines, you know where you can place the vocal emphasis.

Cruise is subtle. He says something stupid to make Moore feel superior, but Moore knows he is not stupid.

```
                CRUISE
    I don't know what that means
    but it sounds pretty bad.
```

When Cruise says, "I don't know what it means . . ." he ends with something that makes us feel superior, which causes the laugh: "But it sounds pretty bad." This is the punch line.

Characterization

Characterizations are distinctive traits or peculiarities that an actor uses to make a character different than normal. In *There's Something About Mary*, Lee Evens fakes being crippled. He wears leg braces to get sympathy from Cameron Diaz. The physical contortions that he goes through when

---

[1] Helitzer, M., *Comedy Writing Secrets*. Cincinnati, OH: Writer's Digest Books, 1987.

he tries to stand up are hilarious. Mike Myers, as Austin Powers, International Man of Mystery, has bad buckteeth and 70's-style clothes to give a comic flair to his character. In *Jack*, Robin Williams gives a characterization of a ten-year-old in a man's body. In *Some Like It Hot*, Jack Lemmon and Tony Curtis impersonate two sexy women to avoid being killed by the mob. In *The Bird Cage*, Gene Hackman's senator dresses up like a woman to avoid reporters.

Absurd Situations

Comedy can take place in absurd or farcical situations. One of the most absurd, farcical, and funny scenes in film is the one in the Marx Brothers' *A Night at the Opera.* We see Groucho in his small shipboard stateroom. A very big steamer trunk sits in the middle of the room. He opens the trunk and out come three male stowaways. Then two maids enter and start to make the bed. Next, an engineer and his very big assistant engineer come in to fix a pipe. A manicurist comes in to do Groucho's nails. Another woman comes in to use the phone, and another maid enters to mop up. Three stewards arrive with trays of food. Fourteen people are packed in this tiny room, all carrying on as if nothing were out of the ordinary. The payoff comes outside the room when a woman opens the door and everybody falls out into the hallway like household junk from an overstuffed closet.

Another absurd situation is portrayed in the film *Being John Malkovich.* John Cusack plays Craig, a puppeteer who finds a "portal" to actually get himself inside John Malkovich's mind and manipulate him. Cameron Diaz plays Cusack's wife, Lotte. Cusack enters Malkovich's mind through the portal to make love with Maxine, played by Catherine Keener. The inanity of the situation creates comedy. In the scene below, Cusack is inside Malkovich's mind. At times, the real Malkovich breaks through and briefly takes control.

```
INT. MALKOVICH'S APARTMENT - NIGHT

(The doorbell rings. Malkovich answers it. Maxine stands
there, dressed in an evening gown.)

                  MALKOVICH AS HIMSELF
         What do you want?

                  KEENER
         I can explain about the por-
         tal, darling.
```

> MALKOVICH AS HIMSELF
> Don't con me, Maxine. We're
> finished. I don't know who the
> hell you people are, but this
> insanity is now over.

> KEENER
> Oh shut up. Craig, darling,
> are you in there?

(Malkovich tenses up, then he shakes his head in an awkward, puppet-like manner. When Malkovich speaks, it seems to be against his will.)

> MALKOVICH AS CRAIG
> (labored)
> Yes. How'd you know it was me?

> KEENER
> Lotte called me. She escaped
> your evil clutches.

> MALKOVICH AS CRAIG
> I see. I'm sorry I did that,
> Maxine, but I really love you
> so much, and I just didn't
> know how else to be with you.

(Keener considers this, then . . .)

> KEENER
> So apparently you can control
> this Malkovich fellow now.

> MALKOVICH AS CRAIG
> (proudly)
> I'm getting better all the
> time.

> KEENER
> I'll say you are. Let's do it
> on his kitchen table, then
> make him eat an omelet off of
> it.

> MALKOVICH AS HIMSELF
> No . . . damn . . . you.

```
          MALKOVICH AS CRAIG
     Oh shut up, you overrated sack
     of shit.
```

Environment

Environment also helps create comedy. In *Sister Act*, Whoopi Goldberg plays a low-rent lounge singer who is hiding from the mob in a convent. The environment of the convent and Whoopi passing as a nun become the source of humor. Paul Hogan, who plays *Crocodile Dundee* and lives with the aborigines in the Northern Territory of Australia, escorts Linda Kozlowski on a tour of the outback. The comedy comes from his putting her on. He uses his watch to tell time, but lets her think he is intuitive and uses the position of the sun. When he visits New York, his naiveté about big city life creates a great deal of comedy. In *City Slickers*, urbanized executive Billy Crystal and his friends Daniel Stern and Bruno Kirby try to find themselves while working on an actual cattle drive. The ranch surroundings help create the humor because the three men are out of their element working cattle and riding horses. In *The Gods Must Be Crazy*, N! Xixi, a bushman who plays himself, lives the same kind of life in the African desert that his ancestors lived for a thousand years. He experiences culture shock when he is forced to leave his home and search for his missing children. The humor comes from the unfamiliarity of this new world and his simplistic approach to dealing with the problems of his new environment. In *Private Benjamin*, Goldie Hawn, a pampered little rich girl, joins the army. Her attitude about military life causes humor.

Comedy Patterns

Comedy often happens in threes. The first time you say something we hear it. The second time we smile. The third time we laugh. In *Comedy Writing Secrets*, Helitzer calls this a "triple." In the scene below, the "Psychiatrist" is actually a mental patient who has sneaked into a psychiatrist's office and is posing as a doctor. The patient is a frightened woman, committed by her husband who is trying to steal her money. The triple helps the joke build the anticipation for the punch line:

```
                PSYCHIATRIST
     You're suffering from a severe
     case of insomnia. Have you
     ever taken a hallucinogenic?

                PATIENT
     Never!
```

                    PSYCHIATRIST
        Why not? I have about 30 or 40
        magic mushrooms before dinner,
        two bottles of Jack Daniels
        after dinner, and two or three
        dozen sleeping pills before
        bedtime.

                    PATIENT
        Does it help?

                    PSYCHIATRIST
        I'll say. I hallucinate all
        night.

Auditioning for Comedy

When you audition for comedy, you have to get a laugh from the casting director, who has probably seen and heard the material performed at least a dozen times before you walk in the door. She knows every joke and punch line in the audition scene by heart. In spite of this, a good comic actor will get a laugh from her. Good comics understand comic delivery, and they seldom wing an audition. They know how to set up the joke and deliver the punch line.

                    GIGI
        (to Jeremiah)
                Then how do you set up a joke
                and deliver a punch line?

JEREMIAH: **That is an important question. Unfortunately, every piece of comedy will be different. There are no absolute answers. First, look at the setup for the joke. Make sure you read all stage directions because sometimes they indicate the setup. Keener's line, "Let's do it on the kitchen table, then make him eat an omelet off of it," sets up the joke for Malkovich. The more seductive Keener is, the greater the setup for Malkovich, who tries to object. The joke happens when Malkovich as himself objects, "NO ... DAMN ... YOU." The greater Malkovich's reaction to eating the omelet off of an unsanitary table, the funnier. The punch line occurs when Malkovich (as Cusack) reacts like he has no control over his own body. Simultaneously, we hear Craig's voice-over saying the line, "Oh shut up, you overrated sack of shit."**

                    GIGI
        (to Jeremiah)
                I am terrible at comedy.

JEREMIAH: **Well-scripted comedy is easier than you think. How would you make the transition on the last line? Everyone in the workshop would do it differently, but the line and the situation help bring out the humor. Your job as an actor is to figure out an effective way to deliver the punch line, then internalize it to make it look spontaneous.**

```
            MALKOVICH AS HIMSELF
No . . . damn . . . you.


            MALKOVICH AS CRAIG
Oh shut up, you overrated sack
of shit.
```

JEREMIAH: **Malkovich delivers the first part with anger and resistance, "No . . . damn . . . you." Then the second part is the transition from Malkovich as himself to Malkovich being controlled by Craig. The audience wants to see the internal and external conflict when Craig takes over. Your job is not to be funny but to be believable. If you make it believable, it will be funny.**

Find the Humor

Understanding humor is not always as simple as it sounds. Anton Chekhov said his play *The Cherry Orchard* had humor in it, and he complained that Stanislavsky missed its comedic elements and directed it solely as a drama. It takes skill to read a script and recognize the fine line between drama and humor and to know how to carry out an author's humorous intention. Even when you think you know where the humor is, the audience will not always laugh in the places you had planned. Once the audience starts to laugh, though, it will usually become your cheering section. It picks up nuances that heighten your comic response. Once laughter happens, it's like feeding chum to sharks. They keep coming.

The Elements of Comedy

The following elements of comedy may help you understand what makes a script or a performance funny. Understanding comedy technique is the first step in learning how to bring the writer's humor to life.

Inappropriate Emotion

In the right situation, an emotion counter to the expected one is funny. In the film *Fried Green Tomatoes*, Kathy Bates plays Evelyn, who has just attended a lecture about putting the magic spark of romance back into her marriage. In the scene below, she waits for her husband to come home.

```
INT. DINING TABLE. EVENING.

Table exquisitely set with Red Roses in a vase. A bottle of
Dom Perignon Champagne is being chilled. A delicious lamb
rib roast finishes the decoration. At the very end of the
table rests several empty boxes of used plastic wrap.

INT. ENTRANCE HALL. EVENING.

Camera tilts slowly up gold high-heeled shoes to Kathy
Bates' legs and continues up her body. She is naked but cov-
ered with plastic wrap. She has a seductive smile on her
face. Ed, her husband, walks in the door. He is shocked.

                    ED
          Evelyn, have you gone insane?
          People can see you.

(Evelyn's smile fades to disappointment.)

                    ED
          What if I had been the paper
          boy or something, Honey. Get
          in there, what are you
          thinking?
```

The humor comes from the response that is counter to the response Bates' character expects. Ed thinks she is acting crazy rather than seductive.

An apparent lack of emotion, or "dead pan," is also funny in humorous situations. An actor with no emotional response is a humorous counterbalance for a big emotional response. This is called playing the "straight man." George Burns was the classic straight man for Gracie Allen. Another excellent example is Dustin Hoffman's brilliant comic performance as La Plant in *Hero*. Dustin is a small-time criminal who is driving to see his ex-wife and visit his son when a jumbo jet crashes in front of him.

```
EXTERIOR. BRIDGE. NIGHT. RAIN.

Hoffman is starting to cross the bridge when a jumbo jet
crashes and blocks the bridge. Hoffman gets out of his car
to investigate. The passengers try to extricate themselves
from the plane but the door is stuck.
```

```
                    PASSENGER
              (from inside)
          Is anybody out there?
```

Hoffman walks over to the rail of the bridge and looks at the crash. He hears the yelling from inside the plane.

```
                    PASSENGER
              (panicked)
          Is anyone there?
```

```
                    HOFFMAN
          What's the problem pal?
```

Dustin Hoffman answers the question in a calm, casual manner. His demeanor is totally inappropriate for the situation. When a plane crashes, you expect a frantic excited response to save lives. Hoffman plays the exact opposite, a give-me-a-cup-of-coffee attitude, rather than one of immediately responding to a catastrophe.

Heightened Emotion

Heightened emotion is used in comedy when the emotional response is larger than normal. An emotion taken to an extreme can be hilarious, and comedy allows you to push your emotions to the limit. In *Blind Date*, Bruce Willis's character takes Kim Bassinger to an art show. She sees her ex-boyfriend, played by John Larroquette, and tries to avoid him. Larroquette approaches her.

```
INT. ART GALLERY - NIGHT
```

```
                    LARROQUETTE
              (friendly)
          Hello Nadia.
```

```
                    BASSINGER
          David, just don't start
          anything.
```

```
                    LARROQUETTE
              (smiling)
          I just came over to say hello.
```

(Reaches out to shake Willis's hand.)

                  LARROQUETTE
Hi, I'm David.

                WILLIS
Walter.

                  LARROQUETTE
Pleasure. She has every right
to be upset with me. I'm
afraid I was so helplessly in
love with her I made a total
asshole of myself.

                WILLIS
Well, apology accepted.

(Willis starts to walk away with Bassinger.)

                WILLIS
Nice to meet you.

(Larroquette walks backwards to block their path.)

                  LARROQUETTE
So, how long have you been
going out with her?

                 BASSINGER
It's none of your business!

                  LARROQUETTE
    (excited)
No no no. I think it is my
business. Considering that
there is not A NIGHT THAT HAS
GONE BY . . .

                 BASSINGER
Stop it . . .

                  LARROQUETTE
    (OUT OF CONTROL)
NOT AN HOUR THAT PASSES . . .

(Larroquette grabs Willis by the lapels and pushes him
backwards.)

```
                    LARROQUETTE
        ARE YOU DRILLING HER? I WANT
        TO KNOW! I JUST WANT TO KNOW!


                    WILLIS
        Hey, watch your mouth.


(Larroquette cocks his arm and throws a punch. Willis
ducks.)


                    LARROQUETTE
        ARE YOU DRILLING HER?


(Larroquette's arm goes through a papier-mâché statue. He is
stuck. Willis and Bassinger exit.)


                    LARROQUETTE
        Nadia wait! Nadia, I just want
        to talk. You son of a bitch.
        I'll find you.
```

To create comedy, John Larroquette uses the inappropriate emotion of heightened anger. His jealousy drives his emotions to an extreme. He tries to punch out his ex-girlfriend's date. The heightened anger makes his performance funny.

Failure

A character is faced with an insurmountable problem, and every time he solves one part of the problem, a bigger problem arises. The more difficult the task, the funnier the failure gets. This is the basis for slapstick. Recall the scene in *The Music Box* where Laurel and Hardy struggle to take a grand piano up a long, narrow flight of stairs. In *There's Something about Mary*, Ben Stiller is about to take his dream girl, Cameron Diaz, to the prom. He has gone to her house to pick her up and needs to use the bathroom, but he zips up his pants so hurriedly that he catches a very personal part of himself in the zipper. He is carried to the ambulance on a stretcher and doesn't get to take his dream date to the prom. Through the rest of the story, which takes place ten years later, every time Stiller tries to get back together with Diaz, something interferes and he fails. The failures are funny and drive the movie.

Character Idiosyncrasies

Physical characteristics like nervousness, a twitch, a stutter, or a speech impediment can be funny if they are done right. In *Rat Race*, Vince

Bieluf has a speech impediment, and he gets his tongue pierced. The inserted stud turns part of his tongue green. The comic twist is that his speech becomes virtually unintelligible. In *There's Something about Mary*, Matt Dillon has a mouth full of false teeth that look like a keyboard, and Chris Elliot's character breaks out in hives whenever he is nervous. At the beginning of the movie Elliot has a clear complexion, and by the end, his face is covered with pimples.

Find and develop character quirks or idiosyncrasies. In character comedy, use a characteristic that works for the character. In the TV series *Married with Children*, Christina Applegate created a stereotypical dumb blond that allows her to have a sleazy attitude toward sex. In the Woody Allen film *Mighty Aphrodite,* one of the comedic characteristics Mira Sorvino creates for her character is a high voice. In the TV series *All in the Family*, Carroll O'Connor created a heavy New York Irish accent for Archie Bunker that helped the audience accept his prejudiced blue-collar attitude. In *Third Rock from the Sun*, French Steward squints his eyes to make his character, Harry, look more like an alien. You can develop comic characteristics just as you would for a stage play and bring them into an audition.

Pain

Pain is often a source of laughter. In the 1933 movie *The Barber Shop*, W. C. Fields is about to shave a man's face. He stretches the chair out in the prone position so that the man can relax and enjoy his shave. When Fields reaches for the hot towel to soak the man's beard, the towel is too hot for Fields to handle. With his cane, he picks up the towel and puts it on the man's face. The man immediately reacts, and W. C. Fields holds him in the chair by his arms. The man flails his legs, trying to extricate himself. The harder he struggles, the funnier it gets. But to evoke laughter in such a situation, the audience has to believe that an actor is not actually causing himself or another actor real harm.

Malapropisms

A malapropism is a humorous misuse of a word that confuses it with one that has a similar sound: as in "I am an entramanure" instead of "I am an entrepreneur." The misused word could be a distorted or made-up word, as in this example, or an actual word used in the wrong context. The term malapropism comes from Mrs. Malaprop, a character in Richard Brinsley Sheridan's eighteenth-century play *The Rivals* who consistently uses the wrong word at the right time. She is always unaware of her mistake and believes she is demonstrating superior knowledge by using these words. The television character Archie Bunker (played by Carroll O'Connor), in *All in the Family*, used a lot of malapropisms. In one scene Archie has just received a doctor's physical and learns that he has a spot on his liver. Archie's friends at the corner bar are discussing his predicament when Archie comes out with a malapropism:

```
              ARCHIE
    They can make a baby in a
    shot glass or something. It's
    what they call artificial
    separation.
```

The malapropism is the word "separation" instead of "insemination." Christina Applegate's Kelly Bundy in *Married with Children* was another TV character known for malapropisms. Don't try to be funny when your character uses malapropisms, because they work best with a straight delivery.

Misunderstandings

One character does not understand his relationship to another character or to a situation. He operates on a false assumption or premise and the audience knows the real situation. For example, an actress cries at references to what she assumes is her dead husband, Harry, but in reality the conversation is about another Harry—a parakeet. The movie *Hero* is built around a misunderstanding about who the hero really is: did Dustin Hoffman or Andy Garcia rescue the passengers from the crashed airliner?

Irony

Irony is a figure of speech in which the real meaning is said in words that carry the opposite meaning. In Shakespeare's *Julius Caesar* Marc Antony is being ironic when he repeatedly refers to Brutus as an "honorable man"—he doesn't mean that at all. Don't confuse irony with sarcasm, which is much the same except that sarcasm is mean-spirited in a petty way. Irony can be serious or funny because of its deliberate contrast between the apparent meaning and the intended meaning.

There is also comic intention behind ironic nicknames such as "Curly" for a bald man, "Shorty" for someone who is six-feet-five, and "Lucky" for a three-legged dog I once knew. In the film *He Said, She Said*, Kevin Bacon and Elizabeth Perkins are both reporters who share a television show and disagree on every subject. They are nevertheless attracted to each other. They are having dinner in a sidewalk cafe when Kevin Bacon's old flame, Ashley Gardner, approaches Bacon to re-establish their relationship. We pick up in the middle of the conversation.

                    GARDNER
               (to Kevin)
          . . . Let's go next week to a
          roller rink.

                    BACON
          But you got to wear that
          dress.

(Gardner leans over the table to kiss Bacon, and her breast
pops out of her dress.)

                    GARDNER
          Oh shit! My tit popped out. I
          hate it when that happens.

(Perkins, caught in the middle, covers her eyes. Gardner
straightens the dress and walks off.)

                    GARDNER
          Bye.

                    PERKINS
          Classy, with a capital K.

The line, "Classy, with a capital K," is ironic. Obviously, Perkins's character means just the opposite, that Gardner's character has no class.

Double Entendre

Double entendre means double meaning. In *Hero*, Dustin
Hoffman crawls out on a ledge to keep Andy Garcia from committing suicide.
Garcia has taken the credit and fame for saving passengers from a crashed jet
airliner, and is overwhelmed with guilt. He can't go on lying to the public, who
think he is a hero. Hoffman, the real hero and small-time criminal, sneaks out
on the ledge because he is smart enough to realize that nobody would ever
believe he is the real hero. He works out a monetary deal with Garcia and con-
vinces him to keep the fame and the reward money.

                    HOFFMAN
          . . . I'm not a nice guy.
          You're the nice guy. Now you
          do your job and be a hero.

> GARCIA
> Are you going to be all right
> with me taking all the credit?

> HOFFMAN
> Hey, I don't take credit. I'm
> a cash kind of guy.

The statement, "I'm a cash kind of guy," is a double entendre on several levels. Garcia is referring to fame. Hoffman is referring to the fact that criminals only take cash. Also, the audience knows that Hoffman was busted earlier for selling stolen credit cards. In *Young Frankenstein,* Marty Feldman, who plays Igor, goes to the front door of the castle, which has very big circular rings for door knockers. Gene Wilder, who plays Dr. Frankenstein, lifts his assistant, played by Teri Garr, to help her out of a wagon. He then turns away from Garr and looks at Feldman, who is knocking on the door.

> WILDER
> What knockers.

> GARR
> Oh, thank you, Doc.

"Knockers" is a double entendre. It has two meaning. The first meaning refers to the familiar device, mounted usually on the front door of a house, that a visitor uses to knock for entrance. The second is a slang word meaning a woman's breasts. Director Mel Brooks cleverly creates comedy by positioning Garr so that Wilder can see her breasts. Then he cleverly has Wilder turn away and say "What knockers" to Feldman, who is standing next to the door knockers. Teri gets the laugh with her matter-of-fact and naive delivery of "Oh, thank you, Doc."

Comedic Dialogue

Comedic dialogue, as we have seen from our earlier discussion, consists of a comedic setup, joke, and punch line. Melvin Helitzer has said "a joke is a story with a surprise ending almost always as its finale." The more cohesive the setups for the jokes, the funnier the punch lines. Well-structured movies go even further and use a preceding punch line to set up the next joke and punch line.

In *Hero,* the overall setup is that Hoffman is a hero who nobody believes could be one. The comedic setup is the misunderstanding about Hoffman's being the hero. In the last scene of the movie, Dustin Hoffman is sitting on a bench at the zoo telling his character's son Joey that he was the actual hero of the plane crash.

> HOFFMAN
> **SETUP:** Now listen, Joey. What I'm going to tell you now is off the record. It doesn't leave the room or whatever this is - zoo . . . Now, what really happened is . . .

(A BAND marches by and drowns out the conversation. After the Band is gone...)

> HOFFMAN
> And that's what really happened.

> SON
> Wow! But you always said keep a low profile.

> HOFFMAN
> Right.

> SON
> You said never stick your neck out.

> HOFFMAN
> Right.

> SON
> **JOKE:** How could you go into a burning plane and save fifty-four people?

> HOFFMAN
> **PUNCH LINE:** Well, I screwed up.

At that moment, another joke occurs when a woman screams, "My daughter fell in the lion's cage!" It is impossible to fall into a lion cage, but we wonder if Hoffman is again going to be the hero. The punch line is created by Hoffman's reluctant decision to save the daughter:

```
           V.O. WOMAN
        (screams)
     JOKE: My daughter fell in the
     lion's cage.


           HOFFMAN
     PUNCH LINE: The zoo keeper.
     Somebody call the zoo keeper.
     Hey, somebody call the zoo
     keeper, for Christ sake.


           V.O. WOMAN
     JOKE: Please, my little girl
     fell in the cage.


(Hoffman looks at his son.)


           HOFFMAN
     PUNCH LINE: Oh, for Christ
     sake. Here watch my shoes.
```

Immediately there is another punch line in the look on the son's face as he watches his father walk out of frame and enter the lion cage:

```
Hoffman slips his shoes off and walks out of frame.

PUNCH LINE: The frame freezes on the bewildered expression
of his son.
```

Misdirection

Comedic dialogue often leads the audience down a certain path so that it carries an image or concept to its natural conclusion. Then the image switches in an unexpected direction. This is called "the right turn." The element of surprise makes us laugh. Here is a typical right-turn story from Gene Perret's *Comedy Step by Step*: "Once I was in a hotel and the walls were kind of thin. The couple in the next room came home very late and were talking kind of loud. So I quickly got a glass and held it to the wall and listened to what they were saying . . . I heard her say to him, 'Take off my dress.' Then she said, 'Take off my slip.' Then she said, 'Take off my bra.' Then she said, 'If I ever catch you wearing them again, I'll divorce you.'"

Absurd Situations or Statements

In an absurd situation, as we discussed earlier, a character finds himself in a highly unlikely predicament. In *After Hours,* Martin Short accidentally locks himself out of his apartment without keys, identification, or money. He must resolve the situation by getting back into his apartment, but every business is closed. These unplanned circumstances become overwhelming for the next several hours, creating a comic situation.

An especially absurd situation, as we have seen, is the one created in *Being John Malkovich.* How can a person get inside the mind of another human being and control him? Impossible. But once the audience accepts the outrageous premise, the movie becomes funny. The absurd situation gives rise to humor and funny circumstances.

Absurd Casting

When you cast George Foreman as a prizefighter, nobody laughs. When you cast Woody Allen as a prizefighter fighting for the heavyweight championship, it's funny because we know he will be killed the instant he climbs into the ring. Another example of absurd casting that is funny is the four-foot-eleven-inch-tall basketball player on a professional basketball team.

The Environment

When the location where the action takes place allows a character to misinterpret information, this creates a humorous situation. In *My Cousin Vinny,* two young men, played by Ralph Macchio and Mitchell Whitfield, are traveling cross-country when they are arrested in a small southern town and accused of robbery. Macchio calls his cousin Vinny, a lawyer played by Joe Pesci, to come down from New York and represent them in court. Pesci arrives and goes to talk to Whitfield, his cousin's friend and alleged accomplice, in a jail cell. Pesci is trying to tell Whitfield that he will be representing him, but the young man doesn't know who he is and misinterprets everything, thinking that Pesci is also a prisoner and wants to have sex with him. The jail environment brings out the humor.

Comic Actors

There are many actors known for their comic roles, including Lucille Ball, Richard Dreyfuss, Jack Nicholson, Tom Hanks, Jack Lemmon, Michael J. Fox, Matthew Broderick, Robin Williams, Dolly Parton, Meg Ryan, Melanie Griffith, Jennifer Love Hewitt, Sigourney Weaver, and many others.

These are all leading actors who have worked in comedy. Watch their movies and study how they do comedy.

Comic Character Actors

Comedic characters are based on physical looks, mannerisms, personality, and the ability for precise comic timing. Danny De Vito and Joe Pesci are character actors whose size and physicality add to the humor of the situations in which they play. De Vito is short, fat, and bald, and Pesci is short and not quite so fat; both speak with some kind of New York accent that makes us laugh at almost everything they say.

Stand-up Comedians

Stand-up is comedy that is usually performed by a lone comedian for nightclub or TV-talk-show audiences. Some comedians who started as stand-ups are Jim Carrey, Woody Allen, Steve Martin, Eddie Murphy, Martin Short, Billy Crystal, Ben Stiller, Chris Rock, Bill Cosby, Jerry Seinfeld, Ellen Degeneres, and Roseanne Barr. They are actors who are able to look as if they are improvising their sketches and jokes without prepared lines. Many of them can do imitations. Eddie Murphy is a stand-up comedian who has successfully played several characters in one movie. Again, closely watch how these actors work.

Physical Comedy or Farce

A farce is a movie, play, or skit that is supposed to be funny. Farce does not have much plot or character, but it is strong on exaggerated, improbable situations in which the humor arises from gross incongruities and jokes ranging from the obvious to the crude. Farce usually includes horseplay such as unusual walks, pratfalls, or stunts that make the actors look funny. The humor is often connected with pain. Chris Farley diving onto and demolishing a coffee table, as he commonly did on *Saturday Night Live*, is farcical. In *There's Something about Mary*, Matt Dillon plays a farcical scene in which he tranquilizes Mary's roommate's (Lyn Shaye) dog with pills so that he can keep it from attacking him. He cradles the sedated dog until he realizes that the dog is comatose. He tries mouth to mouth resuscitation, which doesn't work. He pulls the electrical cord out of a lamp and tries to shock the dog back to life. Instead, he electrocutes the dog, and the wires start a fire. The dog is in flames. Dillon picks up a vase of flowers and throws the water on the dog to put out the fire, and the dog revives. In *Liar Liar*, Jim Carrey has to tell the truth for twenty-four hours. He is defending a client and losing the case because he can't lie. He goes into the restroom, rips his jacket, bounces himself into the wall, slaps himself around, empties the trash can on himself—and then sees that a man is watching him.

> MAN
> What the hell are you doing?

> CARREY
> I'm kicking my ass. Do you
> mind?

Jim Carrey spends a full minute wrestling with himself to exploit the punch line, "I'm kicking my ass. Do you mind?"

In *Moonstruck*, Cher has just made love to Nicholas Cage. The next day she tells him that she is going to marry his brother and can't see him again.

> CHER
> . . . Last night never hap-
> pened, and I'm going to marry
> him. You and I are going to
> take this to our grave.

> CAGE
> I can't do that.

> CHER
> Why not?

> CAGE
> I'm in love with you.

> (Cher slaps Cage across the face. He stands there. She slaps
> him harder.)

> CHER
> Snap out of it.

The slap makes the dialogue humorous. In comedy, action precedes dialogue. When dialogue precedes action, the scene becomes dramatic, not funny. The action makes the line funny.

Mirroring

When one actor does a physical gesture or says a line and the other actor mimics it, it can be funny. This is called mirroring. I once saw a performance of Tom Stoppard's play *Rosencrantz and Gildenstern Are Dead*. The two title actors have just read a letter stating they should be put to death. Rosencrantz starts to cry, and then Gildenstern mirrors him with tears. It was a great bit. The audience not only laughed but applauded. In the film *Duck Soup*, the Marx brothers perform the famous mirror exercise (see Chapter 5). It is a classic bit.

Punching and Undercutting

Punching

Punching is saying a word or a line loudly in order to sell or accentuate the joke. This often includes undercutting the preceding line or phrase. Punching makes the audience more aware of the joke. In *All in the Family*, Archie and Edith Bunker, played by Carroll O'Connor and Jean Stapleton, sing the opening song over the titles. When Stapleton punches the word "when" she goes off tune and creates a laugh. In the following speech directed at Edith, O'Connor was very funny when he punched Archie's last sentence.

```
         O'CONNOR
You're going to have a change
of life. Your going to do it
right now. I'm going to give
you thirty seconds. NOW COME
ON, CHANGE.
```

This is a great technique when reading for situation comedies. Study sitcoms and listen to the laughter to see if the actor has raised his voice and punched the line. Jackie Gleason had a famous line on *The Honeymooners*, which he always punched. He would point his fist at Alice, his wife, played by Audrey Meadows, and say:

```
         GLEASON
ONE OF THESE DAYS, ALICE . . .
JUST ONE OF THESE DAYS.
```

Undercutting

Undercutting is the opposite of punching. When you undercut a line you punch or emphasize the line preceding it—the joke. Actually, undercutting reverses the joke and the punch line. You have a setup, the punch line, then the undercut line, which is often a throwaway. To throw away a line means to de-emphasize it. You speak lower than your normal volume. The undercut line can also be an aside to the audience that gets the laugh. Melvin Helitzer gives this example:

A redneck factory manager to a civil rights investigator.

> CIVIL RIGHTS GUY
> **SETUP:** We've had numerous com-
> plaints.

> REDNECK
> **PUNCH:** WHAT DO YOU MEAN, "AM I
> RESPECTFUL OF EQUAL OPPORTU-
> NITY FOR WOMEN?" OF COURSE I
> AM.

> (then, matter-of-fact)
> **UNDERCUT LINE:** We have lots of
> broads working here.

Rhythm, Tempo, and Pacing

Rhythm is the natural cadence of the dialogue the way it is written. *Tempo* is the speed in which the dialogue is delivered. *Pacing* refers to the
tempo for the scene as a whole. Comedy depends on pacing; if it is too slow or
too fast, the audience can miss the humor. The skill of achieving the right pace
is intuitive in good comic actors. You can learn them by doing stage plays and
sitcoms. It's possible to analyze comedy to death, but you should study it.

Know your character's objective in the scene. Understand the setups for the
jokes and decide how you want to deliver the punch lines. Practice your physical movements by blocking and rehearsing with your props until they feel natural and you can handle them without thinking. Once you have done all this,
then the right rhythm, tempo, and pacing will occur naturally. Rehearsing is a
logical process that allows you to achieve a step-by-step understanding of your
role and to practice your performance.

In TV situation comedies you will have a week of rehearsal. This process is
more like doing a stage play than a film. The dialogue and the blocking will
drive you towards achieving your character's goal. What does your character
want in this scene and how do you try to achieve it? In the following scene,
Gary is a young encyclopedia salesman. Beatrice, a grumpy old lady, has just
slammed the front the door on him. Gary refuses to give up, so he goes to the
back door of the house and knocks again. His goal is to sell encyclopedias.

EXT. BACK DOOR. DAY.

(Gary knocks. Beatrice answers.)

```
              BEATRICE
WHAT  DO  YOU  WANT?


              GARY
I  see  you're  a  sweet,  affec-
tionate,  neighborly  sort,  not
like  your  neighbor  in  the
front.  She  was  a  little
cranky.


              BEATRICE
She  is  not  a  little  cranky.
SHE  IS  VERY  CRANKY.  .  .


              GARY
I  understand.  But  I'm  here  to
make  your  day  as  pleasant  as
possible.


              BEATRICE
Oh  heck.  Would  you  like  a  cup
of  coffee?
```

Harry's objective is to sell his product. Beatrice's objective is to keep from buying his product. She starts off being nasty and even admits she was cranky. At the back door, Gary undercuts Beatrice's anger by being sweet and charming. In comedy, you often decide on your emotions ahead of time in order to get a comic response.

The Comic Pause

The comic pause is often used to set up the surprise in the joke. The comic pause is used by some great comedians. Once the audience catches the joke, the comedian stops and waits. He senses when to continue; if he starts too late, he can lose his audience. The longer the pause, the funnier. The pause is sometimes done with a look to emphasize the joke. Johnny Carson modeled his comic pause after the master, Jack Benny. It is often referred to as "milking the laugh." An interesting example of the comic pause can be see in this story from D. L. Stewart's book *Fathers Are People, Too.*[2]

When you're an only child, you never have anybody to blame. When I was 14 my father came into my room and asked me who had been smoking his cigarettes. I had to tell him it was the dog.

---

[2] Stewart, D. L., *Fathers Are People, Too.* Indianapolis, IN: Bobbs-Merrill, 1983.

In *Comedy Writing Secrets,* Melvin Helitzer makes this joke even funnier by adding two words and a comic pause.

> *. . . my father . . . asked me who had been smoking his cigarettes. I had to tell him the truth . . (pause) . . It was the dog.*

The comic pause adds an element of anticipation to the statement and surprise to the punch line.

Learn Lines Exactly as Written

Memorize comedic material verbatim. Comedy leaves no room for improvisation, unless you are a stand-up comedian and this is your show. Brilliant comedy depends on exact dialogue to make the punch line work.

Rehearsal

Rehearsals are essential for comedy, especially sitcoms, which are similar to stage rehearsals. One major difference between sitcom and stage rehearsals is that rewriting sometimes takes place during rehearsals for a sitcom, where it is easier to see whether or not a joke works. Rewriting can then sometimes improve the humor. The art of comedy is finding and nailing the humor each and every time. This is difficult without an audience, which is the reason why sitcoms prefer to have a live audience present during shooting. When you have an audience, you find the comic moment during your performance based on your audience's response. This allows you to add business as you perfect and develop the role. Planned responses can be changed or modified to accommodate particular audiences. In an audition you need to know when something is funny and be ready to do the business that makes it look like it is happening spontaneously. Rehearsal gives you the confidence to vary the planned response, and allows your own natural spontaneity to evoke the humor.

Lucille Ball was a great comedian who studied her actions in detail in every scene and rehearsed them until they were a part of her. Paul Brownfield and Carla Hill, *Los Angeles Times* staff writers, wrote *First and Still the Funniest,* a fascinating article that gives us a brief description of why Lucille Ball was a great comedian. In one scene, Ball looked like she had just stumbled into a pizza parlor and started flipping pizzas. Brownfield and Hill wrote, "In fact Davis and Carroll, writers for the *I Love Lucy Show,* were walking in Hollywood when they happened by a pizza maker flipping dough in the window at Micelli's. Could Lucy do this? They called Ball at home, and the actress came to the restaurant and began flipping pizzas in plain sight of passersby. 'Buster Keaton once told Lucy know your props'." The brilliance of Lucille Ball was her ability to internalize every stage direction and bring it to life exactly as written.

Physical comedy needs rehearsal. Only when you practice with your props do you get comfortable with the physical action. Then, when you add the dialogue, the material really comes to life. W. C. Fields started out as a juggler, and he would practice so much that his hands bled. I remember watching him do one of his great routines in a Western movie. He steps from a stagecoach holding his cane in his free hand. Stepping off the step causes him to raise his arm, and as his arm goes up, the cane lifts his hat from his head. He looks around to find his hat. It is gone. He steps back onto the stagecoach to look for it. This lowers his arm, and the hat comes down on his head. Inside the stagecoach, he finds his hat back on his head, so he exits and the same thing happens again. He feels his head to see if the hat is there. It is a funny bit that looks simple, but only because Fields had thought it through thoroughly and practiced it until it was perfect.

Comedy is written with a specific result in mind. Find the comic moments and then rehearse them until they become a part of you. Whenever you add an element to the mix—a piece of blocking, a line of dialogue, a bit, a prop, or even a look—only rehearsal makes it work. Lucille Ball worked relentlessly to internalize all her stage business so that everything she did came across as spontaneous second nature. Sometimes you might question doing something in comedy. Don't worry about feeling stupid, and don't judge. Accept the situation, just as the actors did in the Marx Brothers' *A Night at the Opera*, packing fourteen people into a small room. I'm sure anyone would feel strange doing that scene, but don't judge, just enjoy it.

Emotional Ideas

In comedy the writer will often leave emotional hints in the script. Play the comic emotion as written. If a character says to you, "Will you stop crying," you better be crying. For "I love it when you're angry," the more heightened the anger the funnier the line. The writer is telling you how to find the humor. "Stop laughing at me" does not mean that you should stop laughing, it means that you better be laughing. The writer knows that these emotional states bring out her concept of humor. In comedy you are obligated to use those specific emotions and make them believable. Don't judge and don't say, "I don't think my character would laugh or cry here." Trust the material. Do it. Good writers will usually tell you where to start emotionally, either through dialogue or screen directions. Understanding dramatic structure will help you see what the writer is getting at.

Use the writer's emotional hints to heighten the emotions she is writing about. In *Blind Date*, as we saw earlier, John Larroquette's character is so enraged on his line, "Are you drilling her?" that he punches the papier-mâché statue. But now he changes. As Kim Bassinger leaves with Bruce Willis, he becomes sorry: "Nadia wait! Nadia, I just want to talk." Seeing that he has no effect on her, he switches again and verbally attacks Bruce Willis: "You son of a bitch. I'll find you." Determine your character's intention, what he or she is trying to accomplish in the scene. Here, Larroquette is trying to win Bassinger back.

LARROQUETTE
ARE YOU DRILLING HER?

Larroquette's arm goes through a papier-mâché statue. He is stuck. Willis and Bassinger exit.

LARROQUETTE
Nadia wait! Nadia, I just want
to talk. You son of a bitch.
I'll find you.

Comedy is based on character objectives. What does a character want? In one moment, Larroquette wants to kill Willis. What physical actions make this desire come to life? Larroquette tries to punch Willis out. He is in love with Bassinger. Find the emotional value a character is experiencing—sadness, happiness, love, fear, or anger. When Larroquette talks to Bassinger he is loving, but when he talks to Willis he is angry. In comedy acting, do not be afraid to use emotional or physical ideas. They are there for a purpose. (See "Inappropriate Emotion" and "Heightened Emotion" earlier in the chapter for further discussion of the use of emotions in comedy.)

Energy

Energy in comedy comes from an awareness of what is going on in the script. Comedic energy is from the freedom to react to everything, especially on an emotional level, without reservations or judgment.

The Law of Threes

A good example of the "Law of Threes" (defined previously) is found in *Tootsie*. Dustin Hoffman plays an actor who misbehaves with a director and as a result can't get hired. Hoffman stomps into his agent's office, played by Sydney Pollack, and demands to read for a particular part. His agent tells him, "Get some therapy." Later in the story, Hoffman shows up at a restaurant dressed as a woman, and his agent says, "God, I begged you to get some therapy." In the same scene the agent says, "You're psychotic." This last line has been set up for a laugh because the agent has already told Hoffman twice before to get professional help. Below is another "triple" from *Tootsie*.

> HOFFMAN
> . . . I like to make money,
> too.

> POLLACK
> Oh, really? The Harlem theater
> for the blind. Strindberg in
> the park. The people's work-
> shop in Syracuse.

Each statement refers to Hoffman wasting his time on noncommercial theater. Any one of the statements alone would not elicit humor, but when the three thoughts are used in sequence, the last statement gets a laugh.

Asides

An aside is an actor's speech that is intended to be heard by the audience but not by the other actors. When you have an aside, create an imaginary character with whom you can talk. On the stage, turn away from the actors and say it to the audience, but not directly at the audience. The imaginary character helps you to say the line in a more interesting way. Here's a scene done in my workshop to practice delivering an aside.

> ALPHONSE
> I'm offering you one mill for
> your business, but forget your
> staff. They're all losers.

> MIKE
> Bite me.

> (then, aside)
> Did I say that?

Say "Bite me" to the other actor in the scene. Then turn and say, "Did I say that?" in another direction. "Did I say that?" is what you are thinking. The device of an imaginary character helps to convey that thought interestingly to the audience. A film director may ask you to deliver an aside directly to the camera.

Commitment

Be willing to go all the way. Don't be afraid to make yourself look ridiculous. Look at Jim Carrey. He commits totally. He's willing to use anything that comes to him no matter how outrageous.

Attack the Material

Run with your objective. Go for it! Don't be afraid to get angry or be sad or laugh. Make the emotion as full as possible. Don't be kind of angry, be really angry. Make it over-the-top anger, or even angrier. This is called attacking the material. Keep it as truthful as you can. The director can always make it smaller but not necessarily bigger. Have fun. I don't mean laugh at your own character's jokes and antics, but enjoy what you are doing. We could see that Carroll O'Connor loved playing Archie Bunker. If you are not having fun, the audience won't have fun either.

Laughter

When you are acting in sitcoms or live shows, if the audience laughs, wait until the laugh reaches its peak and starts to dissipate before you say your next line. It is okay to laugh as a character reaction, but your laughter cannot be personal. If you laugh at your own jokes, the audience will not laugh. Your job is to make them laugh.

Stand-up comedian Myron Cohen said, "Comedy is a very dangerous business." It should look spontaneous, but good comedy is meticulously planned. Cohen said comedy is dangerous because no matter how meticulously you plan, the audience might not laugh. That, in comedian jargon, is death.

Comedy is a coordinated effort by the actors, the writers, and the director. When we laugh, someone has put a lot of thought into it. When the actors relate and really play off each other, as in *When Harry Met Sally* or *A Few Good Men*, even better comedy than was expected may happen. Or the comedy could be planned out, as in *Hero*, *Blind Date*, or *Being John Malkovich*.

Good comedy can contain a lot of different things. It can be Lucille Ball's planned and internalized stage directions. It can be physical action such as electrocuting the dog in *There's Something about Mary*. It can be Rowan Atkinson in the film *Bean* cleaning the face of Whistler's Mother with paint thinner and removing the paint on a priceless painting. This action was deliberately planned, but the character's stupidity lets us believe that it happened fortuitously.

For a punch line to work, different situations call for different emotional responses. Comedians learn how to make their particular brand of humor work, because they are going only for one thing—laughs. Actors are at a slight disadvantage because comedy has so many different varieties, from farce to black comedy and every variation in between. Your job as an actor is to discover the humor in each piece of material and go with it.

Preparing for the Comedy Audition

Before you go in to audition for a comedy, read the script carefully. Read everything. Read all the screen directions, and look for emotional clues about the character you are reading for.

1. Memorize all your lines if you have the time, but particularly memorize your first line absolutely cold. Become as familiar with the material as you possibly can. Comedy material sometimes calls for a rapid-fire delivery, but make sure you read the lines exactly as written.
2. Determine what emotions the script calls for, where you have to say your speech, and with what emotion.
3. Know where the jokes are.
4. Think of character idiosyncrasies that you can add to your character, such as quirks to heighten the comedy: nervousness, a twitch, a different voice, a laugh, a physical characteristic.
5. What physical actions are necessary to make the material funny?
6. Do you need or can you use props? If you do, keep it simple: a pipe, cigar, glasses, riding crop, or whatever will help you bring the character to life. If possible, you should try to avoid props, but if they are necessary, you should practice with the props until they are second nature.

In the Audition

1. Rehearsal—There are no rehearsals once you are in the audition studio. You will be reading against a casting director. Use the exact dialogue. Limit your blocking and physical movements. Read all the stage directions. Know the setup, the joke, and the punch line. Then strive for a moment-to-moment reality.
2. Comic objective—Decide on a comic objective. Let your character's need drive the scene. What do you want? What do you need? In *Tootsie*, Dustin Hoffman has a reputation as a difficult actor and can't get work. He wants desperately to work, so he auditions for a woman's role on a soap and gets hired. Since he is not a woman, he is forced to respond to men differently than if he were a real woman. In certain scenes he discourages men from coming on to him. If he were a real woman, there would be no humor.

3. In *Blind Date* John Larroquette's character is driven by his love for the character Kim Bassinger plays. This love makes him angry at Bruce Willis's character, who is dating her. In a drama, Larroquette would probably relate in a nice and friendly way to Willis. But this is comedy: if Larroquette doesn't go off the deep end with heightened anger, he doesn't drive the plot, and the scene is not funny. Your job is to make the comedy work.

4. Respond to what the other actor is experiencing and be willing to make adjustments accordingly. In *Blind Date*, Willis and Bassinger want to get away from Larroquette, who actually tries to stop Willis from leaving. Larroquette is relating, but with a comic objective—he wants to kill Willis. Willis relates to this nut case by trying to escape.

5. The Art of Acceptance—Accept the imaginary circumstances and the other characters to help you experience genuine emotion, even during the most absurd situations.

6. The Art of Giving and Receiving—Share your experience with the other actor, and be receptive to all feedback. Be generous by listening and responding and sharing all your impulses with the other actor, no matter how insignificant or crazy they may seem to you. Remember, impulses can't hurt another actor. Give them everything you can emotionally. However, don't touch the casting director.

7. Comic Timing
   a. Know where the humor is in the material.
   b. What line do I punch to sell the joke?
   c. What line do I undercut to sell the joke?
   d. Where can I use inappropriate emotional responses?
   e. Where do I use comic pauses?
   f. Develop character idiosyncrasy.

Summary

1. Read comedy scripts. Study the material
2. Determine what emotions are required by the script. Look for predetermined emotional content. Example: "Stop yelling" or "Stop crying." Be prepared to elicit that emotion.
3. Where can you use inappropriate emotions?
4. Where can you use a comic pause?
5. Know where the setup is, and where the jokes, the punch lines, and undercut lines are. Underline all the punch lines, and double-underline the undercut lines.

6. Think of character idiosyncrasies that you can use—quirks to heighten the comedy. Nervousness, a twitch, a different voice, a laugh, a walk, a physical characteristic.
7. What physical actions do you need to make the material funny?
8. Do you need, or can you use, props? Keep it simple—a pipe, a cigar, reading glasses, riding crop, or whatever can help you bring the character to life. But try to avoid props if possible.

Actor Practice

1. Audition for stage comedies.
2. Join a theater group or improv group.
3. When you're rehearsing comedy on stage, try to give your character a distinctive trait. Play with your physicality and see how the director or the cast responds. This will help you develop a bag of tricks that might come in handy when you audition. You have to feel comfortable with anything you do in an audition, and developing characters on stage will give you that confidence.
4. Watch comedy channels. Tape the standup comedians, and then study how they set up their jokes and punch lines. How do they get laughs?
5. Study the top comedians of our time: Eddie Murphy, Jim Carrey, Robin Williams, Mike Myers, Dana Carvey. Why are they so funny?
6. Get a comedy script and a couple of actor friends and have a table reading. See what other actors do to make something funny. Discuss where the humor is and how to make it work. Ask questions.
7. Tape yourself in a mock audition. Then do it again, only this time like Jim Carrey or Mike Myers as Austin Powers. Play with the material. Learn to be outrageous.
8. Read Melvin Helitzer's *Comedy Writing Secrets*, and Gene Perret's *Comedy Writing Step by Step*. Even though you have no desire to write you can learn a lot about comedy from comedy writers.

16
Conclusion

I get a script. I read it once to see if I want to do it. Then I don't look at it again until the day I shoot.

Robert Ryan

How It Happens

Let's say that you are a teenager who has auditioned for a part in a movie. You meet with the casting director. He likes your reading and calls you back. On your second callback, you meet the producer. A day later you have another callback for the director. The next day you have a fourth callback, and you see some of the competition. Several are actors you recognize. Your first thought is, "How am I going to get cast for the part over these guys?" On this, the final callback, you read with a real veteran, the star. The audition happens so fast you are in and out before you know it. On the way home you go over the interview in your mind, what you shoulda, woulda, coulda done but didn't. You get angry with yourself because you know you could have been better. This was your big chance. Your agent will probably never speak to you again. You might as well pack up and go back to Detroit. You are hyper, waiting to hear something, anything. You check your answering service seventeen times hoping, but nothing. After a week you assume you didn't get the part.

A month later you get a call from your agent to tell you that you got the part. They want you in Camden, New Jersey, by tomorrow morning. You find the script and fly from Burbank to Camden. You try to study the script on the plane, but you fall asleep. You check into your hotel room and you barely doze off when your phone rings. The PA picks you up and drives you to the set. This is a big-budget movie, and everything is happening much too fast. The second AD gives you your sides. Your scene is less than a page of dialogue. As you read it you realize, "Wait, this is my big scene with the star." The second says, "The director always starts with the hard stuff." "But this is my first major film." The second answers, "Hey, lighten up. Don't worry, they're pros."

The Second escorts you into makeup and wardrobe and then to the set. The director is working intently with the director of photography setting up the shot. The star turns to you: "Hey, congratulations." You smile because you don't know what to say. The director approaches and asks, "Are you ready?" You tell him that you just got the call yesterday and didn't have time to work on the script. The star says, "That's the way it always is. You're memorized, right?" You answer, "Yes." The star smiles. "Then we're ready."

Remember the Jimmy Cagney precept of working on film? "Don't bump into the furniture, hit your mark, look them in the eye, and say your lines." This is what every good actor does. When you look another human being in the eye you are forced to relate. Rehearsals for performance happen during the shoot.

To make a creative edit of the film, the film editor needs repetitions of action in a multiple selection of shots and camera angles. The director will know when your experience is truthful. Trust the star; he's a pro. He'll guide you through. No matter how many times you repeat a scene, you never know what this star will experience next. So pay attention to him and look for the five emotions. Is he sad, happy, fearful, loving, or angry? Relating to the other actor puts you in a creative place.

The director decides to cover you first. "This scene," he says, "it happens before the Supreme Court pronounces its sentence on the star, who you know is in jail for a murder he didn't commit." The director senses that you're a bit edgy, and in a calm voice says, "We're going to start off with the scene with you sitting on the stool talking with the star. Just talk to him. You're a talented actor, I trust you. Just talk to him. He's your best friend."

The jail environment of the prison set helps you accept the fact that the star is imprisoned. The AD says, "Roll sound." You get a shot of adrenaline. You look at the star, who is very loving, and this calms you down immediately.

The material reads simply enough, but are you skilled enough to get the maximum emotional mileage out of the scene? Now let's see how the pros do it.

The above is an imaginative and hypothetical description of what might have taken place. The scene, of course, is from the film, *The Hurricane*, the director is the very talented Norman Jewison, and the star is Denzel Washington, one of the most talented actors in the business today. The teenager is played by Vicellous Reon Shannon, who has been working since he was ten years old and has nineteen notable TV appearances. After you see the scene, you know why he beat out the competition. You can learn by watching the movie and studying these actors. Following is how they actually did the scene.

                    JEWISON
          ACTION!

(Shannon slips Washington a cup of coffee between the bars.
Vicellous smiles.)

                    WASHINGTON
                (loving)
          You come a long way little
          brother.

                    SHANNON
                (loving)
          Rubin, I want you to know that
          if this doesn't work I'm gonna
          bust you out of here.

                    WASHINGTON
          You are?

                    SHANNON
          I'm gonna bust you out of
          here.

                    WASHINGTON
          What was the first book you
          ever bought?

                    SHANNON
          Yours.

                    WASHINGTON
          You think that was an acci-
          dent?

                    SHANNON
          No.

                    WASHINGTON
          Me neither. Lester, short for
          Lazarus. He who has risen from
          the dead. Rubin. Genesis
          Chapter twenty-nine, verse 32.
          Behold a Son. You put that
          together and you have, Behold
          a son that has risen from the
          dead. That's no accident. Hate

```
            put me in prison. Love's gonna
            bust me out.
```

(Shannon's face is filled with tears.)

```
                    SHANNON
            Just in case love doesn't. I'm
            gonna bust you out of here.
```

(Washington laughs spontaneously at Shannon's comment. He feels Shannon's pain, and Washington has a hint of sadness in his eyes and voice.)

(Washington then wipes the tears from Shannon's face with his hand. Shannon takes his hand a pulls it towards his face, kissing and holding the hand in a gesture of camaraderie.)

```
                    WASHINGTON
            You already did.

                    DIRECTOR
            CUT!
```

Denzel Washington and Vicellous Reon Shannon are brilliant. Both actors concentrate on the other actor's emotions. Washington and Shannon both express love for each other. Shannon is saddened by Washington's plight and cries. The Art of Not Knowing happens when Shannon cries; and when Washington responds to Shannon, he covers his own pain with a spontaneous laugh when Shannon says "I'm gonna bust you out of here." They are Giving and Receiving when Washington reaches through the bars and wipes Shannon's tears, a courageous move. They share intimacy when Shannon fearlessly responds by receiving and kissing Washington's hand. The bars that separate them add to the realism and create physical conflict. Both actors accept the circumstance, a heightened stake to a life or death. Their acting raises this scene from mediocre drama to an extraordinary piece of work. The actors are not consciously aware that they are practicing the Five Arts of Film Acting. But they are. Again, view the scene in the movie.

The five arts in a single scene. For an honest, unexpected performance, make the other actor more important than what you personally think, and respond to what you see and hear.

The above might not be the exact circumstances under which this scene was actually cast and shot, but it often happens this way.

Summary

Have fun. Enjoy acting. Never complain about the work. You are working and thousands aren't. Appreciate everyone who works in this business. The guy giving tours at Universal might someday turn out to be the most powerful agent in Hollywood. Be kind to everyone.

Afterword

The United States has had more influence on the world than any country since the Roman Empire. The movies of Hollywood have helped spread this influence with their depictions of our culture, particularly our affluence. Some films have a positive affect, like Stanley Kramer's *The Defiant Ones*, in which two escaped prisoners, Sidney Poitier, who is African American, and Tony Curtis, who is white, are chained together. At first, each one wants to kill the other, but they overcome racial prejudice and discover the value of true humanity. Or the effect of films can be negative, as with D. W. Griffith's *The Birth of a Nation*, the 1915 silent film that influenced the revival of the Ku Klux Klan and its evils. Films can offer inspiration, propaganda, comedy, tragedy, evil, or just plain garden-variety entertainment.

Hollywood is the center of the film industry, a business in which good deals are more important than good movies. But good movies do get made in spite of greed and bad taste. I hope that every one of you striving to become an actor will learn and take inspiration from the great performances in the great films. The following are some of the great performances that have a lot to say to you about acting. Look at them and learn:

Ben Kingsley and all the other performances in *Ghandi*. Brando in *On the Waterfront*. Sylvester Stallone gives a wonderful persistence-against-all-odds performance in *Rocky*. Kathy Bates, Jessica Tandy, Mary Stuart Masterson, and Mary Louise Parker in *Fried Green Tomatoes*. Richard Dreyfuss and Holly Hunter in *Once Around*. Cicely Tyson and Paul Winfield in *Sounder*. In *Traffic*, Michael Douglas and Benicio del Toro are realistically honest. Paul Newman is at his best in *The Verdict*. Oprah Winfrey and Whoopi Goldberg in *The Color Purple*. In *Born on the Fourth of July* Tom Cruise gives probably his finest performance. Robert Ryan in *The Set Up*. Daniel Day-Lewis in *My Left Foot*. Glenn Close shows how great she can be in *Fatal Attraction*. Burt Lancaster's tour de force in *Elmer Gantry*. Ernest Borgnine in *Marty*. Watch how Gene Hackman and Denzel Washington push each other's performances in *Crimson Tide*. Sigourney Weaver is exemplary in *Map of the World*. Jimmy Stewart's performance in *It's a Wonderful Life* makes it a classic. Watch Billy Crystal and Meg Ryan in *When Harry Met Sally* to learn about comedy scenes. Jon Voight in *Coming Home*. Morgan Freeman is great in *Shawshank Redemption*. In *Men of Honor, An Officer and a Gentleman,* and *The Last Detail*, Robert De Niro, Louis Gossett Jr., and Jack Nicholson, respectively, show us the epitome of "lifer" enlisted men. In *Men of Honor,* Cuba Gooding Jr. reveals a great portrayal of persistence. Angelina Jolie in *Girl, Interrupted*—Wow! See Al Pacino's emotional power in *Dog Day Afternoon.* In *Henry V,* Kenneth Branagh creates close to a masterpiece. Ellen Burstyn is great in *Requiem for a Dream.* Watch the villainous Doug Hutchison, the guard, in *The Green Mile,* and Ralph Fiennes and all the others in *Schindler's List.* Jon Voight's performance in *Runaway Train . . ..* There are many, many more. Look for them and study them.

A great movie comes out of a talented writer, a dedicated director, and great performances. The force behind each movie is a need inside some unrelenting artist to tell that particular story. That is what drives this art—creative minds who stimulate other creative minds into collaboration. If you are reading this book you probably have the desire to be in the film business in some way. To do that, your desire has to be strong enough to overcome all the insane barriers that the industry sets up.

If you come to Hollywood you may find yourself standing outside one of the studios wondering, how do I get in? Simple—by invitation. What will inspire an invitation? A recognized body of work, such as acting in an independent film that gets critical acclaim, or giving a standout performance in a movie. It could be years of work on small parts to get credibility, or it could be a *tour de force* part in a stage play. Sometimes a name actor prices himself out of a role and you win by default. Humphrey Bogart was not the first choice for *Casablanca.* You could have an agent that hustles and believes in your talent. Maybe you're the right type in the right place at the right time. As you step off the bus at the Hollywood Greyhound bus station, someone might even tap you on the shoulder and say, "Would you like to be in a movie?" It has happened once or twice in the last hundred years, but don't count on it. No one knows the exact formula for how it should be done, but everyone agrees that at the very least it takes hard work and insane persistence.

Go to Hollywood or New York, study, get an agent, work hard. Act every chance you get. Work at your craft. It will not happen overnight. An actor usually puts in ten years before he or she becomes an "overnight" success and makes a good living. There are many thousands of people who tried to be actors and never made it. Not that they weren't talented, but they didn't work hard enough and just gave up too soon. Mike Medavoy, a studio head, said, "You want to be successful, work seven days a week." Nothing succeeds like persistence. If you have an obsessive desire, and you work at your craft both in and out of school, study hard, and never give up, you will eventually get recognition and the invitation to come on in.

This book was written to encourage you in your dreams. That's why I teach. I want you to be successful. Do what's in your heart. Act, direct, write, produce, be a grip, an editor, a camera operator, whatever. There are all kinds of great jobs in the entertainment business. Remember, you have something important to give—Yourself.

Best of luck,
Jeremiah Comey

How to Get in Touch with Jeremiah

Jeremiah teaches several times a week at his studio in Hollywood, California. He can be reached by phone at his office (818) 248-4104.

The Acting Workshop with Jeremiah Comey is a 50-minute video produced by Christine Mehner. It demonstrates one way he works with and teaches beginning actors. Contact Media, Inc. at 1-800-583-0118 to buy a copy.

Bibliography

Barr, Tony. (1982). *Acting for the Camera*. Boston: Allyn & Bacon.

Brestoff, Richard. (1994). *The Camera Smart Actor*. Lyme, NH: Smith & Krause.

Caine, Michael. (1990). *Acting on Film*. New York, London: Applause Theater Books Publishers.

Chekhov, Michael. (1953). *To the Actor*. New York: Harper & Row Publishing.

Cohen, Robert. (1978). *Acting Power*. Palo Alto, California: Mayfield Publishing Company.

Crane, Robert David, and Christopher Fryer. (1975). *Jack Nicholson Face to Face*. New York: M. Evans and Company.

Dmytryk, Edward. (1984). *On Screen Directing*. Boston: Focal Press.

Easty, Edward Dwight. (1981). *On Method Acting*. New York: Ballantine Books, Random House.

Egri, Lajos. (1960). *The Art of Dramatic Writing*. New York: Touchstone Books, Simon & Schuster.

Field, Syd. (1982). *Screenplay*. New York: Dell Publishing.

"First and Still the Funniest." *Los Angeles Times*. January 2, 2002. Sunday's Calendar, p.4.

Goleman, Daniel. (1995). *Emotional Intelligence*. New York: Bantam.

Helitzer, Melvin. (1987). *Comedy Writing Secrets*. Cincinnati, Ohio: Writer's Digest Books. F & W Publications.

Katz, Steven D. (1991). *Film Directing Shot by Shot*. Stoneham, MA: Michael Wiese Productions.

Litwak, Mark. (1986). *Reel Power*. New York: William Morrow and Company.

Lumet, Sidney. (1995). *Making Movies*. New York: Vintage Books.

MacLaine, Shirley. (1995). *My Lucky Stars*. New York: Bantam Books.

Mamet, David. (1999). *True and False*. New York: Vintage Books, Random House.

Mazursky, Paul. (1999). *Show Me the Magic*. New York: Simon & Schuster.

McCarty, John. (1987). *The Films of John Huston*. Secaucus, NJ: Citadel Press.

McKee, Robert. (1997). *Story: Substance, Structure, Style, and the Principles of Screenwriting*. New York: ReganBooks, HarperCollins.

Meisner, Sanford, and Dennis Longwell. (1987). *On Acting*. New York: Random House.

Miller, Allen. (1992). *A Passion for Acting*. New York: Backstage Books.

Morris, Eric, and Joan Hotchkiss. (1979). *No Acting, Please*. New York: Perigee Books.

Perret, Gene. (1982). *Comedy Writing Step by Step*. Hollywood, CA: Samuel French.

Shurtleff, Michael. (1978). *Audition*. New York: Walker and Company.

Spolin, Viola. (1983). *Improvisation for the Theater*. Evanston, IL: Northwestern University Press.

Stanislavsky, Constantine. (1964). *An Actor Prepares*. New York: Routledge.

Stewart, D. L. (1983). *Fathers Are People, Too*. Indianapolis, IN: Bobbs-Merrill.

Truffaut, François, and Helen G. Scott. (1985). *Hitchcock*. New York: Touchstone Books, Simon & Schuster.

Tucker, Patrick. (1994). *Secrets of Screen Acting*. New York: Routledge Press.

Weston, Judith. (1996). *Directing Actors*. Studio City, CA: Michael Wiese Productions.

Videography

There are many more great films, TV series, and videos than those on this list. I have included the ones below principally because I have referred to them in the text as containing fine performances. Using the criteria for good acting that I have talked about in *The Art of Film Acting*, you might find it useful to build on this list.

A Few Good Men. Director: Rob Reiner. Screenwriter: Aaron Sorkin. Actors: Tom Cruise, Demi Moore, Jack Nicholson. Producers: David Brown, Rob Reiner, Andrew Scheinman. 1992.

All in the Family. TV Series. Directors: Paul Bogart, Norman Campbell, Norman Lear, Bud Yorkin, John Rich, Walter C. Miller, Hal Cooper, Wes Kenney, Michael Kidd, Bob LaHenero, Bob Livingston. Various writers: Bob Schiller, Bob Weiskopf, Larry Rhine, Mel Tolkin, Phil Sharp, Lee Kalcheim, Austin Kalish, Rob Reiner. Actors: Carroll O'Connor, Jean Stapleton, Rob Reiner, Sally Struthers. Producer: Norman Lear. Started 1971–1972.

As Good As It Gets. Director: James L. Brooks. Screenwriters: James L. Brooks and Mark L. Anders. Actors: Jack Nicholson, Helen Hunt, Greg Kinnear. Producers: Bridget Johnson and James L. Brooks. 1997.

Barber Shop. Director: Arthur Ripley. Screenwriter: W. C. Fields. Actors: W. C. Fields, Else Cavanna, Cyril Ring. Producer: Mack Sennett. 1933.

Basketball Diaries. Director: Scott Kalvert. Screenwriter: Bryan Goluboff. Actors: Leonardo DiCaprio, Lorraine Bracco, Mark Wahlberg. Producers: Liz Heller, John Bard Manulis. 1995.

A Beautiful Mind. Director: Ron Howard. Screenwriter: Akiva Goldsman. Actors: Russell Crowe, Jennifer Connelly, Ed Harris. Producers: Brian Grazer and Ron Howard. 2001.

Being John Malkovich. Director: Spike Jonze. Screenwriters: Charlie Kaufman and Michael Huhn. Actors: John Cusack, Cameron Diaz, John Malkovich, Catherine Keener. Producers: Steve Golin, Vincent Landay, Sandy Stern, Michael Stipe. 1999.

Blind Date. Director: Blake Edwards. Screenwriter: Dale Launer. Actors: Kim Bassinger, Bruce Willis, John Larroquette. Producer: Tony Adams. 1987.

Bronx Tale. Director: Robert De Niro. Screenwriter: Chazz Palminteri. Actors: Chazz Palminteri, Robert De Niro, Lillo Brancato. Producers: Robert De Niro, Jon Kilik, Jane Rosenthal. 1993.

Casablanca. Director: Michael Curtiz. Screenwriters: Julius and Phillip Epstein and Howard Koch. Actors: Humphrey Bogart, Ingrid Bergman. Producer: Hall B. Wallis. 1942.

City Slickers. Director: Ron Underwood. Screenwriters: Lowell Ganz, Babaloo Mandel. Actors: Billy Crystal, Mitch Ribbins, Daniel Stern, Phil Berquist, Bruno Kirby, Ed Furillo. Producer: Billy Crystal, Irby Smith. 1991.

The Closer. Director: Dimitri Logothetis. Screenwriters: Louis La Ruso and Robert Keats. Actors: Danny Aiello, Dimitri Logothetis. Producer: not listed. 1990.

Crocodile Dundee. Director: Peter Faiman. Screenwriter: Don Cornell, Paul Hogan, Ken Shadie. Actors: Paul Hogan, Micahale J. Dundee, Linda Kozlowski, Sue Charlton. Producer: John Cornell, James Scopt. 1986.

Five Easy Pieces. Director: Bob Rafelson. Screenwriter: Adrien Joyce. Story: Bob Rafelson. Actors: Jack Nicholson, Susan Anspach, Karen Black. Producers: Bob Rafelson, Richard Wechsler. 1970.

Fried Green Tomatoes. Director: Jon Avnet. Screenwriters: Fannie Flagg, Carol Sovieski. Actors: Kathy Bates, Jessica Tandy, Mary Stuart Masterson, Mary Louise Parker, Cicely Tyson. Producers: Jon Avent, Jordan Kerner. 1991.

The Gods Must Be Crazy! Director: Jamie Uys. Screenwriter: Jamie Uys. Actors: N! XIXO, Lena Farugia, Hans Strydom. Producer: Boet Troskie. 1980.

Hero. Director: Stephen Frears. Screenwriter: David Webb Peoples. Actors: Dustin Hoffman, Geena Davis, Andy Garcia. Producer: Laura Ziskin. 1992.

He Said, She Said. Directors: Ken Kwapis, Marisa Silver. Screenwriter: Brian Hohlfield. Actors: Kevin Bacon, Elizabeth Perkins, Ashley Gardner. Producer: Frank Mancuso, Jr. 1991.

The Honeymooners. TV Series. Director: Frank Sapenstein. Screenwriters: Marvin Marx, Walter Stone, Sydney Zelenka, Leonard B. Stern, Andy Russell, Herbert Finn, A. J. Russell. Actors: Audrey Meadows, Jackie Gleason, Art Carney. Producer: Jack Hurdle. Started 1955–1956.

The Hurricane. Director: Norman Jewison. Screenwriters: Armyan Bernstein, Dan Gordon. Actors: Denzel Washington, Deborah Kara Unger, Vicellous Reon Shannon. Producers: Armyan Bernstein, Norman Jewison, John Ketcham, 1999.

I Am Sam. Director: Jessie Nelson. Screenwriters: Kristine Johnson, Jessie Nelson. Actors: Sean Penn, Michelle Pfeiffer, Dakota Fanning. Producers: Marshall Herskovitz, Jessie Nelson, Richard Solomon, Edward Zwick. 2001.

Legends of the Fall. Director: Edward Zwick. Screenwriters: Susan Shilliday, Billy Wittliff. Actors: Brad Pitt, Anthony Hopkins, Aidan Quinn, Julia Ormond. Producers: Marshall Herkovitz, William D. Wittliff, Edward Zwick. 1994.

Liar Liar. Director: Tom Shadyac. Screenwriters: Paul Guay, Stephan Mazur. Actors: Jim Carrey, Maura Tierney, Jennifer Tilly. Producer: Brian Grazer. 1997.

Map of the World. Director: Scott Elliott. Screenwriters: Peter Hedges, Polly Platt. Actors: Sigourney Weaver, Julianne Moore, David Strathairn. Producers: Kathleen Kennedy, Frank Marshall. 1999.

Mighty Aphrodite. Director/Screenwriter: Woody Allen. Actors: Woody Allen, Mira Sorvino. Producer: Robert Greenhut. 1995.

Moonstruck. Director: Norman Jewison. Screenwriter: John Patrick Shanley. Actors: Cher, Nicolas Cage. Producers: Norman Jewison, Patrick J. Palmer. 1987.

My Cousin Vinny. Director: Jonathan Lynn. Screenwriter: Dale Launer. Actors: Joe Pesci, Marisa Tomei, Ralph Macchio, Michael Whitfield. Producers: Paul Schiff, Dale Launer. 1992.

On Golden Pond. Director: Mark Rydell. Screenwriter: Ernest Thompson. Actors: Katharine Hepburn, Henry Fonda, Jane Fonda. Producer: Bruce Gilbert. 1991.

The Pledge. Director: Sean Penn. Screenwriters: Jerzy Kromolowski, Mary Olson Kromolowski. Actors: Jack Nicholson, Robin Wright Penn. Producers: Michael Fitzgerald, Sean Penn, Elie Samaha. 2000.

Raging Bull. Director: Martin Scorsese. Screenwriters: Paul Schrader and Mardik Martin. Actors: Robert De Niro, Cathy Moriarty, Joe Pesci. Producers: Robert Chartoff, Irvin Winkler. 1980.

Sister Act. Director: Emile Ardolino. Screenwriter: Joseph Howard. Actors: Whoopi Goldberg, Maggie Smith, Harvey Keitel. Producer: Teri Schwartz. 1992.

Terms of Endearment. Director/Screenwriter: James L. Brooks: Actors: Shirley MacLaine, Jack Nicholson, Debra Winger. Producer: James L. Brooks. 1983.

There's Something About Mary. Directors: Bobby Farrelly, Peter Farrelly. Screenwriters: Ed Decter, John T. Strauss, Bobby Farrelly, Peter Farrelly. Actors: Ben Stiller, Cameron Diaz, Matt Dillon. Producers: Frank Beddor, Michael Steinberg, Bradley Thomas, Charles B. Wessler. 1989.

Threesome. Director/Screenwriter: Andrew Fleming. Actors: Lara Flynn Boyle, Stephen Baldwin, Josh Charles. Producers: Brad Kervoy, Steven Stabler. 1994.

Tootsie. Director: Sydney Pollack. Screenwriters: Larry Gelbart, Murry Schisgal, Don McGuire. Actors: Dustin Hoffman, Jessica Lange, Teri Garr. Producers: Sydney Pollack, Dick Richards. 1982.

White Palace. Director: Luis Mandoki. Screenwriters: Ted Tally, Alvin Sargent. Actors: Susan Sarandon, James Spader. Producers: Griffin Dunne, Amy Robinson, Mark Rosenberg. 1990.

Young Frankenstein. Director: Mel Brooks. Screenwriters: Mel Brooks, Gene Wilder. Actors: Gene Wilder, Marty Feldman, Teri Garr, Madeline Kahn, Peter Boyle. Producer: Michael Gruskoff. 1974.

Index